The Art of Unit Testing
with Examples in .NET

With Compliments
www.learningconnexions.com
info@learningconnexions.com
0843 523 5765

The Art of Unit Testing

with Examples in .NET

Roy Osherove

MANNING

Greenwich
(74° w. long.)

For online information and ordering of this and other Manning books, please visit www.manning.com. The publisher offers discounts on this book when ordered in quantity. For more information, please contact:

> Special Sales Department
> Manning Publications Co.
> Sound View Court 3B fax: (609) 877-8256
> Greenwich, CT 06830 email: manning@manning.com

©2009 by Manning Publications Co. All rights reserved.

No part of this publication may be reproduced, stored in a retrieval system, or transmitted, in any form or by means electronic, mechanical, photocopying, or otherwise, without prior written permission of the publisher. Figure 3.2 is reproduced with permission from NASA.

Many of the designations used by manufacturers and sellers to distinguish their products are claimed as trademarks. Where those designations appear in the book, and Manning Publications was aware of a trademark claim, the designations have been printed in initial caps or all caps.

♾ Recognizing the importance of preserving what has been written, it is Manning's policy to have the books we publish printed on acid-free paper, and we exert our best efforts to that end. Recognizing also our responsibility to conserve the resources of our planet, Manning books are printed on paper that is at least 15% recycled and processed without the use of elemental chlorine.

Manning Publications Co.	Development Editor:	Nermina Miller
209 Bruce Park Avenue	Copyeditor:	Andy Carroll
Greenwich, CT 06830	Proofreader:	Anna Welles
	Typesetter:	Marija Tudor
	Cover designer:	Leslie Haimes

ISBN: 978-1-933988-27-6

Printed in the United States of America
2 3 4 5 6 7 8 9 10 – MAL – 14 13 12 11 10 09

With Compliments

To my wife, Tal, and my sons,
Itamar and Aviv—my family

Brief contents

PART 1 GETTING STARTED 1
- 1 • The basics of unit testing 3
- 2 • A first unit test 21

PART 2 CORE TECHNIQUES 47
- 3 • Using stubs to break dependencies 49
- 4 • Interaction testing using mock objects 82
- 5 • Isolation (mock object) frameworks 99

PART 3 THE TEST CODE 139
- 6 • Test hierarchies and organization 141
- 7 • The pillars of good tests 171

PART 4 DESIGN AND PROCESS 217
- 8 • Integrating unit testing into the organization 219
- 9 • Working with legacy code 239

Contents

foreword *xv*
preface *xvii*
acknowledgments *xix*
about this book *xx*
about the cover illustration *xxiii*

PART 1 GETTING STARTED 1

1 The basics of unit testing 3

1.1 Unit testing—the classic definition 4
   The importance of writing "good" unit tests 5 ◦ We've all written unit tests (sort of) 5

1.2 Properties of a good unit test 6

1.3 Integration tests 7
   Drawbacks of integration tests compared to automated unit tests 9

1.4 Good unit test—a definition 11

1.5 A simple unit test example 12

1.6 Test-driven development 16

1.7 Summary 19

2 A first unit test 21

2.1 Frameworks for unit testing 22
   What unit-testing frameworks offer 22 ◦ The xUnit frameworks 25

- 2.2 Introducing the LogAn project   25
- 2.3 First steps with NUnit   26
    - Installing NUnit   26 ○ Loading up the solution   26 ○ Using the NUnit attributes in your code   29
- 2.4 Writing our first test   30
    - The Assert class   31 ○ Running our first test with NUnit   32 ○ Fixing our code and passing the test   33 ○ From red to green   33
- 2.5 More NUnit attributes   34
    - Setup and teardown   34 ○ Checking for expected exceptions   36 ○ Ignoring tests   38 ○ Setting test categories   39
- 2.6 Indirect testing of state   40
- 2.7 Summary   44

PART 2 CORE TECHNIQUES   47

3 Using stubs to break dependencies   49

- 3.1 Introducing stubs   50
- 3.2 Identifying a filesystem dependency in LogAn   51
- 3.3 Determining how to easily test LogAnalyzer   52
- 3.4 Refactoring our design to be more testable   55
    - Extract an interface to allow replacing underlying implementation   55 ○ Inject stub implementation into a class under test   58 ○ Receive an interface at the constructor level (constructor injection)   58 ○ Receive an interface as a property get or set   64 ○ Getting a stub just before a method call   66
- 3.5 Variations on refactoring techniques   74
    - Using Extract and Override to create stub results   75
- 3.6 Overcoming the encapsulation problem   77
    - Using internal and [InternalsVisibleTo]   78 ○ Using the [Conditional] attribute   79 ○ Using #if and #endif with conditional compilation   80
- 3.7 Summary   80

4 Interaction testing using mock objects 82

4.1 State-based versus interaction testing 83
4.2 The difference between mocks and stubs 84
4.3 A simple manual mock example 87
4.4 Using a mock and a stub together 89
4.5 One mock per test 94
4.6 Stub chains: stubs that produce mocks or other stubs 95
4.7 The problems with handwritten mocks and stubs 96
4.8 Summary 97

5 Isolation (mock object) frameworks 99

5.1 Why use isolation frameworks? 100
5.2 Dynamically creating a fake object 102

Introducing Rhino Mocks into your tests 102 ○ Replacing a handwritten mock object with a dynamic one 103

5.3 Strict versus nonstrict mock objects 106

Strict mocks 106 ○ Nonstrict mocks 107

5.4 Returning values from fake objects 108
5.5 Creating smart stubs with an isolation framework 110

Creating a stub in Rhino Mocks 110 ○ Combining dynamic stubs and mocks 112

5.6 Parameter constraints for mocks and stubs 115

Checking parameters with string constraints 115 ○ Checking parameter object properties with constraints 118 ○ Executing callbacks for parameter verification 120

5.7 Testing for event-related activities 121

Testing that an event has been subscribed to 122 ○ Triggering events from mocks and stubs 123 ○ Testing whether an event was triggered 124

5.8 Arrange-act-assert syntax for isolation 126
5.9 Current isolation frameworks for .NET 130

NUnit.Mocks 130 ○ NMock 131 ○ NMock2 131 ○ Typemock Isolator 132 ○ Rhino Mocks 132 ○ Moq 134

- 5.10 Advantages of isolation frameworks   134
- 5.11 Traps to avoid when using isolation frameworks   135

    Unreadable test code   135 ○ Verifying the wrong things   136 ○ Having more than one mock per test   136 ○ Overspecifying the tests   136
- 5.12 Summary   137

PART 3 THE TEST CODE   139

6 Test hierarchies and organization   141

- 6.1 Having automated builds run automated tests   142

    Anatomy of an automated build   142 ○ Triggering builds and continuous integration   144 ○ Automated build types   144
- 6.2 Mapping out tests based on speed and type   145

    The human factor of separating unit from integration tests   146 ○ The safe green zone   147
- 6.3 Ensuring tests are part of source control   148
- 6.4 Mapping test classes to code under test   148

    Mapping tests to projects   148 ○ Mapping tests to classes   149 ○ Mapping tests to specific methods   150
- 6.5 Building a test API for your application   150

    Using test class inheritance patterns   151 ○ Creating test utility classes and methods   167 ○ Making your API known to developers   168
- 6.6 Summary   169

7 The pillars of good tests   171

- 7.1 Writing trustworthy tests   172

    Deciding when to remove or change tests   172 ○ Avoiding logic in tests   178 ○ Testing only one thing   179 ○ Making tests easy to run   180 ○ Assuring code coverage   180
- 7.2 Writing maintainable tests   181

    Testing private or protected methods   182 ○ Removing duplication   184 ○ Using setup methods in a maintainable manner   188 ○ Enforcing test isolation   191 ○ Avoiding multiple asserts   198 ○

Avoiding testing multiple aspects of the same object 202 ◦ Avoiding overspecification in tests 205

7.3 **Writing readable tests** 209

Naming unit tests 210 ◦ Naming variables 211 ◦ Asserting yourself with meaning 212 ◦ Separating asserts from actions 214 ◦ Setting up and tearing down 214

7.4 **Summary** 215

PART 4 DESIGN AND PROCESS 217

8 Integrating unit testing into the organization 219

8.1 **Steps to becoming an agent of change** 220

Be prepared for the tough questions 220 ◦ Convince insiders: champions and blockers 220 ◦ Identify possible entry points 222

8.2 **Ways to succeed** 223

Guerrilla implementation (bottom-up) 223 ◦ Convincing management (top-down) 224 ◦ Getting an outside champion 224 ◦ Making progress visible 225 ◦ Aiming for specific goals 227 ◦ Realizing that there will be hurdles 228

8.3 **Ways to fail** 229

Lack of a driving force 229 ◦ Lack of political support 229 ◦ Bad implementations and first impressions 230 ◦ Lack of team support 230

8.4 **Tough questions and answers** 231

How much time will this add to the current process? 231 ◦ Will my QA job be at risk because of this? 233 ◦ How do we know this is actually working? 234 ◦ Is there proof that unit testing helps? 234 ◦ Why is the QA department still finding bugs? 235 ◦ We have lots of code without tests: where do we start? 235 ◦ We work in several languages: is unit testing feasible? 236 ◦ What if we develop a combination of software and hardware? 236 ◦ How can we know we don't have bugs in our tests? 236 ◦ I see in my debugger that my code works fine: why do I need tests? 237 ◦ Must we do TDD-style coding? 237

8.5 **Summary** 238

9 Working with legacy code 239

- 9.1 Where do you start adding tests? 240
- 9.2 Choosing a selection strategy 242
  - Pros and cons of the easy-first strategy 242 ○
  - Pros and cons of the hard-first strategy 243
- 9.3 Writing integration tests before refactoring 244
- 9.4 Important tools for legacy code unit testing 246
  - Isolate dependencies easily with Typemock Isolator 246 ○ Find testability problems with Depender 248 ○ Use JMockit for Java legacy code 248 ○ Use Vise while refactoring your Java code 250 ○ Use FitNesse for acceptance tests before you refactor 251 ○ Read Michael Feathers' book on legacy code 253 ○ Use NDepend to investigate your production code 253 ○ Use ReSharper to navigate and refactor production code 253 ○ Detect duplicate code (and bugs) with Simian 254 ○ Detect threading issues with Typemock Racer 254
- 9.5 Summary 254

Appendix A   Design and testability   256

Appendix B   Extra tools and frameworks   268

Index   284

Foreword

When Roy Osherove told me that he was working on a book about unit testing, I was very happy to hear it. The testing meme has been rising in the industry for years, but there has been a relative dearth of material available about unit testing. When I look at my bookshelf, I see books that are about test-driven development specifically and books about testing in general, but until now there has been no comprehensive reference for unit testing—no book that introduces the topic and guides the reader from first steps to widely accepted best practices. The fact that this is true is stunning. Unit testing isn't a new practice. How did we get to this point?

It's almost a cliché to say that we work in a very young industry, but it's true. Mathematicians laid the foundations of our work less than 100 years ago, but we've only had hardware fast enough to exploit their insights for the last 60 years. There was an initial gap between theory and practice in our industry, and we're only now discovering how it has impacted our field.

In the early days, machine cycles were expensive. We ran programs in batches. Programmers had a scheduled time slot, and they had to punch their programs into decks of cards and walk them to the machine room. If your program wasn't right, you lost your time, so you desk-checked your program with pencil and paper, mentally working out all of the scenarios, all of the edge cases. I doubt the notion of automated unit testing was even imaginable. Why use the machine for testing when you could use it to solve the problems it was meant to solve? Scarcity kept us in the dark.

Later, machines became faster and we became intoxicated with interactive computing. We could just type in code and change it on a whim. The idea of desk-checking code faded away, and we lost some of the discipline of the early years. We knew programming was hard, but that just meant that we had to spend more time at the computer, changing lines and symbols until we found the magical incantation that worked.

We went from scarcity to surplus and missed the middle ground, but now we're regaining it. Automated unit testing marries the discipline of desk-checking with a newfound appreciation for the computer as a development resource. We can write automated tests, in the language we develop in, to check our work—not just once, but as often as we're able to run them. I don't think there is any other practice that's quite as powerful in software development.

As I write this, in 2009, I'm happy to see Roy's book come into print. It's a practical guide that will help you get started and also serve as a great reference as you go about your testing tasks. *The Art of Unit Testing* isn't a book about idealized scenarios. It teaches you how to test code as it exists in the field, how to take advantage of widely used frameworks, and, most importantly, how to write code that's far easier to test.

The Art of Unit Testing is an important title that should have been written years ago, but we weren't ready then. We are ready now. Enjoy.

MICHAEL FEATHERS
SENIOR CONSULTANT
OBJECT MENTOR

Preface

One of the biggest failed projects I worked on had unit tests. Or so I thought. I was leading a group of programmers creating a billing application, and we were doing it in a fully test-driven manner—writing the test, then writing the code, seeing the test fail, making the test pass, refactoring, and starting all over again.

The first few months of the project were great. Things were going well, and we had tests that proved that our code worked. But as time went by, requirements changed. We were forced to change our code to fit those new requirements, and when we did, tests broke and had to be fixed. The code still worked, but the tests we wrote were so brittle that any little change in our code broke them, even though the code was working fine. It became a daunting task to change code in a class or method because we also had to fix all the related unit tests.

Worse yet, some tests became unusable because the people who wrote them left the project and no one knew how to maintain the tests, or what they were testing. The names we gave our unit-testing methods were not clear enough, and we had tests relying on other tests. We ended up throwing out most of the tests less than six months into the project.

The project was a miserable failure because we let the tests we wrote do more harm than good. They took more time to maintain and understand than they saved us in the long run, so we stopped using them. I moved on to other projects, where we did a better job writing our unit tests, and we had some great successes using them, saving huge amounts of debugging and integration time. Ever since that first failed project, I've been compiling best practices for unit tests and using them on subsequent projects. I find a few more best practices with every project I work on.

Understanding how to write unit tests—and how to make them maintainable, readable, and trustworthy—is what this book is about, no matter what language or integrated development environment (IDE) you work with. This book covers the basics of writing a unit test, moves on to the basics of interaction testing, and then introduces best practices for writing, managing, and maintaining unit tests in the real world.

Acknowledgments

A big thank you to Michael Stephens and Nermina Miller at Manning, who were patient with me every step of the long way in writing this book.

Thank you Jim Newkirk, Michael Feathers, Gerard Meszaros, and many others, who provided me with inspiration and the ideas that made this book what it is. And a special thank you to Michael for agreeing to write the foreword to the book.

The following reviewers read the manuscript at various stages during its development. I'd like to thank them for providing valuable feedback: Svetlana Christopher, Wendy Friedlander, Jay Flowers, Jean-Paul S. Boodhoo, Armand du Plessis, James Kovacs, Carlo Bottiglieri, Ken DeLong, Dusty Jewett, Lester Lobo, Alessandro Gallo, Gabor Paller, Eric Raymond, David Laribee, Christian Siegers, Phil Hanna, Josh Cronemeyer, Mark Seemann, Francesco Goggi, Franco Lambardo, Dave Nicolette, and Mohammad Azam. Thanks also to Rod Coffin, who did a technical proofread of the final manuscript shortly before it went to press.

A final word of thanks to the early readers of the book in Manning's Early Access Program for their comments in the online forum. You helped shape the book.

About this book

How to use this book

If you've never written unit tests before, this book is best read from start to finish so you get the full picture. If you already have experience, you should feel comfortable jumping into the chapters as you see fit.

Who should read this book

The book is for anyone who writes code and is interested in learning best practices for unit testing. All the examples are written in C# using Visual Studio 2008, so .NET developers will find the examples particularly useful. But the lessons I teach apply equally to most, if not all, statically typed object-oriented languages (VB.NET, Java, and C++, to name a few). If you're a developer, team lead, QA engineer (who writes code), or novice programmer, this book should suit you well.

Roadmap

The book is divided into four parts.

Part 1 takes you from zero to sixty in writing unit tests. Chapters 1 and 2 cover the basics, such as how to use a testing framework (NUnit), and introduce the basic automated test attributes, such as [SetUp] and [Tear-Down]. They also introduce the ideas of asserts, ignoring tests, and state-based testing.

Part 2 discusses advanced techniques for breaking dependencies: mock objects, stubs, mock frameworks, and patterns for refactoring your code to use them. Chapter 3 introduces the idea of stubs and shows how to manually create and use them. Chapter 4 introduces interaction testing with handwritten mock objects. Chapter 5 merges these two concepts and shows how isolation (mock) frameworks combine these two ideas and allow them to be automated.

Part 3 talks about ways to organize test code, patterns for running and refactoring its structure, and best practices when writing tests. Chapter 6 discusses test hierarchies, how to use test infrastructure APIs, and how to combine tests in the automated build process. Chapter 7 discusses best practices in unit testing for creating maintainable, readable, and trustworthy tests.

Part 4 talks about how to implement change in an organization and how to work on existing code. Chapter 8 discusses problems and solutions you would encounter when trying to introduce unit testing into an organization. It also identifies and answers some questions you might be asked. Chapter 9 talks about introducing unit testing into existing code. It identifies a couple of ways to determine where to begin testing and discusses some tools for testing untestable code.

Finally, there are two appendixes. Appendix A discusses the loaded topic of designing for testability and the other alternatives that exist today. Appendix B has a list of tools you might find useful in your testing efforts.

Code conventions and downloads

You can download the source code for this book from the book's site at www.ArtOfUnitTesting.com, as well as from the publisher's website at www.manning.com/TheArtofUnitTesting.

All source code in listings or in the text is in a `fixed-width font like this` to separate it from ordinary text. In listings, **bold code** indicates code that has changed from the previous example, or that will change in the next example.

Code annotations accompany some of the listings, highlighting important concepts. In some cases, numbered bullets link to explanations that follow in the text.

Software requirements

To use the code in this book, you need at least Visual Studio C# Express (which is free), or a more advanced version of it (Professional or Team Suite, for example). You'll also need NUnit (an open source and free framework) and other tools that will be referenced where they're relevant. All the tools mentioned are either free, open source, or have trial versions you can use freely as you read this book.

Author Online

The purchase of *The Art of Unit Testing* includes free access to a private forum run by Manning Publications where you can make comments about the book, ask technical questions, and receive help from the authors and other users. To access and subscribe to the forum, point your browser to www.manning.com/TheArtofUnitTesting. This page provides information on how to get on the forum once you are registered, what kind of help is available, and the rules of conduct in the forum.

Manning's commitment to our readers is to provide a venue where a meaningful dialogue between individual readers and between readers and the author can take place. It's not a commitment to any specific amount of participation on the part of the author, whose contribution to the book's forum remains voluntary (and unpaid). We suggest you try asking him some challenging questions, lest his interest stray!

The Author Online forum and the archives of previous discussions will be accessible from the publisher's website as long as the book is in print.

About the cover illustration

The figure on the cover of *The Art of Unit Testing* is a "Japonais en Costume de Cérémonie," a Japanese man in ceremonial dress. The illustration is taken from James Prichard's *Natural History of Man*, a book of hand-colored lithographs published in England in 1847. It was found by our cover designer in an antique shop in San Francisco.

Prichard began the research for his study of the natives of the world in 1813. By the time his work was published 34 years later, he had gathered much of the available research about various peoples and nations, and his work became an important foundation for modern ethnological science. Included in Prichard's history were portraits of different human races and tribes in their native dress, taken from original drawings of many artists, most based on first-hand studies.

The lithographs from Prichard's collection, like the other illustrations that appear on our covers, bring to life the richness and variety of dress and tribal customs of two centuries ago. Dress codes have changed since then, and the diversity by region, so rich at the time, has faded away. It is now often hard to tell the inhabitant of one continent from another, not to mention a country or region. Perhaps, trying to view it optimistically, we have traded a cultural and visual diversity for a more varied personal life. Or a more varied and interesting intellectual and technical life.

We at Manning celebrate the inventiveness, the initiative, and, yes, the fun of the computer business with book covers based on the rich diversity of regional life of long ago—brought back to life by picture collections such as Prichard's.

Part 1

Getting started

This part of the book covers the basics of unit testing.

In chapter 1, we'll define what "good" unit testing means and compare it with integration testing, and we'll take a brief look at test-driven development and its role in relation to unit testing.

Then, in chapter 2, we'll take a stab at writing our first unit test using NUnit. We'll get to know NUnit's basic API, how to assert things, and how to run the test in the NUnit test runner.

1
The basics of unit testing

This chapter covers
- *Defining unit testing and integration testing*
- *Exploring a simple unit-testing example*
- *Exploring text-driven development*

There's always a first step: the first time you wrote a program, the first time you failed a project, and the first time you succeeded in what you were trying to accomplish. You never forget your first time, and I hope you won't forget your first tests. You may have already written some tests, and you may even remember them as being bad, awkward, slow, or unmaintainable. (Most people do.) On the other hand, you may have had a great first experience with unit tests, and you're reading this to see what more you might be missing.

This chapter will first analyze the "classic" definition of a unit test and compare it to the concept of integration testing. This distinction is confusing to many. Then we'll look at the pros and cons of each approach and develop a better definition of a "good" unit test. We'll finish up with a look at test-driven development, because it's often associated with unit testing. Throughout the chapter, we'll also touch on various concepts that are explained more thoroughly elsewhere in the book.

Let's begin by defining what a unit test should be.

1.1 Unit testing—the classic definition

Unit testing isn't a new concept in software development. It's been floating around since the early days of the Smalltalk programming language in the 1970s, and it proves itself time and time again as one of the best ways a developer can improve code quality while gaining a deeper understanding of the functional requirements of a class or method.

Kent Beck introduced the concept of unit testing in Smalltalk, and it has carried on into many other programming languages, making unit testing an extremely useful practice in software programming. Before we get too far, we need to define unit testing better. Here's the classic definition, from Wikipedia.

DEFINITION A *unit test* is a piece of a code (usually a method) that invokes another piece of code and checks the correctness of some assumptions afterward. If the assumptions turn out to be wrong, the unit test has failed. A "unit" is a method or function.

Unit testing will be performed against a system under test (SUT).

DEFINITION *SUT* stands for *system under test*, and some people like to use *CUT* (*class under test* or *code under test*). When we test something, we refer to the thing we're testing as the SUT.

This classic definition of a unit test, although technically correct, is hardly enough to enable us to better ourselves as developers. Chances are you already know this and are getting bored reading this definition again, because it appears in any book or website that discusses unit testing. Don't worry. In this book, we'll go beyond the classic definition of unit testing by addressing maintainability, readability, correctness, and more. But this familiar definition, precisely because it is familiar, gives us a shared base from which to extend the idea of a unit test.

No matter what programming language you're using, one of the most difficult aspects of defining a unit test is defining what's meant by a "good" one.

1.1.1 The importance of writing "good" unit tests

Most people who try to unit-test their code either give up at some point or don't actually perform unit tests. Instead, they either rely on system and integration tests to be performed much later in the product lifecycle or they resort to manually testing the code via custom test applications or by using the end product they're developing to invoke their code.

There's no point in writing a bad unit test, unless you're learning how to write a good one and these are your first steps into this field. If you're going to write a unit test badly without realizing it, you may as well not write it at all, and save yourself the trouble it will cause down the road with maintainability and time schedules. By defining what a good unit test is, we can make sure we don't start off with the wrong notion of what we're trying to write.

To succeed in this delicate art of unit testing, it's essential that you not only have a *technical definition* of what unit tests are, but that you describe the *properties* of a good unit test. To understand what a good unit test is, we need to look at what developers do when they're testing something.

How do you make sure that the code works today?

1.1.2 We've all written unit tests (sort of)

You may be surprised to learn this, but you've already implemented some types of unit testing on your own. Have you ever met a developer who has not tested his code before handing it over? Well, neither have I.

You might have used a console application that called the various methods of a class or component, or perhaps some specially created WinForm or WebForm UI (user interface) that checked the functionality of that class or component, or maybe even manual tests run by performing various actions within the real application's UI. The end result is that you've made certain, to a degree, that the code works well enough to pass it on to someone else.

Figure 1.1 shows how most developers test their code. The UI may change, but the pattern is usually the same: using a manual external tool to check something repeatedly, or running the application in full and checking its behavior manually.

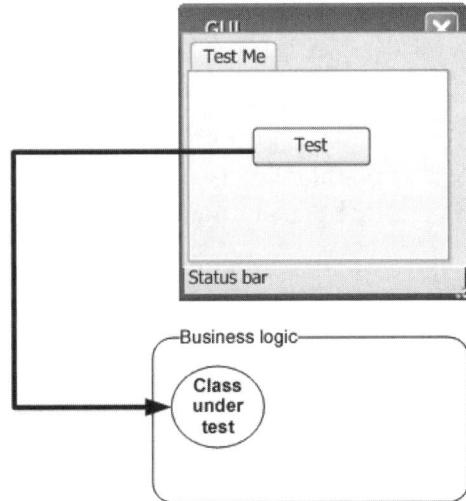

Figure 1.1 In classic testing, developers use a GUI (graphical user interface) to trigger an action on the class they want to test. Then they check the results.

These tests may have been useful, and they may come close to the classic definition of a unit test, but they're far from how we'll define a *good unit test* in this book. That brings us to the first and most important question a developer has to face when defining the qualities of a good unit test: what is a unit test, and what is not.

1.2 Properties of a good unit test

A unit test *should* have the following properties:

- It should be automated and repeatable.
- It should be easy to implement.
- Once it's written, it should remain for future use.
- Anyone should be able to run it.
- It should run at the push of a button.
- It should run quickly.

Many people confuse the act of testing their software with the concept of a unit test. To start off, ask yourself the following questions about the tests you've written up to now:

- Can I run and get results from a unit test I wrote two weeks or months or years ago?

- Can any member of my team run and get the results from unit tests I wrote two months ago?
- Can I run all the unit tests I've written in no more than a few minutes?
- Can I run all the unit tests I've written at the push of a button?
- Can I write a basic unit test in no more than a few minutes?

If you've answered "no" to any of these questions, there's a high probability that what you're implementing isn't a unit test. It's definitely *some* kind of test, and it's as important as a unit test, but it has drawbacks compared to tests that would let you answer "yes" to all of those questions.

"What was I doing until now?" you might ask. You've done *integration testing*.

1.3 Integration tests

What happens when your car breaks down? How do you learn what the problem is, let alone fix it? An engine consists of many parts working together, each relying on the others to help produce the final result: a moving car. If the car stops moving, the fault could be with any of these parts, or more than one. It's the integration of those parts that makes the car move. You could think of the car's movement as the ultimate integration test of these parts. If the test fails, all the parts fail together; if it succeeds, the parts all succeed.

The same thing happens in software. The way most developers test their functionality is through the final functionality of the user interface. Clicking some button triggers a series of events—various classes and components working together to produce the final result. If the test fails, all of these software components fail as a team, and it can be difficult to figure out what caused the failure of the overall operation. (See figure 1.2.)

As defined in *The Complete Guide to Software Testing*, by Bill Hetzel, integration testing is "an orderly progression of testing in which software and/or hardware elements *are combined and tested* until the entire system has been integrated." That definition of integration testing falls

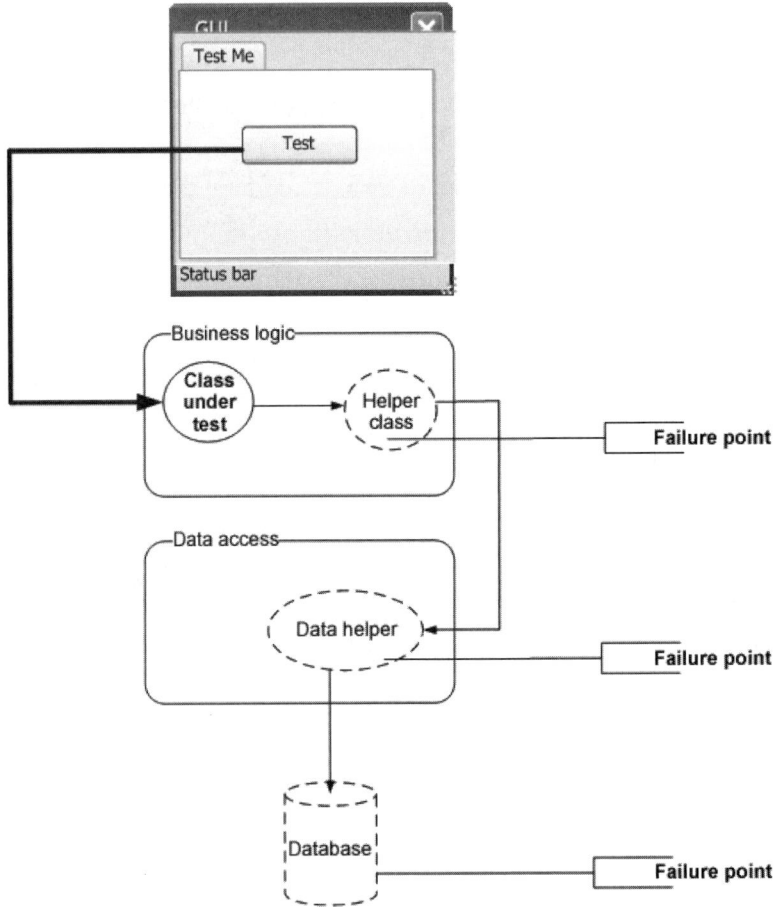

Figure 1.2 You can have many failure points in an integration test. All the units have to work together, and each of them could malfunction, making it harder to find the source of the bug.

a bit short of what many people do all the time, not as part of a system integration test, but as part of development and unit tests.

Here's a better definition of integration testing.

DEFINITION   *Integration testing* means testing two or more dependent software modules as a group.

To summarize: an integration test exercises many units of code that work together to evaluate one or more expected results from the software, whereas a unit test usually exercises and tests only a single unit in isolation.

The questions from the beginning of section 1.2 can help you recognize some of the drawbacks of integration testing. Let's look at them and try to define the qualities we're looking for in a good unit test.

1.3.1 Drawbacks of integration tests compared to automated unit tests

Let's apply the questions from section 1.2 to integration tests, and consider what we want to achieve with real-world unit tests:

- Can I run and get results from the test I wrote two weeks or months or years ago?

  If you can't do that, how would you know whether you broke a feature that you created two weeks ago? Code changes regularly during the life of an application, and if you can't (or won't) run tests for all the previous working features after changing your code, you just might break it without knowing. I call this "accidental bugging," and it seems to occur a lot near the end of a software project, when developers are under pressure to fix existing bugs. Sometimes they introduce new bugs inadvertently as they solve the old ones. Wouldn't it be great to know that you broke something within three minutes of breaking it? We'll see how that can be done later in this book.

  Good tests should be easily executed in their original form, not manually.

DEFINITION A *regression* is a feature that used to work and now doesn't.

- Can any member of my team run and get the results from tests I wrote two months ago?

  This goes with the last point but takes it up a notch. You want to make sure that you don't break someone else's code when you change something. Many developers fear changing *legacy code* in older systems for fear of not knowing what other code depends on what they're changing. In essence, they risk changing the system into an unknown state of stability.

Few things are scarier than not knowing whether the application still works, especially when you didn't write that code. If you knew you weren't breaking anything, you'd be much less afraid of taking on code you're less familiar with because you have that safety net of unit tests.

Good tests can be accessed and run by anyone.

> **DEFINITION** *Legacy code* is defined by Wikipedia as "source code that relates to a no-longer supported or manufactured operating system or other computer technology," but many shops refer to any older version of the application currently under maintenance as legacy code. It often refers to code that's hard to work with, hard to test, and usually even hard to read.
>
> A client of mine once defined legacy code in a down-to-earth way: "code that works." Many people like to define legacy code as "code that has no tests." The book *Working Effectively with Legacy Code* by Michael Feathers uses this as an official definition of legacy code, and it's a definition to be considered while reading this book.

- Can I run all the tests in no more than a few minutes?

  If you can't run your tests quickly (seconds are better than minutes), you'll run them less often (daily, or even weekly or monthly in some places). The problem is that, when you change code, you want to get feedback as early as possible to see if you broke something. The more time between running the tests, the more changes you make to the system, and the (many) more places to search for bugs when you find that you broke something.

  Good tests should run *quickly*.

- Can I run all the tests at the push of a button?

  If you can't, it probably means that you have to configure the machine on which the tests will run so that they run correctly (setting connection strings to the database, for example), or that your unit tests aren't fully automated. If you can't fully automate your unit tests, you'll probably avoid running them repeatedly, as will everyone else on your team.

  No one likes to get bogged down with configuring details to run tests just to make sure that the system still works. As developers, we have more important things to do, like writing more features into the system.

Good tests should be easily executed in their original form, not manually.

- Can I write a basic test in no more than a few minutes?

One of the easiest ways to spot an integration test is that it takes time to prepare correctly and to implement, not just to execute. It takes time to figure out how to write it because of all the internal and sometimes external dependencies. (A database may be considered an external dependency.) If you're not automating the test, dependencies are less of a problem, but you're losing all the benefits of an automated test. The harder it is to write a test, the less likely you are to write more tests, or to focus on anything other than the "big stuff" that you're worried about. One of the strengths of unit tests is that they tend to test every little thing that might break, not only the big stuff. People are often surprised at how many bugs they can find in code they thought was simple and bug free.

When you concentrate only on the big tests, the logic *coverage* that your tests have is smaller. Many parts of the core logic in the code aren't tested (even though you may be covering more components), and there may be many bugs that you haven't considered.

Good tests against the system should be easy and quick to write.

From what we've seen so far about what a unit test is not, and what features need to be present for testing to be useful, we can now start to answer the primary question this chapter poses: what is a good unit test?

1.4 Good unit test—a definition

Now that we've covered the important properties that a unit test should have, let's define unit tests once and for all.

DEFINITION A *unit test* is an automated piece of code that invokes the method or class being tested and then checks some assumptions about the logical behavior of that method or class. A unit test is almost always written using a unit-testing framework. It can be written easily and runs quickly. It's fully automated, trustworthy, readable, and maintainable.

This definition sure looks like a tall order, particularly considering how many developers I've seen implementing unit tests poorly. It makes us take a hard look at the way we, as developers, have implemented testing up until now, compared to how we'd like to implement it. ("Trustworthy, readable, and maintainable" tests are discussed in depth in chapter 7.)

> **DEFINITION** *Logical code* is any piece of code that has some sort of logic in it, small as it may be. It's logical code if it has one or more of the following: an IF statement, a loop, switch or case statements, calculations, or any other type of decision-making code.

Properties (getters/setters in Java) are good examples of code that usually doesn't contain any logic, and so doesn't require testing. But watch out: once you add any check inside the property, you'll want to make sure that logic is being tested.

In the next section, we'll take a look at a simple unit test done entirely in code, without using any unit-testing framework. (We'll look at unit-testing frameworks in chapter 2.)

1.5 A simple unit test example

It's possible to write an automated unit test without using a test framework. In fact, as they have gotten more into the habit of automating their testing, I've seen plenty of developers doing this before discovering test frameworks. In this section, I'll show what writing such a test without a framework can look like, so that you can contrast this with using a framework in chapter 2.

Assume we have a `SimpleParser` class (shown in listing 1.1) that we'd like to test. It has a method named `ParseAndSum` that takes in a string of 0 or more comma-separated numbers. If there are no numbers, it returns 0. If there's a single number, it returns that number as an `int`. If there are multiple numbers, it adds them all up and returns the sum (although, right now, the code can only handle 0 or 1 number).

Listing 1.1 A simple parser class to test

```
public class SimpleParser
    {
        public int ParseAndSum(string numbers)
        {
            if(numbers.Length==0)
            {
                return 0;
            }
            if(!numbers.Contains(","))
            {
                return int.Parse(numbers);
            }
            else
            {
                throw new InvalidOperationException(
"I can only handle 0 or 1 numbers for now!");
            }
        }
    }
```

We can create a simple console application project that has a reference to the assembly containing this class, and we can write a `SimpleParserTests` method as shown in listing 1.2. The test method invokes the *production class* (the class to be tested) and then checks the returned value. If it's not what's expected, it writes to the console. It also catches any exception and writes it to the console.

Listing 1.2 A simple coded method that tests the `SimpleParser` class

```
class SimpleParserTests
    {
        public static void TestReturnsZeroWhenEmptyString()
        {
            try
            {
                SimpleParser p = new SimpleParser();
                int result = p.ParseAndSum(string.Empty);
                if(result!=0)
                {
```

```
            Console.WriteLine(
            @"***SimpleParserTests.TestReturnsZeroWhenEmptyString:
            -------
            Parse and sum should have returned 0 on an empty string");
                }
            }
            catch (Exception e)
            {
                Console.WriteLine(e);
            }
        }
    }
```

Next, we can invoke the tests we've written by using a simple `Main` method run inside a console application in this project, as seen in listing 1.3. The `Main` method is used here as a simple test runner, which invokes the tests one by one, letting them write out to the console. Because it's an executable, this can be run without human intervention (assuming the tests don't pop up any interactive user dialogs).

Listing 1.3 Running coded tests via a simple console application

```
public static void Main(string[] args)
        {
            try
            {
                SimpleParserTests.TestReturnsZeroWhenEmptyString();
            }
            catch (Exception e)
            {
                Console.WriteLine(e);
            }
        }
```

It's the test method's responsibility to catch any exceptions that occur and write them to the console, so that they don't interfere with the running of subsequent methods. We can then add more method calls into the `Main` method as we add more and more tests to the project. Each test is responsible for writing the problem output (if there's a problem) to the console screen.

Obviously, this is an ad hoc way of writing such a test. If you were writing multiple tests like this, you might want to have a generic `ShowProblem` method that all tests could use, which would format the errors consistently. You could also add special helper methods that would help check on various things like null objects, empty strings, and so on, so that you don't need to write the same long lines of code in many tests.

Listing 1.4 shows what this test would look like with a slightly more generic `ShowProblem` method.

Listing 1.4 Using a more generic implementation of the `ShowProblem` method

```
public class TestUtil
    {
        public static void ShowProblem(string test,string message )
        {
            string msg = string.Format(@"
---{0}---
     {1}
--------------------
", test, message);
            Console.WriteLine(msg);
        }
    }

public static void TestReturnsZeroWhenEmptyString()
        {
            //use .NET's reflection API to get the current
                                                    method's name
            // it's possible to hard code this,
            //but it's a useful technique to know
            string testName = MethodBase.GetCurrentMethod().Name;
            try
            {
                SimpleParser p = new SimpleParser();
                int result = p.ParseAndSum(string.Empty);
                if(result!=0)
                {
                //Calling the helper method
                    TestUtil.ShowProblem(testName,
"Parse and sum should have returned 0 on an empty string");
```

```
            }
        }
        catch (Exception e)
        {
            TestUtil.ShowProblem(testName, e.ToString());
        }
    }
```

Unit-testing frameworks can help make helper methods more generic like this, so tests are written more easily. We'll talk about that in chapter 2. But before we get there, I'd like to discuss one important matter: not just *how* you write a unit test, but *when* during the development process you write it. That's where test-driven development comes into play.

1.6 Test-driven development

Once we know how to write structured, maintainable, and solid tests with a unit-testing framework, the next question is when to write the tests. Many people feel that the best time to write unit tests for software is after the software has been written, but a growing number of people prefer writing unit tests *before* the production code is written. This approach is called test-first or test-driven development (TDD).

> **NOTE** There are many different views on exactly what test-driven development means. Some say it's test-first development, and some say it means you have a lot of tests. Some say it's a way of designing, and others feel it could be a way to drive your code's behavior with only some design. For a more complete look at the different views people have of TDD, see "The various meanings of TDD" on my blog (http://weblogs.asp.net/rosherove/archive/2007/10/08/the-various-meanings-of-tdd.aspx). In this book, TDD means test-first development, with design taking a secondary role in the technique (which isn't discussed in this book).

Figures 1.3 and 1.4 show the differences between traditional coding and test-driven development.

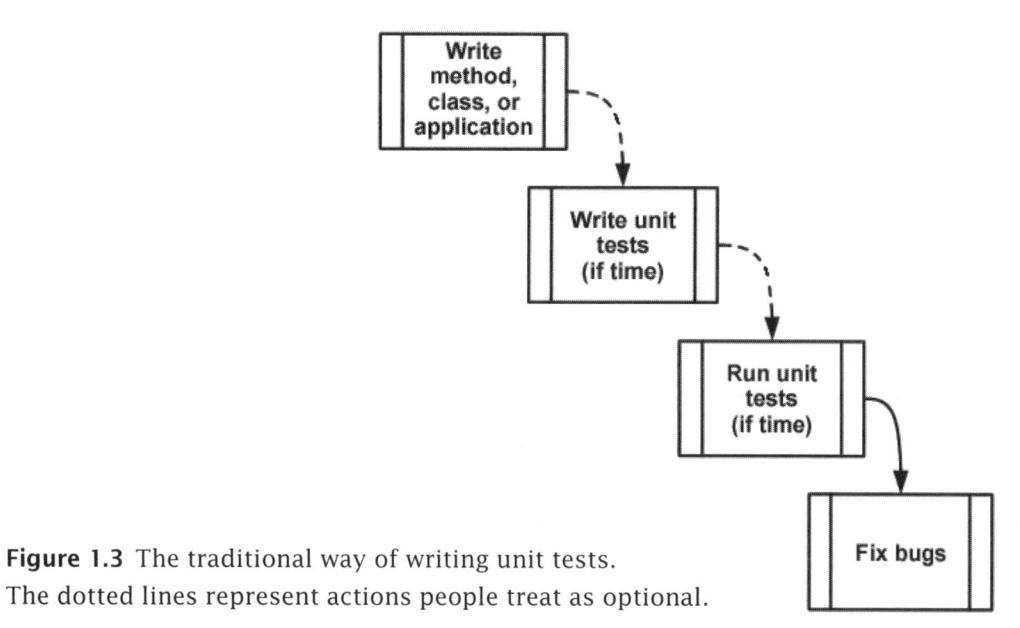

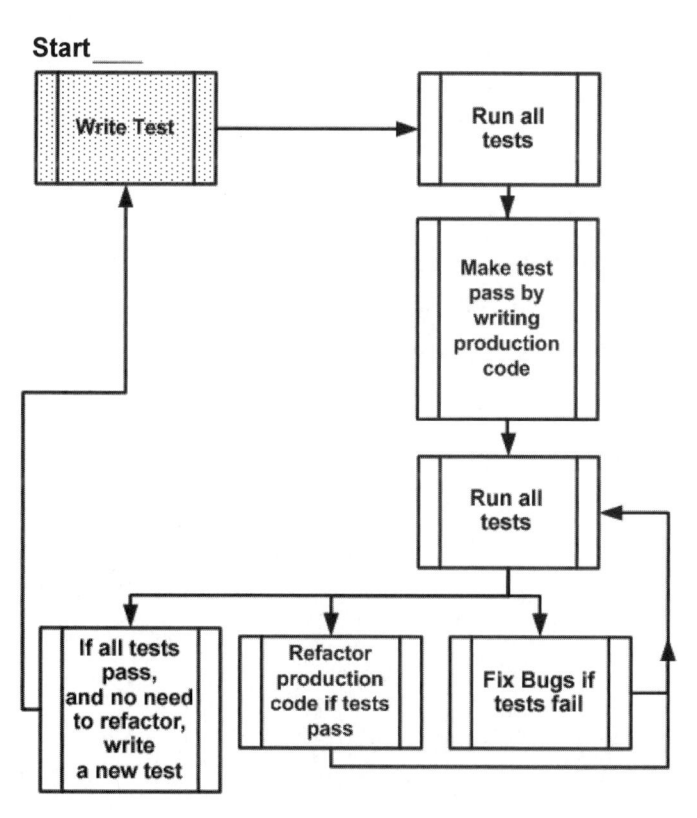

Figure 1.3 The traditional way of writing unit tests. The dotted lines represent actions people treat as optional.

Figure 1.4 Test-driven development—a bird's-eye view. Notice the spiral nature of the process: write test, write code, refactor, write next test. It shows the incremental nature of TDD: small steps lead to a quality end result.

Test-driven development is different from traditional development, as figure 1.4 shows. You begin by writing a test that fails; then you move on to creating the production code, seeing the test pass, and continuing on to either refactor your code or to create another failing test.

This book focuses on the technique of writing good unit tests, rather than on test-driven development, but I'm a big fan of doing test-driven development. I've written several major applications and frameworks using TDD, have managed teams that utilize it, and have taught more than a hundred courses and workshops on TDD and unit-testing techniques. Throughout my career, I've found TDD to be helpful in creating quality code, quality tests, and better designs for the code I was writing. I am convinced that it can work to your benefit, but it's not without a price (time to learn, time to implement, and more). It's definitely worth the admission price, though.

It's important to realize that TDD doesn't ensure project success or tests that are robust or maintainable. It's quite easy to get caught up in the technique of TDD and not pay attention to the way unit tests are written: their naming, how maintainable or readable they are, and whether they test the right things or might have bugs. That's why I'm writing this book.

The technique of test-driven development is quite simple:

1 *Write a failing test to prove code or functionality is missing from the end product.*

    The test is written *as if* the production code were already working, so the test failing means there's a bug in the production code. For example, if I wanted to add a new feature to a calculator class that remembers the `LastSum` value, I would write a test that verifies that `LastSum` is indeed a number. The test will fail because we haven't implemented that functionality yet.

2 *Make the test pass by writing production code that meets the expectations of your test.*

    It should be written as simply as possible.

3 *Refactor your code.*

    When the test passes, you're free to move on to the next unit test or to *refactor* your code to make it more readable, to remove code duplication, and so on.

Refactoring can be done after writing several tests or after writing each test. It's an important practice, because it ensures your code gets easier to read and maintain, while still passing all of the previously written tests.

DEFINITION   *Refactoring* means changing a piece of code without changing its functionality. If you've ever renamed a method, you've done refactoring. If you've ever split a large method into multiple smaller method calls, you've refactored your code. The code still does the same thing, but it becomes easier to maintain, read, debug, and change.

The preceding steps sound technical, but there's a lot of wisdom behind them. Done correctly, TDD can make your code quality soar, decrease the number of bugs, raise your confidence in the code, shorten the time it takes to find bugs, improve your code's design, and keep your manager happier. If TDD is done incorrectly, it can cause your project schedule to slip, waste your time, lower your motivation, and lower your code quality. It's a double-edged sword, and many people find this out the hard way.

1.7 Summary

In this chapter, we defined a good unit test as one that has these qualities:

- It's an automated piece of code that invokes a different method and then checks some assumptions on the logical behavior of that method or class.
- It's written using a unit-testing framework.
- It can be written easily.
- It runs quickly.
- It can be executed repeatedly by anyone on the development team.

To understand what a *unit* is, we had to figure out what sort of testing we've done until now. We identified that type of testing as integration testing because it tests a set of units that depend on each other.

The difference between unit tests and integration tests is important to recognize. You'll be using that knowledge in your day-to-day life as a developer when deciding where to place your tests, what kind of tests to write when, and which option is better for a specific problem. It will also help you identify how to fix problems with tests that are already causing you headaches.

We also looked at the cons of doing integration testing without a framework behind it: this kind of testing is hard to write and automate, slow to run, and needs configuration. Although you do want to have integration tests in a project, unit tests can provide a lot of value earlier in the process, when bugs are smaller and easier to find, and there's less code to skim through.

Lastly, we talked about test-driven development, how it's different from traditional coding, and what its basic benefits are. TDD helps you make sure that the code coverage of your test code (how much of the code your tests exercise) is very high (close to 100 percent of *logical* code). It helps you make sure that your tests can be trusted by making sure that they fail when the production code isn't there, and that they pass when the production code works. TDD also has many other benefits, such as aiding in design, reducing complexity, and helping you tackle hard problems step by step. But you can't do TDD without knowing how to write good tests.

If you write tests *after* writing the code, you assume the test is OK because it passes, when it could be that you have bugs in your tests. Trust me—finding bugs in your *tests* is one of the most frustrating things you can imagine. It's important that you don't let your tests get to that state, and TDD is one of the best ways I know to keep that possibility close to zero.

In the next chapter, we'll start writing our first unit tests using NUnit, the de facto unit-testing framework for .NET developers.

A first unit test

This chapter covers

- *Exploring unit-testing frameworks in .NET*
- *Writing our first test with NUnit*
- *Working with the NUnit attributes*
- *Understanding indirect state testing*

When I first started writing unit tests with a real unit-testing framework, there was little documentation, and the frameworks I worked with did not have proper examples. (I was mostly coding in VB 5 and 6 at the time.) It was a challenge learning to work with them, and I started out writing rather poor tests. Fortunately, times have changed.

This chapter will get you started writing tests even if you have no idea where to start. It will get you well on your way to writing real-world unit tests with a framework called NUnit—a .NET unit-testing framework. It's my favorite framework in .NET for unit testing because it's easy to use, easy to remember, and has lots of great features.

There are other frameworks in .NET, including some with more features, but NUnit is where I always start. I sometimes then expand to a different framework if the need arises. We'll look at how NUnit works, its syntax, and how to run it and get feedback when the test fails or passes. To accomplish this, I'll introduce a small software project that we'll use throughout the book to explore the testing techniques and best practices.

First, we need to look at what a unit-testing framework is, and at what it enables us to do that we couldn't and wouldn't have done without it.

2.1 Frameworks for unit testing

Consider the advantages an integrated development environment (IDE) gives you as a developer. Unit-testing frameworks offer similar advantages for testing.

To this day, in many IDEs for other environments (such as Unix), the steps involved in getting a final binary output from your code aren't as simple, and may require manually calling other external tools to do parts of this big task. When using a modern IDE like Visual Studio .NET or Eclipse for Java, you do all your coding tasks within that environment, in a structured manner. You write the code, you compile it, you build any resources (like graphics and text) into it, and you create the final binary—all that building and compiling with no more than a couple of keystrokes.

Doing things completely manually would be error-prone and time-consuming, and people would defer doing that as much as possible. These problems are alleviated by tooling. In the same way, unit-testing frameworks help developers write tests more quickly with a set of known APIs, execute those tests automatically, and review the results of those tests easily.

2.1.1 What unit-testing frameworks offer

Up to now, the tests you've done were limited:

- *They were not structured.*

  You had to reinvent the wheel every time you wanted to test a feature. One test might look like a console application, another uses a UI form, and another uses a web form. You don't have that time to spend on testing, and the tests fail the "easy to implement" requirement.

- *They were not repeatable.*

  Neither you nor your team members could run the tests you'd written in the past. That breaks the "repeatedly" requirement and prevents you from finding regression bugs. With a framework, you can more easily and automatically write tests that are repeatable.

- *They were not on all your code.*

    The tests didn't test all the code that matters. That means all the code with logic in it, because each and every one of those could contain a potential bug. (Property getters and setters don't count as logic, unless you have some sort of logic inside them.) If it were easier to write the tests, you'd be more inclined to write more of them, and get better coverage.

In short, what you've been missing is a *framework* for writing, running, and reviewing unit tests and their results. Figure 2.1 shows the areas in software development where a unit-testing framework has influence.

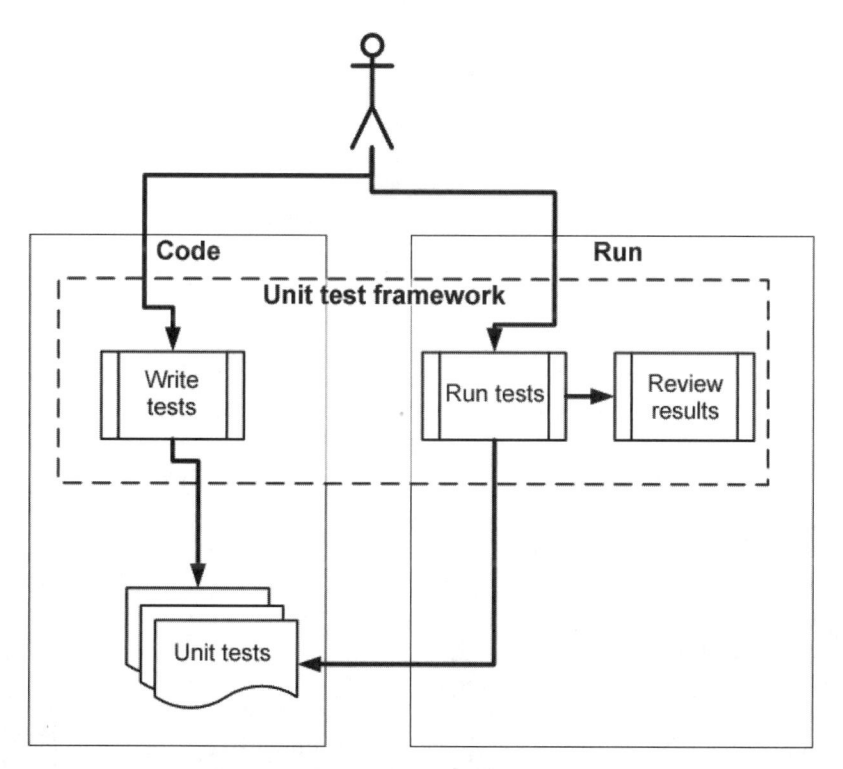

Figure 2.1 Unit tests are written as code, using libraries from the unit-testing framework. Then the tests are run from a separate unit-testing tool, and the results are reviewed (either in the UI or as text) by the developer or an automated build process.

Table 2.1 How unit-testing frameworks help developers write and execute tests, and review results

Unit-testing practice	How the framework helps
Write tests easily and in a structured manner.	Framework supplies the developer with a class library that holds • base classes or interfaces to inherit. • attributes to place in your code to note your tests to run. • assert classes that have special assert methods you invoke to verify your code.
Execute one or all of the unit tests.	Framework provides a test runner (a console or GUI tool) that • identifies tests in your code. • runs tests automatically. • indicates status while running. • can be automated by command line.
Review the results of the test runs.	The test-runners will usually provide information such as • how many tests ran. • how many tests didn't run. • how many tests failed. • which tests failed. • the reason tests failed. • the ASSERT message you wrote. • the code location that failed. • possibly a full stack trace of any exceptions that caused the test to fail, and will let you go to the various method calls inside the call stack.

Unit-testing frameworks are code libraries and modules that help developers unit-test their code, as outlined in table 2.1. They also have another side—running the tests as part of an automated build, which I cover in later chapters.

At the time of this writing, there are more than 150 unit-testing frameworks out there—practically one for every programming language in public use. A good list can be found at http://www.xprogramming.com. Consider that .NET, alone, has at least 9 different unit-testing frameworks; among these, NUnit is the de facto standard.

NOTE Using a unit-testing framework doesn't ensure that the tests we write are *readable*, *maintainable*, or *trustworthy*, or that they cover all the logic we'd like to test. We'll look at how to ensure that our unit tests have these properties in chapter 7 and in various other places throughout this book.

2.1.2 The xUnit frameworks

Collectively, these unit-testing frameworks are called the *xUnit frameworks*, because their names usually start with the first letters of the language for which they were built. You might have CppUnit for C++, JUnit for Java, NUnit for .NET, and HUnit for the Haskell programming language. Not all of them follow these naming guidelines, but most of them do.

In this book, we'll be using NUnit, a .NET unit-testing framework that makes it easy to write tests, run them, and get the results. NUnit started out as a direct port of the ubiquitous JUnit for Java, and has since made tremendous strides in its design and usability, setting it apart from its parent and breathing new life into an ecosystem of test frameworks that's changing more and more. The concepts we'll be looking at will be understandable to Java and C++ developers alike.

2.2 Introducing the LogAn project

The project that we'll use for testing in this book will be simple at first, and will only contain one class. As the book moves along, we'll extend that project with new classes and features. We'll call it the LogAn project (short for "log and notification").

Here's the scenario. Your company has many internal products it uses to monitor its applications at customer sites. All these products write log files and place them in a special directory. The log files are written in a proprietary format that your company has come up with that can't be parsed by any existing third-party tools. You're tasked with building a product, LogAn, that can analyze these log files and find various special cases and events in them. When it finds these cases and events, it should alert the appropriate parties.

In this book, we'll write tests that verify LogAn's parsing, event-recognition, and notification abilities. Before we get started testing our project, though, we'll look at how to write a unit test with NUnit. The first step is installing it.

2.3 First steps with NUnit

As with any new tool, you'll need to install it first. Because NUnit is open source and freely downloadable, this task should be rather simple. Then we'll see how to start writing a test with NUnit, use the various built-in attributes that NUnit ships with, and run our test and get some real results.

2.3.1 Installing NUnit

You can download NUnit from www.NUnit.org or www.NUnit.com. NUnit is free to use and is an open source product, so you can get the source code for NUnit, compile it yourself, and use the source freely within the limits of the open source license. (See the license.txt file in the program directory for license details.)

> **NOTE** At the time of writing, the latest version of NUnit is 2.2.8. The examples in this book should be compatible with most future versions of the framework.

To install NUnit, run the setup program you downloaded. The installer will place a shortcut to the GUI part of the NUnit runner on your desktop, but the main program files should reside in a directory named something like c:\Program Files\NUnit-Net-2.0 2.2.8. If you double-click the NUnit desktop icon, you'll see the unit test runner shown in figure 2.2.

We'll be using this GUI to run our tests shortly.

2.3.2 Loading up the solution

If you have the book's code on your machine, load up the ArtOfUnit-Testing.sln solution from the Code folder inside Visual Studio 2008.

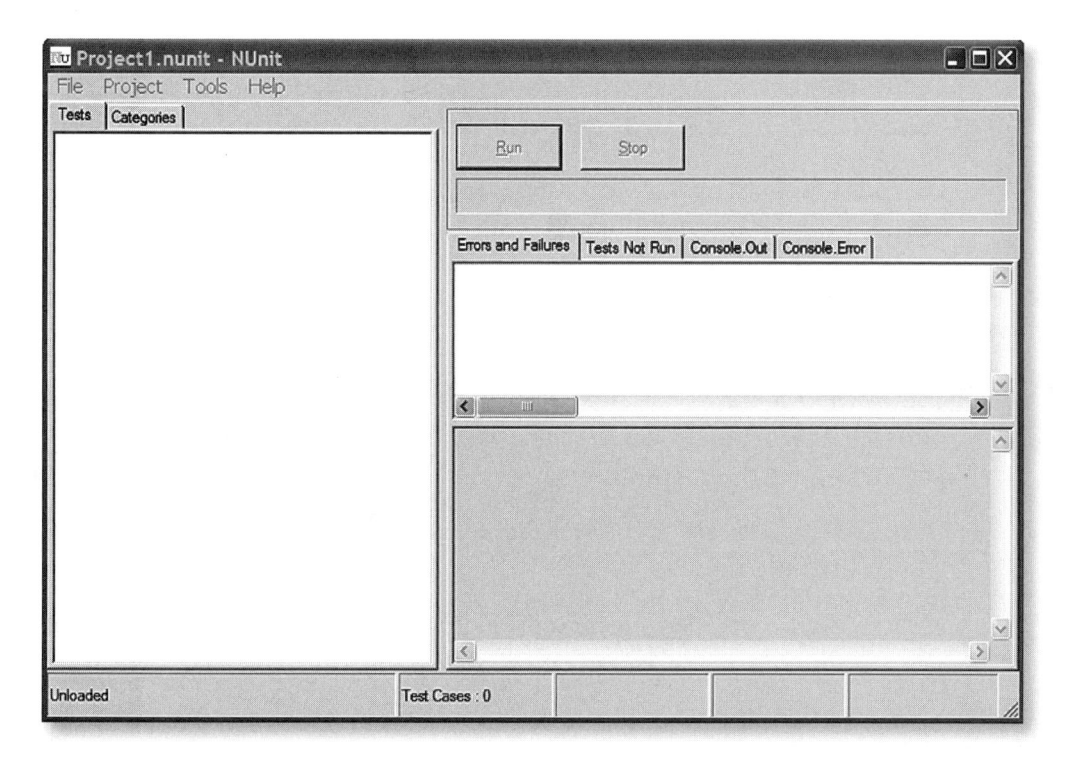

Figure 2.2 The NUnit GUI is divided into three main parts: the tree listing the tests on the left, messages and errors at the top right, and stack trace information at the bottom right.

> **NOTE** The C# Express Edition of Visual Studio 2008 (or above) is fine for use with this book.

We'll begin by testing the following simple class with one method (the unit we're testing) inside it:

```
public class LogAnalyzer
{
    public bool IsValidLogFileName(string fileName)
    {
        if(!fileName.EndsWith(".SLF"))
        {
            return false;
        }
```

```
        return true;
    }
}
```

This method may not seem complicated, but we'll test it to make sure it works. In the real world, you'll want to test any method that contains logic, even if it seems to be simple. Logic can fail, and we want to know when it does. In the following chapters, we'll test more complicated scenarios and logic.

The method looks at the file extension to determine whether a file is a valid log file or not. Our first test will be to send in a valid filename, and make sure the method returns true.

Here are the first steps for writing an automated test for the IsValid-LogFileName method:

1. Add a new class library project to the solution, which will contain your test classes.
2. To that library, add a new class that will hold your test methods.
3. Add a new method to the preceding test case named IsValid-LogFileName.

We'll touch more on test-naming and arrangement standards later in the book, but the basic rules are listed in table 2.2.

Table 2.2 Basic rules for placing and naming tests

Object to be tested	Object to create on the testing side
Project	Create a test project named [ProjectUnderTest].Tests.
Class	For each class, create at least one class with the name [ClassName]Tests.
Method	For each method, create at least one test method with the following name: [MethodName]_[StateUnderTest]_[ExpectedBehavior].

For example, the name for our LogAn test project would be AOUT.Logan.Tests (with AOUT standing for Art of Unit Testing). The name for the `LogAnalyzer` test class would be `LogAnalyzerTests`.

Here are the three parts of the test method name:

- `MethodName`—The name of the method you're testing
- `StateUnderTest`—The conditions used to produce the expected behavior
- `ExpectedBehavior`—What you expect the tested method to do under the specified conditions

In our test of the `IsValidLogFileName` method, the state or condition is that we're sending the method a valid filename, and the expected behavior is that the method will return a `true` value. Our test method name might be `IsValidFileName_validFile_ReturnsTrue()`.

We haven't used the NUnit test framework yet, but we're close. We still need to add a reference to the project under test for the new testing project. Do this by right-clicking on the test project and selecting Add Reference. Then select the Projects tab and select the LogAn project.

The next thing to learn is how to mark the test method to be loaded and run by NUnit automatically.

2.3.3 Using the NUnit attributes in your code

NUnit uses an attribute scheme to recognize and load tests. Just like bookmarks in a book, these attributes help the framework identify the important parts in the assembly that it loads, and which parts are tests that need to be invoked.

NUnit provides an assembly that contains these special attributes. You just need to add a reference in your test project (not in your production code!) to the NUnit.Framework assembly. You can find it under the .NET tab in the Add Reference dialog box. Type `Nunit` and you'll see several assemblies starting with that name; add nunit.framework.

NUnit needs at least two attributes to know what to run:

- `[TestFixture]` —The `[TestFixture]` attribute denotes a class that holds automated NUnit tests. (If you replace the word "Fixture" with "Class", it makes much more sense.) Put this attribute on your new `LogAnalyzerTests` class.
- `[Test]` —The `[Test]` attribute can be put on a method to denote it as an automated test to be invoked. Put this attribute on your new test method.

When you're done, your test code should look like this:

```
[TestFixture]
 public class LogAnalyzerTests
 {
    [Test]
    public void IsValidFileName_validFile_ReturnsTrue()
    {

    }
 }
```

TIP NUnit requires test methods to be void and accept no parameters.

At this point, you've marked your class and a method to be run. Now, whatever code you put inside your test method will be invoked by NUnit whenever you want.

2.4 Writing our first test

How do we test our code? A unit test usually comprises three main actions:

- *Arrange* objects, creating and setting them up as necessary.
- *Act* on an object.
- *Assert* that something is as expected.

Here's a simple piece of code that does all three, with the assert part performed by the NUnit framework's `Assert` class:

```
[Test]
 public void IsValidFileName_validFile_ReturnsTrue()
 {
     //arrange
     LogAnalyzer analyzer = new LogAnalyzer();

     //act
     bool result = analyzer.IsValidLogFileName("whatever.slf");

     //assert
     Assert.IsTrue(result, "filename should be valid!");
 }
```

Before we go on, you'll need to know a little more about the `Assert` class, because it's an important part of writing unit tests.

2.4.1 The Assert class

The `Assert` class has static methods and is located in the NUnit.Framework namespace. It's the bridge between your code and the NUnit framework, and its purpose is to declare that a specific assumption is supposed to exist. If the arguments that are passed into the `Assert` class turn out to be different than what we're asserting, NUnit will realize the test has failed and will alert us. We can optionally tell the `Assert` class what message to alert us with if the assertion fails.

The `Assert` class has many methods, with the main one being `Assert.IsTrue (some Boolean expression)`, which verifies a Boolean condition. But there are many other methods.

This one verifies that an expected object or value is the same as the actual one:

`Assert.AreEqual(expectedObject, actualObject, message);`

Here's an example:

`Assert.AreEqual(2, 1+1, "Math is broken");`

This one verifies that the two arguments reference the same object:

`Assert.AreSame(expectedObject, actualObject, message);`

Here's an example:

```
Assert.AreSame(int.Parse("1"),int.Parse("1"),
   "this test should fail").
```

`Assert` is simple to learn, use, and remember.

Now that we've covered the basics of the API, let's run a test

2.4.2 Running our first test with NUnit

It's time to run our first test and see if it passes or not. To do that, we need to have a build assembly (a .dll file in this case) that we can give to NUnit to inspect. After you build the project, locate the path to the assembly file that was built.

Then, load up the NUnit GUI and select File > Open. Enter the name of your test's assembly. You'll see your single test and the class and namespace hierarchy of your project on the left, as shown in figure 2.3. Click the Run button to run your tests. The tests are automatically grouped by namespace (assembly, typename) so you can pick and choose to run only by specific types or namespaces. (You'll usually want to run all of the tests to get better feedback on failures.)

As you can see, we have a failing test, which might suggest that there's a bug in the code. It's time to fix the code and see the test pass.

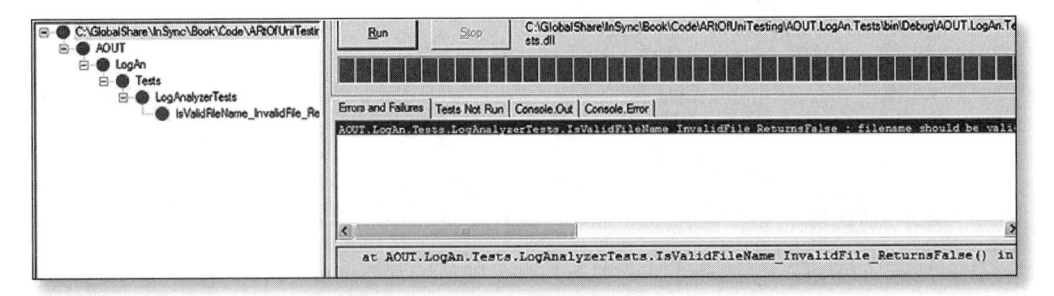

Figure 2.3 NUnit test failures are shown in three places: the test hierarchy on the left becomes red, the progress bar at the top becomes red, and any errors are shown on the right.

2.4.3 Fixing our code and passing the test

A quick look through the code reveals that we're testing for an uppercase filename extension, and our test is sending in a lowercase filename extension, which makes our code return `false` instead of `true`. Our test could also have failed if our code threw an exception of any kind. An unhandled exception in your code is considered a failure, unless your code is *supposed* to throw an exception under specific circumstances. (We'll see how to test for deliberate exceptions in section 2.5.2.)

If we fix the `if` statement in the production code to look like this, we can make the test pass:

```
if(!fileName.ToLower().EndsWith(".slf"))
```

But this is a sign that the name of our test may need changing, and that we need another test to make sure that sending in an uppercase extension works. (We know that it works now, but who's to say that some programmer working on this feature won't break it in the future?) A better name for our current test might be `IsValidFileName_validFileLowerCased_ReturnsTrue()`.

If you rebuild the solution now, you'll find that NUnit's GUI can detect that the assembly has changed, and it will automatically reload the assembly in the GUI. If you rerun the tests, you'll see that the test passes with flying (green) colors.

2.4.4 From red to green

NUnit's GUI is built with a simple idea in mind: all the tests should pass in order to get the "green" light to go ahead. If even one of the tests fails, you'll see a red light on the top progress bar to let you know that something isn't right with the system (or your tests).

The red-green concept is prevalent throughout the unit-testing world, and especially in test-driven development (TDD). Its mantra is "Red-Green-Refactor," meaning that you start with a failing test, then pass it, and then make your code readable and more maintainable.

2.5 More NUnit attributes

Now that you've seen how easy it is to create unit tests that run automatically, we'll look at how to set up the initial state for each test, and how to remove any garbage that's left by your test.

A unit test has specific points in its lifecycle that you'll want to have control over. Running the test is only one of them, and there are special setup methods that run before each test run, as we'll see in the next section.

2.5.1 Setup and teardown

For unit tests, it's important that any leftover data or instances from previous tests are destroyed and that the state for the new test is recreated as if no tests have been run before. If you have leftover state from a previous test, you might find that your test fails, but only if it's run after a different test, and it passes other times. Locating that kind of dependency bug between tests is difficult and time-consuming, and I don't recommend it to anyone. Having tests that are totally independent of each other is one of the best practices I will be covering in part 2 of this book.

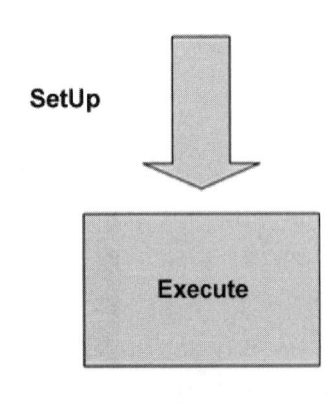

In NUnit, there are special attributes that allow easier control of setting up and clearing out state before and after tests. These are the [SetUp] and [TearDown] action attributes. Figure 2.4 shows the process of running a test with setup and teardown actions.

For now, make sure that each test you write uses a new instance of the class under test, so that no leftover state will mess up your tests.

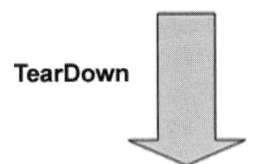

Figure 2.4 NUnit performs setup and teardown actions before each and every test method.

More NUnit attributes

We can take control of what happens in the setup and teardown steps by using two NUnit attributes:

- [SetUp]—This attribute can be put on a method, just like a [Test] attribute, and it causes NUnit to run that setup method each time it runs any of the tests in your class.
- [TearDown]—This attribute denotes a method to be executed once after each test in your class has executed.

Listing 2.1 shows how we can use the [SetUp] and [TearDown] attributes to make sure that each test receives a new instance of LogAnalyzer, while also saving some repetitive typing.

Listing 2.1 Using [SetUp] and [TearDown] attributes

```
using NUnit.Framework;

namespace AOUT.LogAn.Tests
{
   [TestFixture]
    public class LogAnalyzerTests
    {
        private LogAnalyzer m_analyzer=null;

        [SetUp]
        public void Setup()
        {
            m_analyzer = new LogAnalyzer();
        }

        [Test]
         public void IsValidFileName_validFileLowerCased_ReturnsTrue()
            {
              bool result =
   m_analyzer.IsValidLogFileName("whatever.slf");

              Assert.IsTrue(result, "filename should be valid!");
            }

   [Test]
    public void IsValidFileName_validFileUpperCased_ReturnsTrue()
     {
```

```
            bool result = 
    m_analyzer.IsValidLogFileName("whatever.SLF");

            Assert.IsTrue(result, "filename should be valid!");
        }

        [TearDown]
         public void TearDown()
         {
            m_analyzer = null;
         }
    }
}
```

You can think of the setup and teardown methods as constructors and destructors for the tests in your class. You can only have one of each in any test class, and each one will be performed once for each test in your class. In listing 2.1 we have two unit tests, so the execution path for NUnit will be something like that shown in figure 2.5.

NUnit contains several other attributes to help with setup and cleanup of state. For example, [TestFixtureSetUp] and [TestFixtureTearDown] allow setting up state once before all the tests in a specific *class* run, and once after all the tests have been run (once per test fixture). This is useful when setting up or cleaning up takes a long time, and you want to only do it once per fixture. You'll need to be cautious about using these attributes. You may find that you're sharing state between tests if you're not careful.

Next, we'll look at how we can test that an exception is thrown by our code when it should be.

2.5.2 Checking for expected exceptions

One common testing scenario is making sure that the correct exception is thrown from the tested method when it should be.

Let's assume that our method should throw an ArgumentException when we send in an empty filename. If our code doesn't throw an exception, it means our test should fail. We're going to test the method logic in listing 2.2.

More NUnit attributes   37

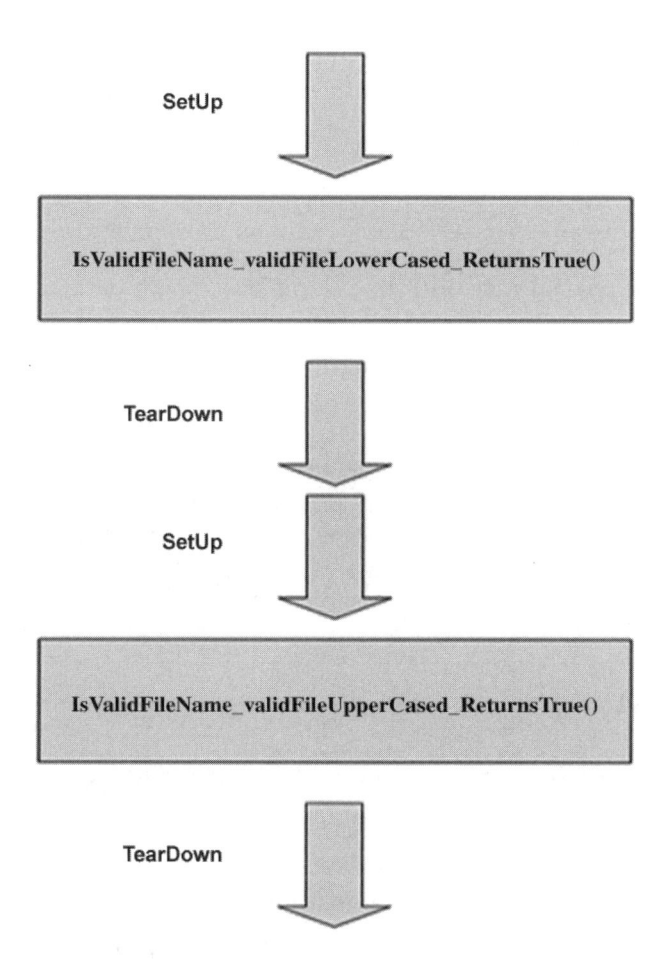

```
         SetUp
           ↓
┌──────────────────────────────────────┐
│ IsValidFileName_validFileLowerCased_ReturnsTrue() │
└──────────────────────────────────────┘

        TearDown
           ↓

         SetUp
           ↓
┌──────────────────────────────────────┐
│ IsValidFileName_validFileUpperCased_ReturnsTrue() │
└──────────────────────────────────────┘

        TearDown
           ↓
```

Figure 2.5 How NUnit calls `SetUp` and `TearDown` with multiple unit tests in the same class: each test is preceded by running `SetUp` and followed by a `TearDown` method run.

Listing 2.2 The `LogAnalyzer` filename-validation logic we'd like to test

```
public class LogAnalyzer
    {
        public bool IsValidLogFileName(string fileName)
        {
            if(String.IsNullOrEmpty(fileName))
            {
                throw new ArgumentException("No filename provided!");
            }
            if(!fileName.EndsWith(".SLF"))
            {
```

```
            return false;
        }
        return true;
    }
}
```

There's a special attribute in NUnit that helps us test exceptions: the `[ExpectedException]` attribute. Here's what a test that checks for the appearance of an exception might look like:

```
[Test]
[ExpectedException(typeof(ArgumentException),
  ExpectedMessage ="No filename provided!")]
    public void IsValidFileName_EmptyFileName_ThrowsException()
    {
        m_analyzer.IsValidLogFileName(string.Empty);
    }
```

There are several important things to note here:

- The expected exception message is provided as a parameter to the `[ExpectedException]` attribute.
- There's no `Assert` call in the test itself. The `[ExpectedException]` attribute contains the assert within it.
- There's no point getting the value of the Boolean result from the method because the method call is supposed to trigger an exception.

Given the method in listing 2.2 and the test for it, this test should pass. Had our method *not* thrown an `ArgumentException`, or had the exception's message been different than the one expected, our test would have failed—saying either that an exception was not thrown or that the message was different than expected.

2.5.3 Ignoring tests

Sometimes you'll have tests that are broken and you still need to check in your code to the main source tree. In those rare cases (and they should be rare!), you can put an `[Ignore]` attribute on tests that are broken because of a problem in the test, not in the code.

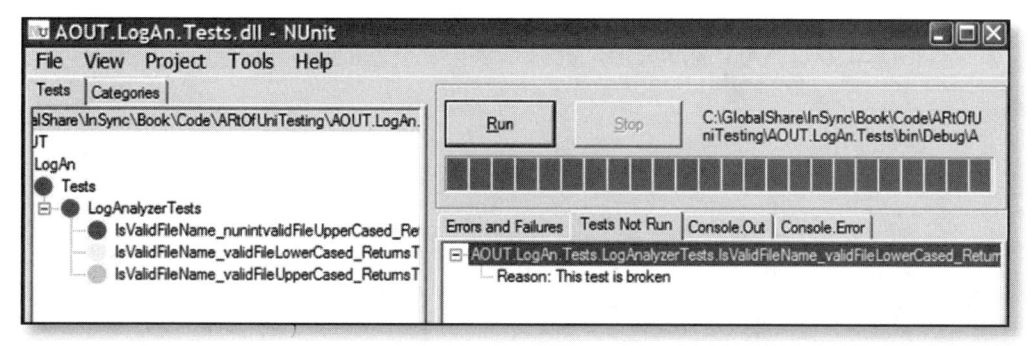

Figure 2.6 In NUnit, an ignored test is marked in yellow (the middle test), and the reason for not running the test is listed under the Tests Not Run tab on the right.

It can look like this:

```
[Test]
[Ignore("there is a problem with this test")]
 public void IsValidFileName_ValidFile_ReturnsTrue()
 {
 /// ...
 }
```

Running this test in the NUnit GUI will produce a result like that shown in figure 2.6.

What happens when you want to have tests running not by a namespace but by some other type of grouping? That's where test categories come in.

2.5.4 Setting test categories

You can set up your tests to run under specific test categories, such as slow tests and fast tests. You do this by using NUnit's [Category] attribute:

```
[Test]
[Category("Fast Tests")]
 public void IsValidFileName_ValidFile_ReturnsTrue()
 {
 /// ...
 }
```

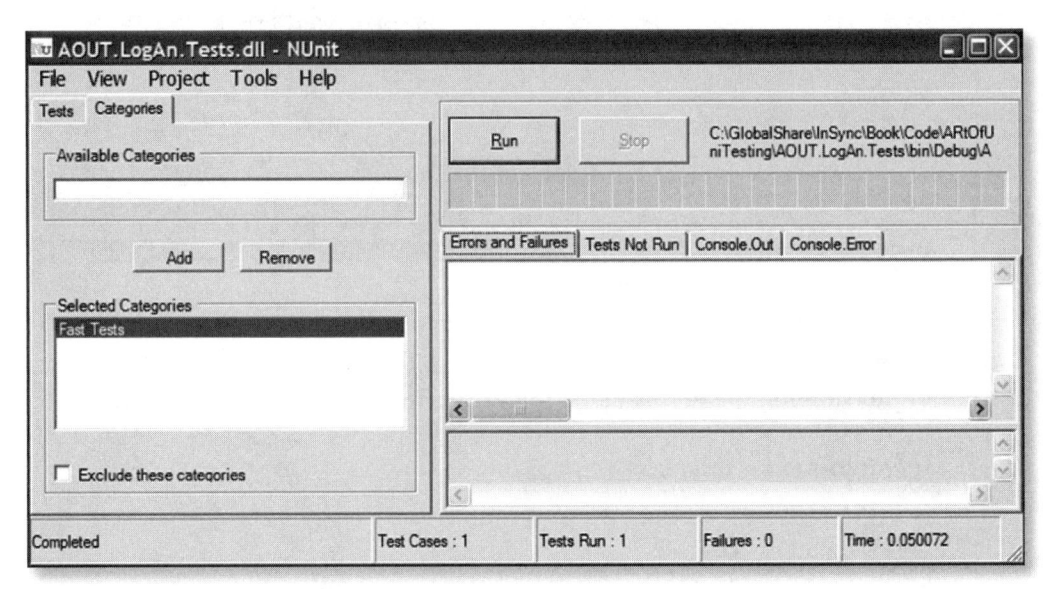

Figure 2.7 You can set up categories of tests in the code base and then choose a particular category to be run from the NUnit GUI.

When you load your test assembly again in NUnit, you can see them organized by categories instead of namespaces. Switch to the Categories tab in NUnit, and double-click the category you'd like to run so that it moves into the lower Selected Categories pane. Then click the Run button. Figure 2.7 shows what the screen might look like after you select the Categories tab.

So far, we've run simple tests against methods that return some value as a result. What if our method doesn't return a value, but changes some state in the object?

2.6 Indirect testing of state

Throughout this chapter and the next, we'll be using state-based testing methods in our unit tests.

DEFINITION   *State-based testing* (also called *state verification*) determines whether the exercised method worked correctly by examining the state of the system under test and its collaborators (dependencies) after the method is exercised.

Let's consider a simple state-based testing example using the `LogAnalyzer` class, which we can't test simply by calling one method in our test. Listing 2.3 shows the code for this class.

Listing 2.3 Testing the property value by calling `IsValidLogFileName`

```
public class LogAnalyzer
    {
        private bool wasLastFileNameValid;

        public bool WasLastFileNameValid
        {
            get { return wasLastFileNameValid; }
            set { wasLastFileNameValid = value; }
        }

        public bool IsValidLogFileName(string fileName)
        {
            if (!fileName.ToLower().EndsWith(".slf"))
            {
                wasLastFileNameValid=false;
                return false;
            }

            wasLastFileNameValid = true;   ⟵  Saves state of result
            return true;                        for later assertions
        }
    }
```

As you can see in this code, `LogAnalyzer` remembers what the last outcome of a validation check was. Because the logic depends on having another method invoked first, we can't simply test this functionality by writing a test that gets a return value from a method; we have to use alternative means to see if the logic works.

First, we have to identify where the logic we're testing is located. Is it in the new property called `wasLastFileNameValid`? Not really; it's in the `IsValidLogFileName` method, so our test should start with the name of that method. Listing 2.4 shows a simple test to see if the outcome is remembered.

Listing 2.4 Testing a class by calling a method and checking the value of a property

```
[Test]
public void IsValidLogFileName_ValidName_RemembersTrue()
{
    LogAnalyzer3 log = new LogAnalyzer3();
    log.IsValidLogFileName("somefile.slf");
    Assert.IsTrue(log.WasLastFileNameValid);
}
```
⮠ Asserts on property value, not return value

Notice that we're testing the functionality of the `IsValidLogFileName` method by asserting against code in a different location than the piece of code under test.

Listing 2.5 shows another example (that will be used again in chapter 3). This one looks into the functionality of a built-in memory calculator. (Take a look at Calculator.cs under CH3 and CalculatorTests.cs in the book's sample code.)

Listing 2.5 The `Add()` and `Sum()` methods

```
public class Calculator
    {
        private int sum=0;

        public void Add(int number)
        {
         sum+=number;
        }

        public int Sum()
        {
            int temp = sum;
            sum = 0;
            return temp;
        }
    }
```

The `Calculator` class works a lot like the pocket calculator you know and love. You can click a number, then click Add, then click another number, then click Add again, and so on. When you're done, you can click Equals and you'll get the total so far.

Where do you start testing the Sum() function? You should always consider the simplest test to begin with, such as testing that Sum() returns 0 by default. This is shown in listing 2.6.

Listing 2.6 The simplest test for Calculator's Sum()

```
[Test]
 public void Sum_NoAddCalls_DefaultsToZero()
 {
        Calculator calc = new Calculator();
        int lastSum = calc.Sum();              ◁──── Asserts on default
        Assert.AreEqual(0,lastSum);                  return value
 }
```

We can't write any other test without first invoking the Add() method, so our next test will have to call Add() and assert against the number returned from Sum(). Listing 2.7 shows our test class with this new test.

Listing 2.7 The two tests, with the second one calling the Add() method

```
[SetUp]
        public void Setup()
        {
           calc = new Calculator();
        }

        [Test]
        public void Sum_NoAddCalls_DefaultsToZero()
        {
            int lastSum = calc.Sum();
            Assert.AreEqual(0,lastSum);
        }

        [Test]
        public void Add_CalledOnce_SavesNumberForSum()
        {
           calc.Add(1);                    ◁──── Tests the Add() method
           int lastSum = calc.Sum();             indirectly by checking return
           Assert.AreEqual(1,lastSum);           value from Sum()
        }
```

Notice that this time the tests initialize the `Calculator` object in a `[SetUp]`-related method. This is a good idea, because it saves time writing the tests, makes the code smaller, and makes sure `Calculator` is always initialized the same way. It's also better for test maintainability, because if the constructor for `Calculator` changes, you only need to change the initialization in one place instead of going through each test and changing the `new` call.

So far, so good. But what happens when the method we're testing depends on an external resource, such as the filesystem, a database, a web service, or anything else that's hard for us to control? That's when we start creating test stubs, fake objects, and mock objects, which are discussed in the next few chapters.

2.7 Summary

In this chapter, we looked at using NUnit to write simple tests against simple code. We used the `[SetUp]` and `[TearDown]` attributes to make sure our tests always use new and untouched state. We used `[Ignore]` to skip tests that need to be fixed. Test categories can help us group tests in a logical way rather than by class and namespace, and `[ExpectedException]` helps us make sure our code throws exceptions when it should. Finally, we looked at what happens when we aren't facing a simple method with a return value, and we need to test the end state of an object. This attribute is handy, and you'll use it in many of your future tests.

This isn't enough though. Most test code has to deal with far more difficult coding issues. The next couple of chapters will give you some more basic tools for writing unit tests. You'll need to pick and choose from these tools when you write tests for various difficult scenarios you'll come across.

Finally, keep the following points in mind:

- It's common practice to have one test class per tested class, one test project per tested project, and at least one test method per tested method.

- Name your tests clearly using the following model: [MethodUnderTest]_[Scenario]_[ExpectedBehavior].
- Use the `[SetUp]` and `[TearDown]` attributes to reuse code in your tests, such as code for creating and initializing objects all your tests use.
- Don't use `[SetUp]` and `[TearDown]` to initialize or destroy objects that aren't shared *throughout* the test class in all the tests, because it makes the tests less understandable. Someone reading your code won't know which tests use the logic inside the setup method and which don't.

In the next chapter, we'll look at more real-world scenarios, where the code to be tested is a little more realistic than what you've seen so far. It has dependencies and testability problems, and we'll start discussing the notion of integration tests versus unit tests, and what that means to us as developers who write tests and want to ensure our code's quality.

Part 2

Core techniques

Having covered the basics in previous chapters, we'll now introduce the core testing and refactoring techniques that are necessary for writing tests in the real world.

In chapter 3, we'll begin by learning about stubs and how they help us break dependencies. We'll go over refactoring techniques that make code more testable, and we'll learn about seams in the process.

Then, in chapter 4, we'll move on to mock objects and interaction testing and look at how mock objects differ from stubs.

Lastly, in chapter 5, we'll look at isolation frameworks (also known as mock object frameworks) and how they solve some of the repetitive coding involved in handwritten mocks and stubs. Chapter 5 also compares the leading isolation frameworks in .NET and uses Rhino Mocks for examples, showing its API in common use cases.

3
Using stubs to break dependencies

This chapter covers
- *Defining stubs*
- *Refactoring code to use stubs*
- *Overcoming encapsulation problems in code*
- *Exploring best practices when using stubs*

In the previous chapter, we wrote our first unit test using NUnit and explored the different testing attributes that are available, such as `[ExpectedException]`, `[SetUp]`, and `[TearDown]`. We also built tests for simple use cases, where all we had to check on were simple return values from simple objects.

In this chapter, we'll take a look at more realistic examples where the object under test relies on another object over which we have no control (or which doesn't work yet). That object could be a web service, the time of day, threading, or many other things. The important point is that our test can't control what that dependency returns to our code under test or how it behaves (if we wanted to simulate an exception, for example). That's when we use *stubs*.

3.1 Introducing stubs

Flying people into space presents interesting challenges to engineers and astronauts, one of the more difficult being how to make sure the astronaut is ready to go into space and operate all the machinery. A full *integration test* for a space shuttle would require being in space, and that's obviously not a safe way to test astronauts. That's why NASA has full simulators that mimic the surroundings of a space shuttle's control deck, which removes the external dependency of having to be in outer space.

DEFINITION   An *external dependency* is an object in your system that your code under test interacts with, and over which you have no control. (Common examples are filesystems, threads, memory, time, and so on.)

Controlling external dependencies in your code is the topic that this chapter, and most of this book, will be dealing with. In programming, we use *stubs* to get around the problem of external dependencies.

DEFINITION   A *stub* is a controllable replacement for an existing dependency (or *collaborator*) in the system. By using a stub, you can test your code without dealing with the dependency directly.

Let's look at a real example and make things a bit more complicated for our `LogAnalyzer` class, introduced in the previous chapters. We'll try to untangle a dependency against the filesystem.

> **Test pattern names**
>
> *xUnit Test Patterns* by Gerard Meszaros is a classic pattern reference book for unit testing. It defines patterns for things we fake in our tests in at least five ways, which I feel confuses people (although it's detailed). In this book, I chose to use only three definitions for fake things in tests: fakes, stubs, and mocks. I feel that this simplification of terms makes it easy for readers to digest the patterns, and that there's no need to know more than those three to get started and write great tests. In various places in the book, though, I will refer to the pattern names used in *xUnit Test Patterns* so that you can easily refer to that definition if you'd like.

3.2 Identifying a filesystem dependency in LogAn

Our `LogAnalyzer` class application can be configured to handle multiple log filename extensions using a special adapter for each file. For the sake of simplicity, let's assume that the allowed filenames are stored somewhere on disk as a configuration setting for the application, and that the `IsValidLogFileName` method looks like this:

```
public bool IsValidLogFileName(string fileName)
    {
    //read through the configuration file
    //return true if configuration says extension is supported.
    }
```

The problem that arises, as depicted in figure 3.1, is that, once this test depends on the filesystem, we're performing an integration test, and we have all the associated problems: integration tests are slower to run, they need configuration, they test multiple things, and so on.

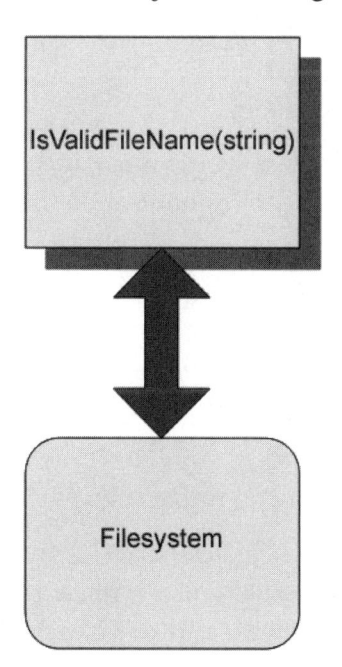

This is the essence of *test-inhibiting* design: the code has some dependency on an external resource, which might break the test even though the code's logic is perfectly valid. In legacy systems, a single class or method might have many dependencies on external resources over which your test code has little, if any, control. Chapter 9 touches more on this subject.

Figure 3.1 Our method has a direct dependency on the filesystem. Our design of the object model under test inhibits us from testing it as a unit test; it promotes integration testing.

3.3 Determining how to easily test LogAnalyzer

"There is no object-oriented problem that cannot be solved by adding a layer of indirection, except, of course, too many layers of indirection." I like this quote (from a friend of mine) because a lot of the "art" in the art of unit testing is about finding the right place to add or use a layer of indirection to test the code base.

You can't test something? Add a layer that wraps up the calls to that something, and then mimic that layer in your tests. Or make that something replaceable (so that it is itself a layer of indirection). The art also involves figuring out when a layer of indirection already exists instead of having to invent it, or knowing when not to use it because it complicates things too much. But let's take it one step at a time.

The only way we can write a test for this code, as it is, is to have a configuration file in the filesystem. Because we're trying to avoid these kinds of dependencies, we want our code to be easily testable without resorting to integration testing.

If we look at the astronaut analogy we started out with, we can see that there's a definite pattern for breaking the dependency:

1 Find the *interface* or *API* that the object under test works against. In the astronaut example, this was the joysticks and monitors of the space shuttle, as depicted in figure 3.2.
2 Replace the *underlying implementation* of that interface with something that you have control over. This involved hooking up the various shuttle monitors, joysticks, and buttons to a control room where test engineers were able to control what the space shuttle *interface* was showing to the astronauts under test.

Transferring this pattern to our code requires more steps:

1 Find the *interface* that the method under test works against. (In this case, "interface" isn't used in the pure object-oriented sense; it refers to the defined method or class being collaborated with.) In our LogAn project, this is the filesystem configuration file.

Figure 3.2 A space shuttle simulator has realistic joysticks and screens to simulate the outside world. (Photo courtesy of NASA)

2   If the interface is *directly connected* to our method under test (as in this case—we're calling directly into the filesystem), make the code testable by adding a level of indirection to the interface. In our example, moving the direct call to the filesystem to a separate class (such as `FileExtensionManager`) would be one way to add a level of indirection. We'll also look at others. (Figure 3.3 shows how the design might look after this step.)

3   Replace the *underlying implementation* of that interactive interface with something that you have control over. In our case, we'll replace the instance of the class that our method calls (`FileExtensionManager`) with a stub class that we can control (`StubExtensionManager`), giving our test code control over external dependencies.

Our replacement instance will *not* talk to the filesystem at all, which breaks the dependency on the filesystem. Because we aren't testing the class that talks to the filesystem, but the code that calls this class, it's OK if that stub class doesn't do anything but make happy noises when running inside the test. Figure 3.4 shows the design after this alteration.

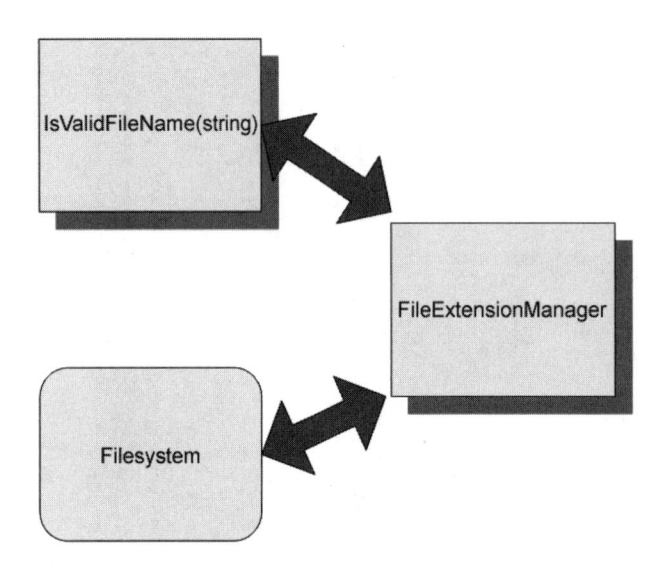

Figure 3.3 Introducing a layer of indirection to avoid a direct dependency on the filesystem. The code that calls the filesystem is separated into a `FileExtensionManager` class, which will later be replaced with a stub in our test.

In figure 3.4, I've added a new interface into the mix. This new interface will allow the object model to abstract away the operations of what a `FileExtensionManager` class does, and will allow the test to create a stub that looks like a `FileExtensionManager`. You'll see more on this method in the next section.

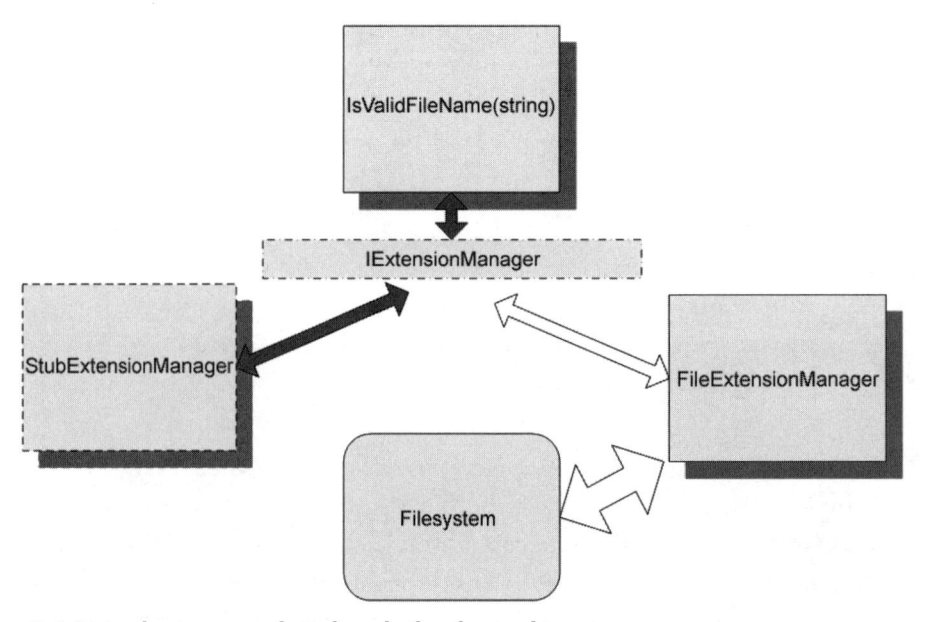

Figure 3.4 Introducing a stub to break the dependency

We've looked at one way of introducing testability into our code base—by creating a new interface. Now let's look at the idea of code *refactoring* and introducing *seams* into our code.

3.4 Refactoring our design to be more testable

I'm going to introduce two new terms that will be used throughout the book: *refactoring* and *seams*.

DEFINITION   *Refactoring* is the act of changing the code's design without breaking existing functionality.

DEFINITION   *Seams* are places in your code where you can plug in different functionality, such as stub classes. (See Michael Feathers' book, *Working Effectively with Legacy Code*, for more about seams.)

If we want to break the dependency between our code under test and the filesystem, we can use common design patterns, refactorings, and techniques, and introduce one or more *seams* into the code. We just need to make sure that the resulting code does exactly the same thing. Here are some techniques for breaking dependencies:

- Extract an interface to allow replacing underlying implementation.
- Inject stub implementation into a class under test.
- Receive an interface at the constructor level.
- Receive an interface as a property get or set.
- Get a stub just before a method call.

We'll look at each of these.

3.4.1 Extract an interface to allow replacing underlying implementation

In this technique, we need to break out the code that touches the filesystem into a separate class. That way we can easily distinguish it and later replace the call to that class from our tested function (as was shown in figure 3.3). Listing 3.1 shows the places where we need to change the code.

Listing 3.1 Extracting a class that touches the filesystem, and calling it

```
public bool IsValidLogFileName(string fileName)
{
    FileExtensionManager mgr =
            new FileExtensionManager();
    return mgr.IsValid(fileName);                    ◁──── Uses the extracted class
}

class FileExtensionManager
    {
        public bool IsValid(string fileName)
        {                                                  Defines the
        //read some file here                              extracted class
        }
    }
```

Next, we can tell our class under test that, instead of using the concrete `FileExtensionManager` class, it will deal with some form of `ExtensionManager`, without knowing its concrete implementation. In .NET, this could be accomplished by either using a base class or an interface that `FileExtensionManager` would extend.

Listing 3.2 shows the use of a new interface in our design to make it more testable. Figure 3.4 showed a diagram of this implementation.

Listing 3.2 Extracting an interface from a known class

```
public class FileExtensionManager : IExtensionManager     ◁──┐ Implements
    {                                                        │ the interface
        public bool IsValid(string fileName)
        {
        ...
        }
    }
public interface IExtensionManager
    {                                                         Defines the
        bool IsValid (string fileName);                       new interface
    }

//the method under test:
public bool IsValidLogFileName(string fileName)
```

```
    {
        IExtensionManager mgr =
                new FileExtensionManager();      ◁──┐  Defines variable
        return mgr.IsValid(fileName);                  as the type of
    }                                                  the interface
```

We've simply created an interface with one `IsValid` (string) method, and made `FileExtensionManager` implement that interface. It still works exactly the same way, only now we can replace the "real" manager with our own "stub" manager to support our test.

We still haven't created the stub extension manager, so let's create that right now. It's shown in listing 3.3.

Listing 3.3 Simple stub code that always returns `true`

```
public class StubExtensionManager:IExtensionManager     ◁──┐
    {                                                          Implements
        public bool IsValid(string fileName)                   IExtensionManager
        {
            return true;
        }
    }
```

This stub extension manager will always return `true`, no matter what the file extension is. We can use it in our tests to make sure that no test will ever have a dependency on the filesystem, but also so we can create new and bizarre scenarios where we can simulate serious system errors like making the stub manager throw an `OutOfMemoryException` and seeing how the system deals with it. Later in this chapter, we'll add configurability to the stub class so it can emulate many things and be used by multiple tests.

Now we have an interface and two classes implementing it, but our method under test still calls the real implementation directly:

```
public bool IsValidLogFileName(string fileName)
        {
            IExtensionManager mgr = new FileExtensionManager();
```

```
        return mgr.IsValid(fileName);
}
```

We somehow have to tell our method to talk to our implementation rather than the original implementation of `IExtensionManager`. We need to introduce a *seam* into the code, where we can plug in our stub.

3.4.2 Inject stub implementation into a class under test

There are several proven ways to create interface-based seams in our code—places where we can inject an implementation of an interface into a class to be used in its methods. Here are some of the most notable ways:

- Receive an interface at the constructor level and save it in a field for later use.
- Receive an interface as a property get or set and save it in a field for later use.
- Receive an interface just before the call in the method under test using
  - a parameter to the method (*parameter injection*).
  - a factory class.
  - a local factory method.
  - variations on the preceding techniques.

The parameter injection method is trivial: you send in an instance of a (fake) dependency to the method in question by adding a parameter to the method signature.

Let's go through the rest of the possible solutions one by one and see why you'd want to use each.

3.4.3 Receive an interface at the constructor level (constructor injection)

In this scenario, we add a new constructor (or a new parameter to an existing constructor) that will accept an object of the interface type we extracted earlier (`IExtensionManager`). The constructor then sets a local field of the interface type in the class for later use by our method or any other. Figure 3.5 shows the flow of the stub injection.

Refactoring our design to be more testable

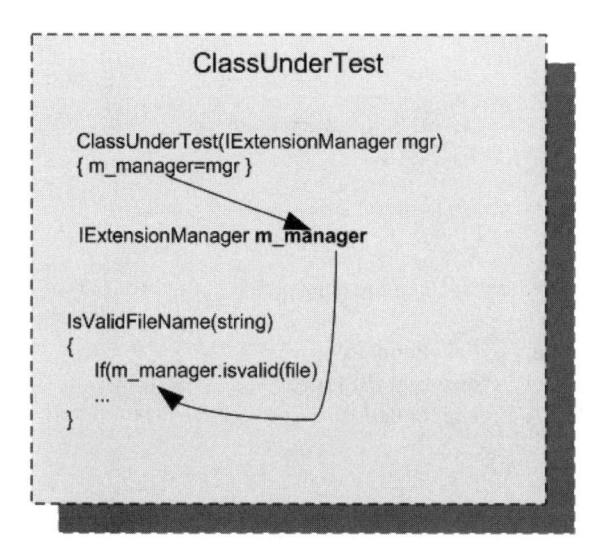

Figure 3.5 Flow of injection via a constructor

Listing 3.4 shows how we could write a test for our `LogAnalyzer` class using a constructor injection technique.

Listing 3.4 Injecting our stub using constructor injection

```
public class LogAnalyzer                  ◁──── Defines production code
    {
        private IExtensionManager manager;

        public LogAnalyzer ()
        {
            manager = new FileExtensionManager();   ◁──┐ Creates object
        }                                              │ in production code
        public LogAnalyzer(IExtensionManager mgr)   ◁──┐
        {                                              │
            manager = mgr;                             │ Defines constructor
        }                                              │ that can be called by tests

        public bool IsValidLogFileName(string fileName)
        {
            return manager.IsValid(fileName);
        }
    }

    public interface IExtensionManager
        {
```

```csharp
        bool IsValid(string fileName);
    }

    [TestFixture]                              // Defines test code
    public class LogAnalyzerTests
    {
        [Test]
        public void
IsValidFileName_NameShorterThan6CharsButSupportedExtension_ReturnsFalse()
        {
            StubExtensionManager myFakeManager =
                    new StubExtensionManager();              // Sets up stub
            myFakeManager.ShouldExtensionBeValid             // to return true
                                    = true;

            //create analyzer and inject stub
            LogAnalyzer log =
                new LogAnalyzer (myFakeManager);     // Sends in stub

            //Assert logic assuming extension is supported
            bool result = log.IsValidLogFileName("short.ext");
            Assert.IsFalse(result,
                "File name with less than 5 chars should have failed
                the method, even if the extension is supported");
        }
    }

    internal class StubExtensionManager : IExtensionManager
    {
        public bool ShouldExtensionBeValid;             // Defines stub
                                                        // that uses
        public bool IsValid(string fileName)            // simplest
        {                                               // mechanism
            return ShouldExtensionBeValid;              // possible
        }
    }
```

> **NOTE** The stub analyzer is located in the same file as the test code because currently the stub is used only from within this test class. It's far easier to locate, read, and maintain a stub in the same file than in a different one. If, later on, I have an additional class that needs to use this stub, I can move it to another file easily.

Notice that the test in listing 3.4 tests some domain logic that's built *on top* of the call to the `FileExtensionManager`. The domain logic in `IsValidLogFileName` should make sure that the extension is supported, and that the filename is long enough to be considered.

You'll also notice that the stub object in listing 3.4 can be configured by the test code as to what Boolean value to return when its method is called. Configuring the stub from the test means the stub class's source code can be reused in more than one test case, with the test setting the values for the stub before using it on the object under test. This also helps the readability of the test code, because the reader of the code can read the test and find everything she needs to know in one place. Readability is an important aspect of writing unit tests, and we'll cover it in detail later in the book, particularly in chapter 7.

Another thing to note is that, by using parameters in the constructor, we're in effect making the parameters non-optional dependencies (assuming this is the only constructor), which is a design choice. The user of the type will have to send in arguments for any specific dependencies that are needed.

Problems with constructor injection

Problems can arise from using constructors to inject implementations. If your code under test requires more than one stub to work correctly without dependencies, adding more and more constructors (or more and more constructor parameters) becomes a hassle, and it can even make the code less readable and less maintainable.

For example, suppose `LogAnalyzer` also had a dependency on a web service and a logging service in addition to the file extension manager. The constructor might look like this:

```
public LogAnalyzer(IExtensionManager mgr, ILog logger, IWebService
    service)
{
    //    this constructor can be called by tests
        manager = mgr;
       log= logger;
       svc= service;
}
```

One solution to these problems is to create a special class that contains all the values needed to initialize a class, and to have only one parameter to the method: that class type. That way, you only pass around one object with all the relevant dependencies. (This is also known as a *parameter object refactoring*.) This can get out of hand pretty quickly, with dozens of properties on an object; but it's possible.

Another possible solution to these problems is using inversion of control (IoC) containers. You can think of IoC containers as "smart factories" for your objects (although they are much more than that). A couple of well-known containers of this type are Spring.NET and Castle Windsor. Both provide special factory methods that take in the type of object you'd like to create and any dependencies that it needs, and then initialize the object using special configurable rules such as what constructor to call, what properties to set in what order, and so on. They're powerful when put to use on a complicated composite object hierarchy where creating an object requires creating and initializing objects several levels down the line. If your class needs an `ILogger` interface at its constructor, for example, you can configure such a container object to always return the same `ILogger` object that you give it, when resolving this interface requirement. The end result of using containers is usually simpler handling and retrieving of objects, and less worry about the dependencies or maintaining the constructors.

> **TIP** Some of the more popular containers in the .NET world are Castle Windsor, Microsoft Unity, and Spring.NET. There are also many up-and-coming container implementations, such as Autofac, Ninject, and StructureMap, which use a more fluent interface API, so look at them when you read more about this topic. Dealing with containers is beyond the scope of this book, but you can start reading about them with Scott Hanselman's list: http://www.hanselman.com/blog/ListOfNETDependencyInjectionContainersIOC.aspx.

Now, imagine that you have 50 tests against your constructor, and you find another dependency you had not considered, such as a factory service for creating special objects that works against a database. You'd have to create an interface for that dependency and add it as a parameter to the current constructor, and you'd also have to change the call in

50 other tests that initialize the code. At this point, your constructor could use a facelift. Whatever logic it does have is beginning to be hidden by the many parameters. Fortunately, using property getters and setters can solve this problem easily, as we'll see in section 3.4.4.

When you should use constructor injection

My experience is that using constructor arguments to initialize objects can make your testing code more cumbersome unless you're using helper frameworks such as IoC containers for object creation. Every time you add another dependency to the class under test, you have to create a new constructor that takes all the other arguments plus a new one, make sure it calls the other constructors correctly, and make sure other users of this class initialize it with the new constructor.

On the other hand, using parameters in constructors is a great way to signify to the user of your API that these parameters are non-optional. They have to be sent in when creating the object.

If you want these dependencies to be optional, refer to the next section. It discusses using property getters and setters, which is a much more relaxed way to define optional dependencies than, say, adding different constructors to the class for each dependency.

There are people who disagree with my approach and define constructor arguments as non-optional arguments, using properties strictly for optional ones. That way, the semantics of the class also imply the proper usage of that class. I agree somewhat with this approach; my problem is with its maintainability.

> TIP   You'll find that dilemmas about what method to use in which situation are common in the world of unit testing. This is a wonderful thing. Always question your assumptions; you might learn something new.

If you choose to use constructor injection, you'll probably also want to use IoC containers. This would be a great solution if all code in the world were using IoC containers, but most people don't know what the Inversion of Control principle is, let alone what tools you can use to make it a reality. The future of unit testing will likely see more and more use of these frameworks. As that happens, we'll see clearer and clearer guidelines on how to design classes that have dependencies, or we'll see tools that solve the dependency injection problem without needing to use constructors at all.

In any case, constructor parameters are just one way to go. Properties are often used as well.

3.4.4 Receive an interface as a property get or set

In this scenario, we add a property get and set for each dependency we'd like to inject. We then use this dependency when we need it in our code under test. Figure 3.6 shows the flow of injection with properties.

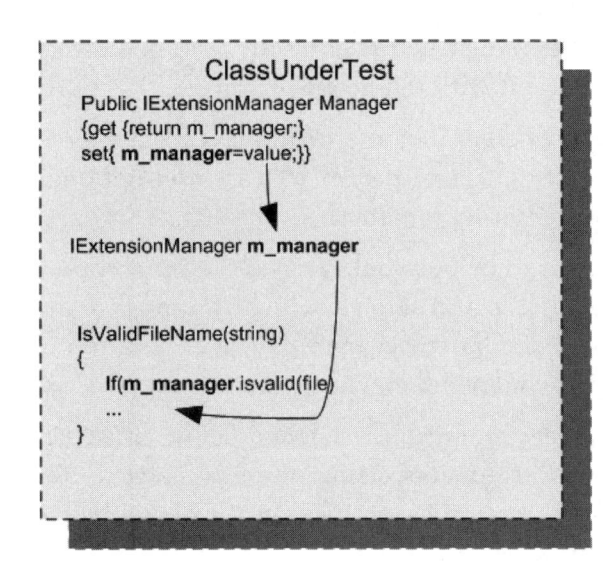

Figure 3.6 Using properties to inject dependencies. This is much simpler than using a constructor because each test can set only the properties that it needs to get the test underway.

Using this technique (also called *dependency injection*, a term that can also be used to describe the other techniques in this chapter), our test code would look quite similar to that in section 3.4.3, which used constructor injection. But this code, shown in listing 3.5, is more readable and simpler to achieve.

Listing 3.5 Injecting a stub by adding property setters to the class under test

```
public class LogAnalyzer
    {
        private IExtensionManager manager;

        public LogAnalyzer ()
```

```
        {
    manager = new FileExtensionManager();
        }

        public IExtensionManager ExtensionManager
        {                                            ⎫ Allows setting
            get { return manager; }                  ⎬ dependency
            set { manager = value; }                 ⎭ via a property
        }

        public bool IsValidLogFileName(string fileName)
        {
            return manager.IsValid(fileName);
        }
    }

        [Test]
        Public void
IsValidFileName_NameShorterThan6CharsButSupportedExtension_ReturnsFalse()
        {
            //set up the stub to use, make sure it returns true
            ...

            //create analyzer and inject stub
            LogAnalyzer log =                                        ⎫ Injects stub
                new LogAnalyzer ();                                  ⎬
            log.ExtensionManager=someFakeManagerCreatedEarlier;  ←   ⎭

            //Assert logic assuming extension is supported
            ...
        }
    }
```

Like constructor injection, property injection has an effect on the API design in terms of defining which dependencies are required and which aren't. By using properties, you're effectively saying, "This dependency isn't required to operate this type."

When you should use property injection

Use this technique when you want to signify that a dependency of the class under test is optional, or if the dependency has a default instance created that doesn't create any problems during the test.

3.4.5 Getting a stub just before a method call

This section deals with a scenario where you get an instance of an object just before you do any operations with it, instead of getting it via a constructor or a property. The difference is that the object initiating the stub request in this situation is the code under test; in previous sections, the stub instance was set by code external to the code under test before the test started.

Use a factory class

In this scenario, we go back to the basics, where a class initializes the manager in its constructor, but it gets the instance from a factory class. The Factory pattern is a design that allows another class to be responsible for creating objects.

Our tests will configure the factory class (which, in this case, uses a static method to return an instance of an object that implements `IExtensionManager`) to return a stub instead of the real implementation. Figure 3.7 shows this.

This is a clean design, and many object-oriented systems use factory classes to return instances of objects. But most systems don't allow

```
ClassUnderTest                              FactoryClass

ClassUnderTest(I)                           Static IExtensionManager Create()
{ m_manager= FactoryClass.Create(); }       {
                                                return manager;
IExtensionManager m_manager                 }

                                            IExtensionManager manager

IsValidFileName(string)                     Static SetManager(IExtensionManager mgr)
{                                           {
    If(m_manager.Isvalid(file))                 manager= mgr;
    ...                                         ...
}                                           }
                                                                            Test
```

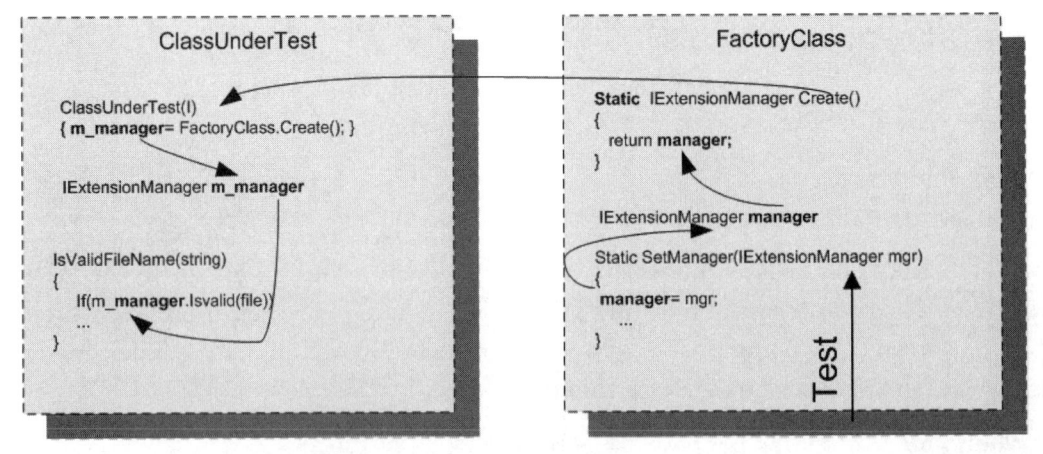

Figure 3.7 A test configures the factory class to return a stub object. The class under test uses the factory class to get that instance, which in production code would return an object that isn't a stub.

anyone outside the factory class to change the instance being returned, in order to protect the encapsulated design of this class.

In this case, I've added a new setter method (our new seam) to the factory class so that our tests will have more control over what instance gets returned. Once you introduce statics into test code, you might also need to reset the factory state before or after each test run, so that other tests won't be affected by the configuration.

This technique produces test code that's easy to read, and there's a clear separation of concerns between the classes. Each one is responsible for a different action.

Listing 3.6 shows code that uses the factory class in `LogAnalyzer` (and also includes the tests).

Listing 3.6 Setting a factory class to return a stub when the test is running

```
public class LogAnalyzer
    {
        private IExtensionManager manager;

        public LogAnalyzer ()                        Uses factory in
        {                                            production code
            manager = ExtensionManagerFactory.Create();
        }

        public bool IsValidLogFileName(string fileName)
        {
            return manager.IsValid(fileName)
                && Path.GetFileNameWithoutExtension(fileName).Length>5;
        }
    }

        [Test]
         Public void
IsValidFileName_NameShorterThan6CharsButSupportedExtension_ReturnsFalse()
        {
            //set up the stub to use, make sure it returns true
            ...
```

```
                ExtensionManagerFactory
                            .SetManager(myFakeManager);     ◁──┐
            //create analyzer and inject stub                  │
            LogAnalyzer log =                                  Sets stub into
                new LogAnalyzer ();                            factory class
                                                               for this test
            //Assert logic assuming extension is supported
            ...
        }
    }

Class ExtensionManagerFactory
{
    Private IExtensionManager customManager=null;
    Public IExtensionManager Create()
    {
        If(customManager!=null)
return customManager;                     Defines factory that can use
        Return new FileExtensionManager();        and return custom manager
    }
    Public void SetManager(IExtensionManager mgr)
    {
        customManager = mgr;
    }

}
```

The implementation of the factory class can vary greatly, and the examples shown here represent only the simplest illustration. For more examples of factories, read about the factory method and the Abstract Factory Design patterns in the classic book *Design Patterns*, by the Gang of Four (Erich Gamma, Richard Helm, Ralph Johnson, and John M. Vlissides).

The only thing you need to make sure of is that, once you use these patterns, you add a seam to the factories you make so that they can return your stubs instead of the default implementations. Many systems have a global #debug switch that, when turned on, causes seams to automatically send in fake or testable objects instead of default implementations. Setting this up can be hard work, but it's worth it when it's time to test the system.

Hiding seams in release mode

What if you don't want the seams to be visible in release mode? There are several ways to achieve that. In .NET, for example, you can put the seam statements (the added constructor, setter, or factory setter) under a conditional compilation argument, like this:

```
#if DEBUG
    MyConstructor(IExtensionManager mgr)
    {...}
#endif
```

There's also a special attribute in .NET that can be used for these purposes:

```
[Conditional("DEBUG")]
MyConstructor(IExtensionManager mgr)
{...}
```

When you should use conditional compilation

First, you need to realize that we're dealing with a different layer depth here than the previous sections. At each different depth, we're faking (or stubbing) a different object. Table 3.1 shows three layer depths that are used inside the code to return stubs.

Table 3.1 Layers of code that can be faked

Code under test	Possible action
Layer depth 1: the `FileExtensionManager` variable inside the class	Add a constructor argument that will be used as the dependency. A member in the class under test is now fake; all other code remains unchanged.
Layer depth 2: the dependency returned from the factory class into the class under test	Tell the factory class to return your fake dependency by setting a property. The member inside the factory class is fake; the class under test isn't changed at all.
Layer depth 3: the factory class that returns the dependency	Replace the instance of the factory class with a fake factory that returns your fake dependency. The factory is a fake, which also returns a fake; the class under test isn't changed.

The thing to understand about layers of indirection is that the deeper you go down the rabbit hole (down the code-base execution call stack) the better manipulation power you have over the code under test, because you create stubs that are in charge of more things down the line. But there's also a bad side to this: the further you go down the layers, the harder the test will be to understand, and the harder it will be to find the right place to put your seam. The trick is to find the right balance between complexity and manipulation power so that your tests remain readable but you get full control of the situation under test.

For the scenario in listing 3.6 (using a factory), adding a constructor-level argument would complicate things when we already have a good possible target layer for our seam—the factory at depth 2. Layer 2 is the simplest to use here because the changes it requires in the code are minimal:

- *Layer 1 (faking a member in the class under test)*

    You would need to add a constructor, set the class in the constructor, set its parameters from the test, and worry about future uses of that API in the production code. This method would change the semantics of using the class under test, which is best avoided unless you have a good reason.

- *Layer 2 (faking a member in a factory class)*

    This method is easy. Add a setter to the factory and set it to a fake dependency of your choice. There's no changing of the semantics of the code base, everything stays the same, and the code is dead simple. The only con is that this method requires that you understand who calls the factory and when, which means you need to do some research before you can implement this easily. Understanding a code base you've never seen is a daunting task, but it still seems more reasonable than the other options.

- *Layer 3 (faking the factory class)*

    You would need to create your own version of a factory class, which may or may not have an interface. This means also creating an interface for it. Then you would need to create your fake factory instance, tell it to return your fake dependency class (a fake returning a fake—take note!), and then set the fake factory class on the class under test. A fake returning a fake is always a bit of a mind-boggling scenario, which is best avoided because it makes the test less understandable.

Use a local factory method (Extract and Override)

This method doesn't reside in any of the layers listed in table 3.1; it creates a whole new layer of indirection close to the surface of the code under test. The closer we get to the surface of the code, the less we need to muck around with changing dependencies. In this case, the class under test is also a dependency of sorts that we need to manipulate.

In this scenario, we use a local *virtual* method in the class under test as a factory to get the instance of the extension manager. Because the method is marked as *virtual*, it can be overridden in a derived class, which creates our seam. We inject a stub into the class by *inheriting* a new class from the class under test, *overriding* the virtual factory method, and finally returning whatever instance the new class is configured to return in the overriding method. The tests are then performed on the new derived class. The factory method could also be called a stub method that returns a stub object. Figure 3.8 shows the flow of object instances.

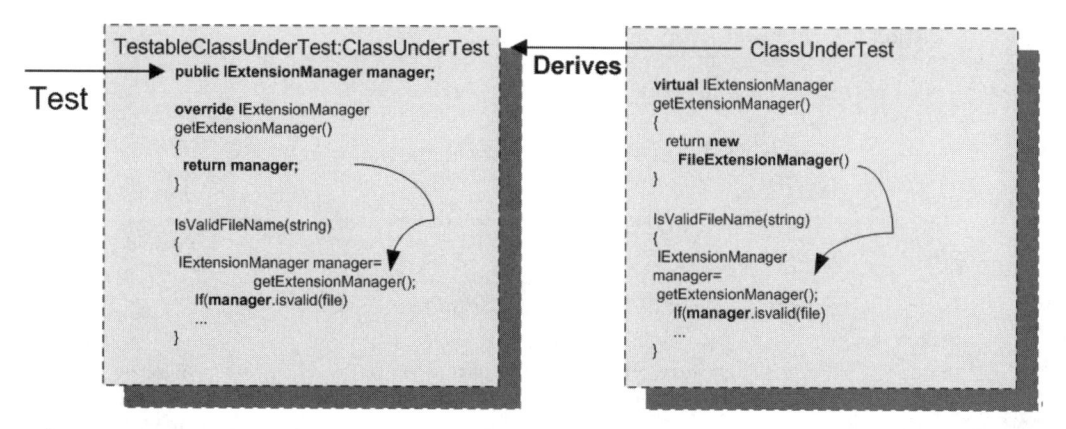

Figure 3.8 We inherit from the class under test so we can override its virtual factory method and return whatever object instance we want, as long as it implements `IExtensionManager`. Then we perform our tests against the newly derived class.

Here are the steps for using a factory method in your tests.

- In the class under test,
  - add a virtual factory method that returns the real instance.
  - use the factory method in your code, as usual.
- In your test project, create a new class:
  - Set the new class to inherit from the class under test.
  - Create a public field (no need for property get or set) of the interface type you want to replace (`IExtensionManager`).
  - Override the virtual factory method.
  - Return the public field.
- In your test code,
  - create an instance of a stub class that implements the required interface (`IExtensionManager`).
  - create an instance of the *newly derived class*, *not* of the class under test.
  - configure the new instance's public field (which you created earlier) and set it to the stub you've instantiated in your test.

When you test your class now, your production code will be using your stub through the overridden factory method.

Listing 3.7 shows what the code might look like when using this method.

Listing 3.7 Faking a factory method

```
public class LogAnalyzerUsingFactoryMethod
    {
        public bool IsValidLogFileName(string fileName)
        {
            return GetManager().IsValid(fileName);     ◁── Uses virtual GetManager() method
        }

        protected virtual IExtensionManager GetManager()
        {
            return new FileExtensionManager();          ◁── Returns hardcoded value
        }
    }

[TestFixture]
    public class LogAnalyzerTests
```

```
{
   [Test]
    public void overrideTest()
    {
        StubExtensionManager stub = new StubExtensionManager();
        stub.ShouldExtensionBeValid = true;

        TestableLogAnalyzer logan =
                new TestableLogAnalyzer();
        logan.Manager=stub;
        bool result = logan.IsValidLogFileName("file.ext");
        Assert.IsFalse(result,
   "File name should be too short to be considered valid");
    }
}

class  TestableLogAnalyzer
                    :LogAnalyzerUsingFactoryMethod
{
    public IExtensionManager Manager;

    protected override IExtensionManager GetManager()
    {
        return Manager;
    }
}
internal class StubExtensionManager : IExtensionManager
{
    //no change from the previous samples
    ...
}
```

Creates instance of class derived from class under test

Returns what we tell it to

The technique we're using here is called *Extract and Override,* and you'll find it extremely easy to use once you've done it a couple of times. It's a powerful technique, and one I will put to other uses throughout this book.

TIP You can learn more about this dependency-breaking technique and others in a book I have found to be worth its weight in gold: *Working Effectively with Legacy Code* by Michael Feathers.

Extract and Override is a powerful technique because it lets you directly replace the dependency without going down the rabbit hole (changing dependencies deep inside the call stack). That makes it quick and clean to perform, and it almost corrupts your good sense of object-oriented aesthetics, leading you to code that might have fewer interfaces but more virtual methods. I like to call this method "ex-crack and override" because it's such a hard habit to let go of once you know it.

When you should use this method

Extract and Override is great for simulating *inputs* into your code under test, but it's cumbersome when you want to verify interactions that are coming *out of* the code under test into your dependency.

For example, it's great if your test code calls a web service and gets a *return value*, and you'd like to simulate your own return value. But it gets bad quickly if you want to test that your code *calls out* to the web service correctly. That requires lots of manual coding, and mock frameworks are better suited for such tasks (as you'll see in the next chapter). Extract and Override is good if you'd like to simulate return values or simulate whole interfaces as return values, but not for checking interactions between objects.

I use this technique a lot when I need to simulate inputs into my code under test, because it helps keep the changes to the semantics of the code base (new interfaces, constructors, and so on) a little more manageable. You need to make fewer of them to get the code into a testable state. The only times I don't use this technique is when the code base clearly shows that there's a path already laid out for me: there's already an interface ready to be faked or there's already a place where a seam can be injected. When these things don't exist, and the class itself isn't sealed (or can be made nonsealed without too much resentment from your peers), I check out this technique first, and only after that move on to more complicated options.

3.5 Variations on refactoring techniques

There are many variations on the preceding simple techniques to introduce *seams* into source code. For example, instead of adding a parameter to a constructor, you can add it directly to the method under test. Instead of sending in an interface, you could send a base class, and so on. Each variation has its own strengths and weaknesses.

One of the reasons you may want to avoid using a base class instead of an interface is that a base class from the production code may already have (and probably has) built-in production dependencies that you'll have to know about and override. This makes implementing derived classes for testing harder than implementing an interface, which lets you know exactly what the underlying implementation is and gives you full control over it.

In chapter 4, we'll look at techniques that can help you avoid writing manual stub classes that implement interfaces, and instead use frameworks that can help do this at runtime.

But for now, let's look at another way to gain control over the code under test *without* using interfaces. You've already seen one way of doing this in the previous pages, but this method is so effective it deserves a discussion of its own.

3.5.1 Using Extract and Override to create stub results

You've already seen an example of Extract and Override in section 3.4.5. We derive from the class under test so that we can override a virtual method and force it to return our stub.

But why stop there? What if you're unable or unwilling to add a new interface every time you need control over some behavior in your code

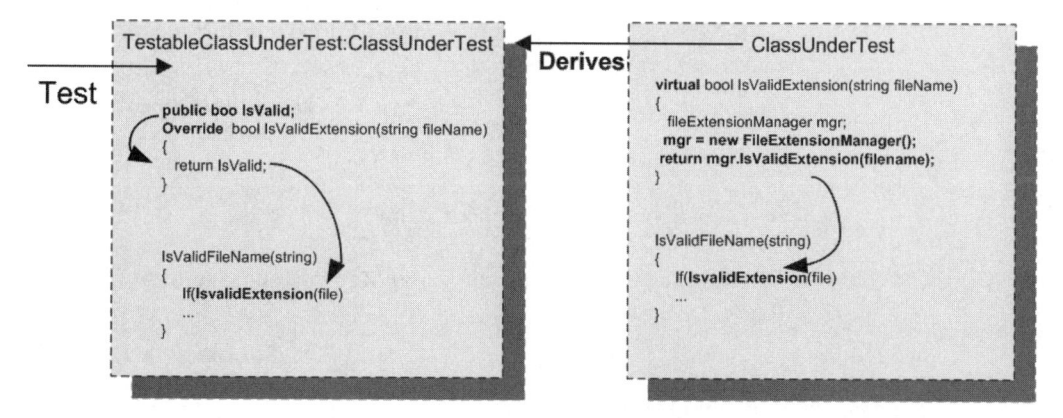

Figure 3.9 Using Extract and Override to return a logical result instead of calling an actual dependency. This uses a simple fake result instead of a stub.

under test? In those cases, Extract and Override can help simplify things, because it doesn't require writing and introducing new interfaces—just deriving from the class under test and overriding some behavior in the class.

Figure 3.9 shows another way we could have forced the code under test to always return true about the validity of the file extension.

In the class under test, instead of *virtualizing* a factory method, we *virtualize* the calculation result. This means that, in our derived class, we override the method and return whatever value we want, without needing to create an interface or a new stub. We simply inherit and override the method to return the desired result.

Listing 3.8 shows how our code might look using this technique.

Listing 3.8 Returning a result rather than a stub object from an extracted method

```
public class LogAnalyzerUsingFactoryMethod
   {
       public bool IsValidLogFileName(string fileName)
       {
           int len = fileName.Length;
           return this.IsValid(fileName) && len>5;
       }

       protected virtual bool IsValid(string fileName)
       {
            FileExtensionManager mgr = new FileExtensionManager();
           return mgr.IsValid(fileName);              ⟵ Returns result from real dependency
       }
   }

   [Test]
       public void overrideTestWithoutStub()
       {
           TestableLogAnalyzer logan = new TestableLogAnalyzer();
           logan.IsSupported = true;                  ⟵ Sets fake result value

           bool result =
 logan.IsValidLogFileName("file.ext");
           Assert.IsFalse(result,"...");
       }
```

```
class TestableLogAnalyzer: LogAnalyzerUsingFactoryMethod
    {
        public bool IsSupported;

        protected override bool IsValid(string fileName)
        {
            return IsSupported;
        }
    }
```
Returns fake value that was set by the test

When you should use Extract and Override

The basic motivation for using this technique is the same as for the method discussed in section 3.4.5. This technique is even simpler than the previous one. If I can, I use this technique over the previous one.

By now, you may be thinking to yourself that adding all these constructors, setters, and factories for the sake of testing is problematic. It breaks some serious object-oriented principles, especially the idea of encapsulation, which says, "Hide everything that the user of your class doesn't need to see." That's our next topic. (Appendix A also deals with testability and design issues.)

3.6 Overcoming the encapsulation problem

Some people feel that opening up the design to make it more testable is a bad thing because it hurts the object-oriented principles the design is based on. I can wholeheartedly say to those people, "Don't be silly." Object-oriented techniques are there to enforce some constraints on the end user of the API (the end user being the programmer who will use your object model) so that the object model is used properly and is protected from unforeseen ways of usage. Object orientation also has a lot to do with reuse of code and the single-responsibility principle (which requires that each class has only a single responsibility).

When we write unit tests for our code, we are adding another end user (the test) to the object model. That end user is just as important as the original one, but it has different goals when using the model. The test has specific requirements from the object model that seem to defy the basic logic behind a couple of object-oriented principles, mainly *encapsulation*. Encapsulating those external dependencies somewhere without allowing anyone to change them, having private constructors or sealed classes, having nonvirtual methods that can't be overridden: all these are classic signs of overprotective design. (Security-related designs are a special case that I forgive.) The problem is that the second end user of the API, the test, needs them as a feature in the code. I call the design that emerges from designing with testability in mind testable object-oriented design (TOOD), and you'll hear more about TOOD in Appendix A.

The concept of *testable designs* conflicts in places with the concept of object-oriented design. If you really need to consolidate these two worlds (to have your cake and eat it too), here are a few tips and tricks you can use to make sure that the extra constructors and setters don't show up in release mode or at least don't play a part in release mode.

> **TIP** A good place to look at design objectives that adhere more to the idea of testable design is Bob Martin's timeless SOLID design series of articles. SOLID stands for Single Responsibility Principle, Open Closed Principle, Liskov Substitution Principle, Interface Segregation Principle, and Dependency Inversion Principles. These principles can be found at http://butunclebob.com/ArticleS.UncleBob.PrinciplesOfOod.

3.6.1 Using internal and [InternalsVisibleTo]

If you dislike adding a public constructor to your class that everyone can see, you can make it `internal` instead of `public`. You can then expose all `internal` related members and methods to your test assembly by using the `[InternalsVisibleTo]` assembly-level attribute. Listing 3.9 shows this more clearly.

Listing 3.9 Exposing internals to the tests assembly

```
public class LogAnalyzer
    {
    ...
    internal LogAnalyzer (IExtensionManager extentionMgr)
        {
            manager = extentionMgr;
        }
```

```
    ...
}

using System.Runtime.CompilerServices;
[assembly:
        InternalsVisibleTo("AOUT.CH3.Logan.Tests")]
```

Such code can usually be found in `AssemblyInfo.cs` files. Using `internal` is a good solution if you have no other way of making things public to the test code.

3.6.2 Using the [Conditional] attribute

The `System.Diagnostics.ConditionalAttribute` attribute is notable in its non-intuitive action. When you put this attribute on a method, you initialize the attribute with the string signifying a conditional build parameter that's passed in as part of the build. (`DEBUG` and `RELEASE` are the two most common ones, and Visual Studio uses them by default according to your build type.)

If the build flag is *not* present during the build, the *callers* to the annotated method won't be included in the build. For example, this method will have all the callers to it removed during a release build, but the method itself will stay on:

```
[Conditional ("DEBUG")]
public void DoSomething()
{
}
```

You can use this attribute on methods (but not on constructors) that you only want called in certain debug modes.

> **NOTE** These annotated methods won't be hidden from the production code, which is different from how the next technique we'll discuss behaves.

It's important to note that using conditional compilation constructs in your production code can reduce its readability and increase its "spaghetti-ness." Beware!

3.6.3 Using #if and #endif with conditional compilation

Putting your methods or special test-only constructors between `#if` and `#endif` constructs will make sure they only compile when that build flag is set, as shown in listing 3.10.

Listing 3.10 Using special build flags

```
#if DEBUG
        public LogAnalyzer (IExtensionManager extensionMgr)
        {
            manager = extensionMgr;
        }
#endif
...
#if DEBUG
        [Test]
        public void
IsValidFileName_NameLessThan6SupportedExtension_False()
        {
...
            //create analyzer and inject stub
            LogAnalyzer log =
                new LogAnalyzer (myFakeManager);
            ...
        }
#endif
```

This method is commonly used, but it can lead to code that looks messy. Consider using the `[InternalsVisibleTo]` attribute where you can, for clarity.

3.7 Summary

We started writing simple tests in the first couple of chapters, but we have dependencies in our tests that we need to find a way to override. We learned how to stub out those dependencies in this chapter, using interfaces and inheritance.

A stub can be injected into your code in many different ways. The real trick is to locate the right layer of indirection, or to create one, and then use it as a *seam* from which you can inject your stub into running code.

The deeper you go down the layers of interactions, the harder it will be to understand the test, and to understand the code under test and its deep interactions with other objects. The closer you are to the surface of the object under test, the easier your test will be to understand and manage, but you may also be giving up some of your power to manipulate the environment of the object under test.

Learn the different ways of injecting a stub into your code. When you master them, you'll be in a much better position to pick and choose which method you want to use when.

The Extract and Override method is great for simulating inputs into the code under test, but if you're also testing interactions between objects (the topic of the next chapter), be sure to have it return an interface rather than an arbitrary return value. It will make your testing life easier.

Testable object-oriented design (TOOD) can present some interesting advantages over classic object-oriented design, such as allowing maintainability while still permitting tests to be written against the code base. If you really need them, there are several ways of hiding your testable design in release mode, such as the `[InternalsVisibleTo]` and the `[Conditional]` attributes.

In chapter 4, we'll take a look at some other issues relating to dependencies, and find ways to resolve them: how to avoid writing manual stubs for interfaces, and how to test the interaction between objects as part of your unit tests.

4
Interaction testing using mock objects

This chapter covers

- *Defining interaction testing*
- *Understanding mock objects*
- *Differentiating mocks and stubs*
- *Exploring mock object best practices*

In the previous chapter, we solved the problem of testing code that depends on other objects to run correctly. We used stubs to make sure that the code under test received all the inputs it needed so that we could test its logic independently.

In this chapter, we'll look at how you test whether an object calls other objects correctly. The object being called may not return any result or save any state, but it has complex logic that needs to result in correct calls to other objects. Using the approach we've employed so far won't do here, because there's no externalized API that we can use to check if something has changed in the object under test. How do you test that your object interacts with other objects correctly? We'll use mock objects.

The first thing we need to do is define what interaction testing is, and how it's different from the testing we've done so far—state-based testing.

4.1 State-based versus interaction testing

We defined state-based testing in section 2.6 of chapter 2. Let's define interaction testing, and then look at how we use it in our unit tests.

DEFINITION *Interaction testing* is testing how an object sends input to or receives input from other objects—how that object *interacts* with other objects.

You can also think of interaction testing as being "action-driven testing," and state-based testing as being "result-driven testing." *Action-driven* means that you test a particular action an object takes (such as sending a message to another object). *Result-driven* means you test that some end result is now true (that a property value has changed, for example). It's usually preferable to check the end results of objects, not their particular actions. But sometimes interactions between objects are the end result. That's when we need to test the interaction itself (where the end result of calling a method on the object under test is that the object then calls another object, such as a web service).

Interaction testing, in one form or another, has existed since the first days of unit testing. Back then, there weren't any names or patterns for it, but people still needed to know if one object called another object correctly.

Let's look at an example of the two types of testing. Say you have a watering system, and you have given your system specific instructions on when to water the tree in your yard: how many times a day and what quantity of water each time. Here's how you'd test that it's working correctly:

- *State-based testing*—Run the system for a specific amount of time (say 12 hours), and at the end of that time, check the state of the tree being irrigated. Is the land moist enough, is the tree doing well, are its leaves green, and so on. It may be quite a difficult test to perform, but assuming you can do it, you can find out if your watering system works.
- *Interaction testing*—At the end of the irrigation hose, set up a device that records when irrigation starts and stops, and how much water flows through the device. At the end of the day, check that the device

has been called the right number of times, with the correct quantity of water each time, and don't worry about checking the tree. In fact, you don't even need a tree to check that the system works. You can go further and modify the system clock on the irrigation unit, so that it thinks that the time to irrigate has arrived, and it will irrigate whenever you choose. That way, you don't have to wait (for 12 hours in this example) to find out whether it works.

Sometimes state-based testing is the best way to go because interaction testing is too difficult to pull off. That's the case with crash test dummies: a car is crashed into a standing target at a specific speed, and after the crash, both car and dummies' states are checked to determine the outcomes. Running this sort of test as an interaction test in a lab can be too complicated, and a real-world state-based test is called for. (People are working on simulating crashes with computers, but it's still not close to testing the real thing.)

Now, back to the irrigation system. What is that device that records the irrigation information? It's a fake water hose, or a stub, you could say. But it's a smarter breed of stub—a stub that records the calls made to it. That's partly what a mock object is.

DEFINITION A *mock object* is a fake object in the system that decides whether the unit test has passed or failed. It does so by verifying whether the object under test interacted as expected with the fake object. There's usually no more than one mock per test.

A mock object may not sound much different from a stub, but the differences are large enough to warrant discussion and special syntax in various frameworks, as you'll see in chapter 5. Let's look at exactly what the difference is.

4.2 The difference between mocks and stubs

The distinction between mocks and stubs is important because a lot of today's tools and frameworks (as well as articles) use these terms to describe different things. There's a lot of confusion about what each term means, and many people seem to use them interchangeably. Once

Figure 4.1 When using a stub, the assert is performed on the class under test. The stub aids in making sure the test runs smoothly.

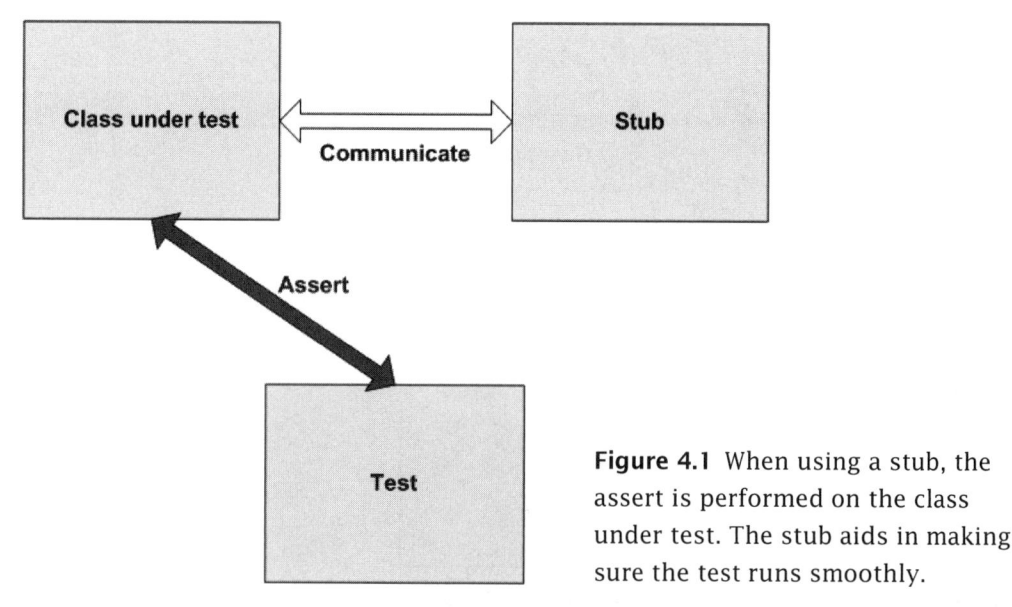

you understand the differences, you can evaluate the world of tools, frameworks, and APIs more carefully and understand more clearly what each does.

At first glance, the difference between mocks and stubs may seem small or nonexistent. The distinction is subtle, but important, because many of the mock object frameworks that we'll deal with in the next chapters use these terms to describe different behaviors in the framework. The basic difference is that stubs can't fail tests, and mocks can.

Stubs replace an object so that we can test another object without problems. Figure 4.1 shows the interaction between the stub and the class under test.

The easiest way to tell we're dealing with a stub is to notice that the stub can never fail the test. The asserts the test uses are always against the class under test.

On the other hand, the test will use a mock object to verify whether the test failed or not. Figure 4.2 shows the interaction between a test and a mock object. Notice that the assert is performed on the mock.

Again, the mock object is the object we use to see if the test failed or not.

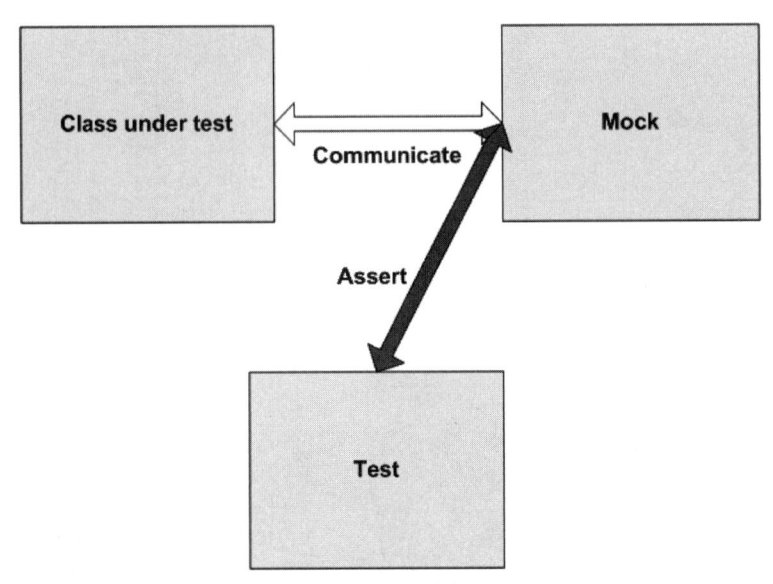

Figure 4.2 The class under test communicates with the mock object, and all communication is recorded in the mock. The test uses the mock object to verify that the test passes.

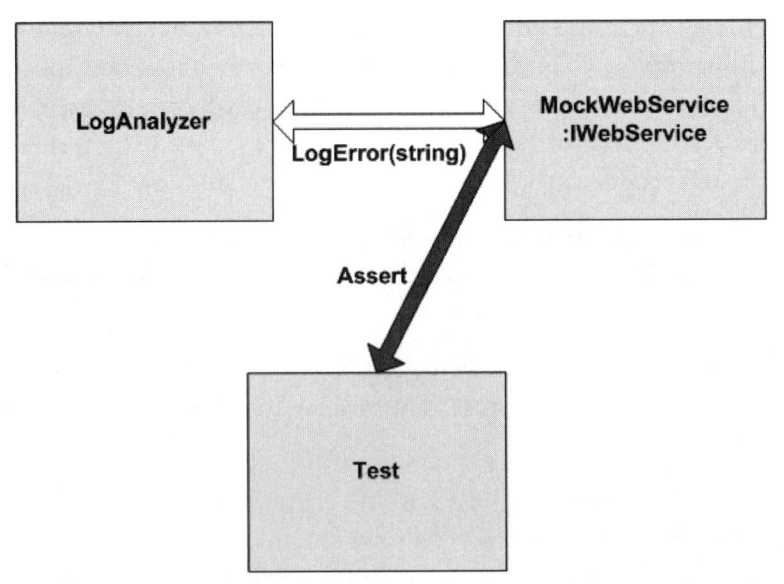

Figure 4.3 Our test will create a `MockWebService` to record messages that `LogAnalyzer` will send. It will then assert against the `MockWebService`.

Let's look at these ideas in action by building our own mock object.

4.3 A simple manual mock example

Creating and using a mock object is much like using a stub, except that a mock will do a little more than a stub: it will save the history of communication, which will later be verified.

Let's add a new requirement to our `LogAnalyzer` class. This time, it will have to interact with an external web service that will receive an error message whenever the `LogAnalyzer` encounters a filename whose length is too short.

Unfortunately, the web service we'd like to test against is still not fully functional, and even if it were, it would take too long to use it as part of our tests. Because of that, we'll refactor our design and create a new interface for which we can later create a mock object. The interface will have the methods we'll need to call on our web service, and nothing else.

Figure 4.3 shows how our `MockWebService` will fit into the test.

First off, let's extract a simple interface that we can use in our code under test, instead of talking directly to the web service:

```
public interface IWebService
{
    void LogError(string message);
}
```

This interface will serve us when we want to create stubs as well as mocks. It will let us avoid an external dependency we have no control over.

Next, we'll create the mock object itself. It may look like a stub, but it contains one extra bit of code that makes it a mock object.

```
public class MockService:IWebService
{
    public string LastError;

    public void LogError(string message)
    {
```

```
            LastError = message;
    }
}
```

Our mock implements an interface, as a stub does, but it saves some state for later, so that our test can then assert and verify that our mock was called correctly.

> **NOTE** According to *xUnit Test Patterns* by Gerard Meszaros, this would be called a Test Spy.

Listing 4.1 shows what the test might look like.

Listing 4.1 Testing the `LogAnalyzer` with a mock object

```
[Test]
 public void Analyze_TooShortFileName_CallsWebService()
  {
     MockService mockService = new MockService();
     LogAnalyzer log = new LogAnalyzer(mockService);
     string tooShortFileName="abc.ext";
     log.Analyze(tooShortFileName);

        Assert.AreEqual("Filename too short:abc.ext",    ⟵  Asserts against
                    mockService.LastError);                  mock object
 }

 public class LogAnalyzer
 {
    private IWebService service;

    public LogAnalyzer(IWebService service)
    {
        this.service = service;
    }

    public void Analyze(string fileName)
    {
        if(fileName.Length<8)
        {
            service.LogError("Filename too short:"      ⟵  Logs error in
                    + fileName);                            production code
        }
    }
}
```

Notice how the assert is performed against the mock object, and not against the `LogAnalyzer` class. That's because we're testing the interaction between `LogAnalyzer` and the web service. We still use the same dependency injection techniques from chapter 3, but this time the mock object (used instead of a stub) also makes or breaks the test.

Also notice that we aren't writing the tests directly inside the mock object code. There are a couple of reasons for this:

- We'd like to be able to reuse the mock object in other test cases, with other asserts on the message.
- If the assert were put inside the mock object, whoever reads the test would have no idea what we're asserting. We'd be hiding essential information from the test code, which hinders the readability and maintainability of the test.

In your tests, you might find that you need to replace more than one object. We'll look at combining mocks and stubs next.

4.4 Using a mock and a stub together

Let's consider a more elaborate problem. This time our `LogAnalyzer` not only needs to talk to a web service, but if the web service throws an error, `LogAnalyzer` has to log the error to a different external dependency, sending it by email to the web service administrator, as shown in figure 4.4.

Here's the logic we'd like to test inside `LogAnalyzer`:

```
if(fileName.Length<8)
{
   try
   {
     service.LogError("Filename too short:" + fileName);
   }
   catch (Exception e)
   {
       email.SendEmail("a","subject",e.Message);
   }
}
```

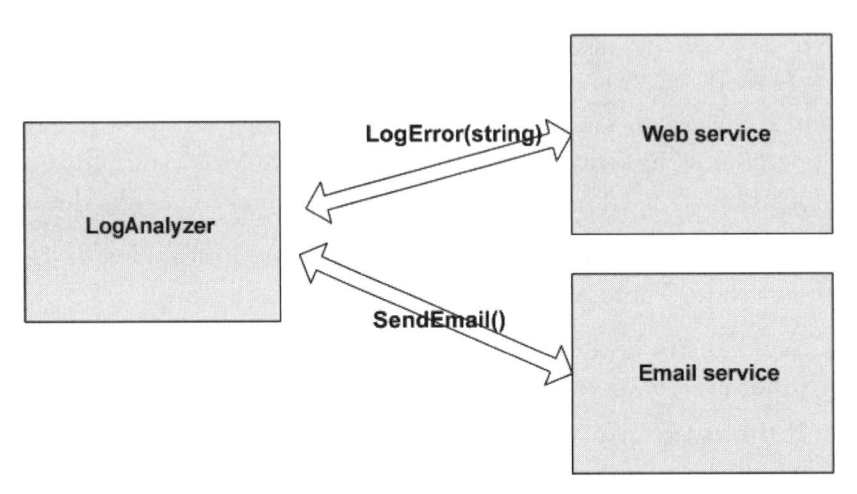

Figure 4.4 `LogAnalyzer` has two external dependencies: web service and email service. We need to test `LogAnalyzer`'s logic when calling them.

Notice that there's logic here that only applies to interacting with external objects; there's no end result returned to the caller. How do you test that `LogAnalyzer` calls the email service correctly when the web service throws an exception?

Here are the questions we're faced with:

- How can we replace the web service?
- How can we simulate an exception from the web service so that we can test the call to the email service?
- How will we know that the email service was called correctly or at all?

We can deal with the first two questions by using a stub for the web service. To solve the third problem, we can use a mock object for the email service.

DEFINITION   A *fake* is a generic term that can be used to describe either a stub or a mock object (handwritten or otherwise), because they both look like the real object. Whether a fake is a stub or a mock depends on how it's used in the current test. If it's used to check an interaction (asserted against), it's a *mock object*. Otherwise, it's a *stub*.

In our test, we'll have two fakes. One will be the email service mock, which we'll use to verify that the correct parameters were sent to the email service. The other will be a stub that we'll use to simulate an exception thrown from the web service. It's a stub because we won't be using the web service fake to verify the test result, only to make sure the test runs correctly. The email service is a mock because we'll assert against it that it was called correctly. Figure 4.5 shows this visually.

Here's the interface for the email service, followed by the mock email service:

```
public interface IEmailService
    {
        void SendEmail(string to, string subject, string body);
    }
```

Listing 4.2 shows the code that implements figure 4.5.

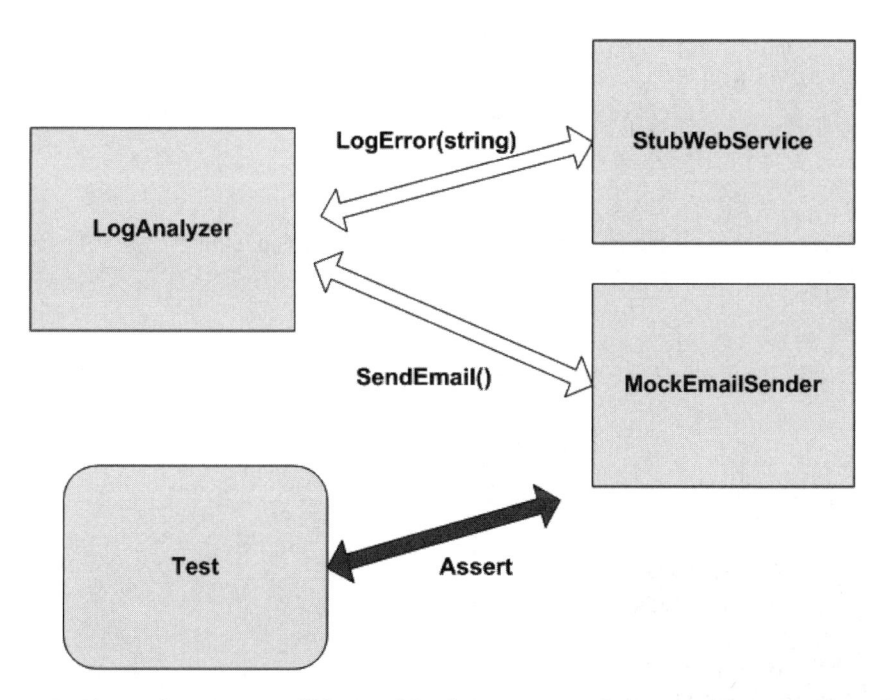

Figure 4.5 The web service will be stubbed out to simulate an exception; then the email sender will be mocked to see if it was called correctly. The whole test will be about how `LogAnalyzer` interacts with other objects.

Listing 4.2 Testing the LogAnalyzer with a mock and a stub

```
public class LogAnalyzer2
    {
        private IWebService service;
        private IEmailService email;

        public IWebService Service
        {
            get { return service; }
            set { service = value; }
        }

        public IEmailService Email
        {
            get { return email; }
            set { email = value; }
        }

    public void Analyze(string fileName)
        {
            if(fileName.Length<8)
            {
                try
                {
                service.LogError("Filename too short:" + fileName);
                }
                catch (Exception e)
                {
                    email.SendEmail("a","subject",e.Message);
                }
            }
        }
    }

    [TestFixture]
     public class LogAnalyzer2Tests
     {
        [Test]
         public void Analyze_WebServiceThrows_SendsEmail()
         {
            StubService stubService = new StubService();
```

```
            stubService.ToThrow=  new Exception("fake exception");

            MockEmailService mockEmail = new MockEmailService();

            LogAnalyzer2 log = new LogAnalyzer2();
        //we use setters instead of
        //constructor parameters for easier coding
            log.Service = stubService                ◄──┐
            log.Email=mockEmail;                        ❶ Using properties instead
                                                          of constructor injection
            string tooShortFileName="abc.ext";
            log.Analyze(tooShortFileName);

            Assert.AreEqual("a",mockEmail.To);
            Assert.AreEqual("fake exception",mockEmail.Body);
            Assert.AreEqual("subject",mockEmail.Subject);
        }
    }

    public class StubService:IWebService
    {
        public Exception ToThrow;
        public void LogError(string message)
        {
            if(ToThrow!=null)
            {
                throw ToThrow;
            }
        }
    }

    public class MockEmailService:IEmailService
    {
        public string To;
        public string Subject;
        public string Body;

        public void SendEmail(string to,
                              string subject,
                              string body)
        {
            To = to;
```

```
            Subject = subject;
            Body = body;
        }
    }
```

Note that the public properties ❶ we've added will be used instead of a constructor. We'll use these setters to set the stub and mock, which will make the code easier to read and maintain.

This code raises some interesting questions:

- Why are we doing several asserts in a single test? How easy would it be to separate this test into three different tests with one assert each? Could the three asserts be combined into a single logical test?
- It can be quite tedious to create manual mocks and stubs for each test or test class. How can we overcome that?
- Couldn't we have used the `MockService` from listing 4.1 as a stub?

We'll explore answers to these questions in the rest of this and the next chapter.

One important thing to consider is how many mocks and stubs you can use in a test.

4.5 One mock per test

In a test where you test only one thing (which is how I recommend you write tests), there should be no more than one mock object. All other fake objects will act as stubs. Having more than one mock per test usually means you're testing more than one thing, and this can lead to complicated or brittle tests. (Look for more on this in chapter 7.)

If you follow this guideline, when you get to more complicated tests, you can always ask yourself, "Which one is my mock object?" Once you've identified it, you can leave the others as stubs and not worry about assertions against them.

Next, we'll deal with a more complex scenario: using a stub to return a stub or a mock that will be used by the application.

4.6 Stub chains: stubs that produce mocks or other stubs

One of the most common scamming techniques online these days follows a simple path. A fake email is sent to a massive number of recipients. The fake email is from a fake bank or online service claiming that the potential customer needs to have a balance checked or to change some account details on the online site.

All the links in the email point to a fake site. It looks exactly like the real thing, but its only purpose is to collect data from innocent customers of that business. This simple "chain of lies" is known as a "phishing" attack, and is more lucrative that you'd imagine. Most people respond instinctively to these emails and do what's asked. Consequently, it's one of the biggest threats to identity theft in the world.

How does this "chain of lies" matter to us? Sometimes we want to have a fake component return another fake component, producing our own little chain of stubs in our tests, so that we can end up collecting some data during our test. A stub leads to a mock object that records data.

The design of many systems under test allows for complex object chains to be created. It's not uncommon to find code like this:

```
IServiceFactory factory = GetServiceFactory();
IService service = factory.GetService();
```

Or like this:

```
String connstring =
GlobalUtil.Configuration.DBConfiguration.ConnectionString;
```

Suppose you wanted to replace the connection string with one of your own during a test. You could set up the `Configuration` property of the `GlobalUtil` object to be a stub object. Then, you could set the `DBConfiguration` property on that object to be another stub object, and so on.

It's a powerful technique, but you need to ask yourself whether it might not be better to refactor your code to do something like this:

```
String connstring =GetConnectionString();
Protected virtual string GetConnectionString()
{
    Return GlobalUtil.Configuration.DBConfiguration.ConnectionString;
}
```

You could then override the virtual method as described in section 3.4.5 in chapter 3. This can make the code easier to read and maintain, and it doesn't require adding new interfaces to insert two more stubs into the system.

> **TIP** Another good way to avoid call chains is to create special wrapper classes around the API that simplify using and testing it. For more about this method, see Michael Feathers' book, *Working Effectively with Legacy Code*. The pattern is called "Adapt Parameter" in that book.

Handwritten mocks and stubs have benefits, but they also have their share of problems. Let's take a look at them.

4.7 The problems with handwritten mocks and stubs

There are several issues that crop up when using manual mocks and stubs:

- It takes time to write the mocks and stubs.
- It's difficult to write stubs and mocks for classes and interfaces that have many methods, properties, and events.
- To save state for multiple calls of a mock method, you need to write a lot of boilerplate code to save the data.
- If you want to verify all parameters on a method call, you need to write multiple asserts. If the first assert fails, the others will never run, because a failed assert throws an exception.
- It's hard to reuse mock and stub code for other tests.

These problems are inherent in manually written mocks and stubs. Fortunately, there are other ways to create mocks and stubs, as you'll see in the next chapter.

4.8 Summary

This chapter covered the distinction between stub and mock objects. A mock object is like a stub, but it also helps you to assert something in your test. A stub, on the other hand, can never fail your test and is strictly there to simulate various situations. This distinction is important because many of the mock object frameworks you'll see in the next chapter have these definitions engrained in them, and you'll need to know when to use which.

Combining stubs and mocks in the same test is a powerful technique, but you must take care to have no more than one mock in each test. The rest of the fake objects should be stubs that can't break your test. Following this practice can lead to more maintainable tests that break less often when internal code changes.

Stubs that produce other stubs or mocks can be a powerful way to inject fake dependencies into code that uses other objects to get its data. It's a great technique to use with factory classes and methods. You can even have stubs that return other stubs that return other stubs and so on, but at some point you'll wonder if it's all worth it. In that case, take a look at the techniques described in chapter 3 for injecting stubs into your design. (Only one mock framework currently allows stubbing a full call chain in one line of code—creating stubs that return stubs—and that's Typemock Isolator.)

One of the most common problems encountered by people who write tests is using mocks too much in their tests. You should rarely verify calls to fake objects that are used both as mocks and as stubs in the same test. (This is quite a narrow corner case. You verify a function was called. Because it's still a function, it must return some value, and because you're faking that method, you'll need to tell the test what that value will be. This value is the part in the test that's a stub, because it has nothing to do with asserting whether the test passes or fails.) If you see "verify" and "stub" on the same variable in the same test, you most likely are overspecifying your test, which will make it more brittle.

You can have multiple stubs in a test, because a class may have multiple dependencies. Just make sure your test remains readable. Structure your code nicely so the reader of the test understands what's going on.

You may find that writing manual mocks and stubs is inconvenient for large interfaces or for complicated interaction-testing scenarios. It is, and there are better ways to do this, as we'll see in the next chapter. But often you'll find that handwritten mocks and stubs still beat frameworks for simplicity and readability. The art lies in when you use which.

Our next chapter deals with mock object frameworks, which allow you to automatically create, at runtime, stub or mock objects and use them with at least the same power as manual mocks and stubs, if not more.

5
Isolation (mock object) frameworks

This chapter covers

- Understanding isolation frameworks
- Defining fake objects
- Using Rhino Mocks to create stubs and mocks
- Surveying advanced use cases for mocks and stubs
- Exploring arrange-act-assert and record-and-replay syntax
- Avoiding common misuses of isolation frameworks

In the previous chapter, we looked at writing mocks and stubs manually and saw the challenges involved. In this chapter, we'll look at some elegant solutions for these problems in the form of a *mock object framework*—a reusable library that can create and configure stub and mock objects *at runtime*. These objects are usually referred to as *dynamic stubs* and *dynamic mocks*.

We'll start this chapter off with an overview of mock object frameworks (or isolation frameworks—the word *mock* is too overloaded already) and what they can do for us. We'll then take a closer look at one specific framework: Rhino Mocks. We'll see how we can use it to test various things and to create stubs, mocks, and other interesting things.

Later in this chapter, we'll contrast Rhino Mocks with other frameworks currently available to .NET developers, and we'll finish with a list of things to watch out for when using such frameworks in your tests.

Let's start at the beginning: What are isolation frameworks?

5.1 Why use isolation frameworks?

We'll start with a basic definition.

DEFINITION   An *isolation framework* is a set of programmable APIs that make creating mock and stub objects much easier. Isolation frameworks save the developer from the need to write repetitive code to test or simulate object interactions.

This definition may sound a bit bland, but it needs to be generic in order to include the various isolation frameworks out there.

Isolation frameworks exist for most languages that have a unit-testing framework associated with them. For example, C++ has mockpp and other frameworks, and Java has jMock and EasyMock, among others. .NET has NMock, Moq, Typemock Isolator, and Rhino Mocks.

Using isolation frameworks instead of writing mocks and stubs manually, as in previous chapters, has several advantages that make developing more elaborate and complex tests easier, faster, and less error-prone.

The best way to understand the value of an isolation framework is to see a problem and solution. One problem that might occur when using handwritten mocks and stubs is repetitive code.

Assume you have an interface a little more complicated than the ones shown so far:

```
public interface IComplicatedInterface
    {
        void Method1(string a, string b, bool c, int x, object o);
        void Method2(string b, bool c, int x, object o);
        void Method3(bool c, int x, object o);
    }
```

Creating a handwritten stub or mock for this interface may be time-consuming, because we'd need to remember the parameters on a per-method basis, as listing 5.1 shows.

Listing 5.1 Implementing complicated interfaces with handwritten stubs

```
class MytestableComplicatedInterface:IComplicatedInterface
    {
        public string meth1_a;
        public string meth1_b,meth2_b;
        public bool meth1_c,meth2_c,meth3_c;
        public int meth1_x,meth2_x,meth3_x;
        public int meth1_0,meth2_0,meth3_0;

        public void Method1(string a,
string b, bool c,
int x, object o)
        {
            meth1_a = a;
            meth1_b = b;
            meth1_c = c;
            meth1_x = x;
            meth1_0 = 0;
        }

        public void Method2(string b, bool c, int x, object o)
        {
            meth2_b = b;
            meth2_c = c;
            meth2_x = x;
            meth2_0 = 0;
        }

        public void Method3(bool c, int x, object o)
        {
            meth3_c = c;
            meth3_x = x;
            meth3_0 = 0;
        }
    }
```

Not only is this test time-consuming and cumbersome to write, what happens if we want to test that a method is called many times? Or if we want it to return a specific value based on the parameters it receives, or to remember all the values for all the method calls on the same method (the parameter history)? The code gets ugly fast.

Using an isolation framework, the code for doing this becomes trivial, readable, and much shorter, as you'll see when you create your first dynamic mock object.

> **NOTE** The word *fake* was introduced in chapter 4 as a generic term for either a stub or a mock.

5.2 Dynamically creating a fake object

Let's define *dynamic fake objects*, and how they're different from regular mocks.

> **DEFINITION** A *dynamic fake object* is any stub or mock that's created at runtime without needing to use a handwritten implementation of an interface or subclass.

Using dynamic fakes removes the need to hand-code classes that implement interfaces or that derive from other classes, because this can be generated for the developer at runtime by a simple line of code.

5.2.1 Introducing Rhino Mocks into your tests

In this chapter, we'll use Rhino Mocks, an isolation framework that's open source and freely downloadable from http://ayende.com. It's simple and quick to use, with little overhead in learning how to use the API. I'll walk you through a few examples, and then we'll explore other frameworks and discuss the differences among them.

The only thing you'll need to do to use Rhino Mocks, after downloading and unzipping it, (assuming you have NUnit installed on your machine) is to add a reference to the Rhino.Mocks.Dll. In the Add Reference dialog of the test project, click Browse, and locate the downloaded DLL file (which you can get from http://www.ayende.com/projects/rhino-mocks/downloads.aspx).

Rhino Mocks allows us to create and use fakes in two different ways. The first one is the *record-and-replay* model, and is the one you'll be seeing most in this chapter. The other is the *arrange-act-assert* model, which I'll be discussing near the end of this chapter.

Rhino Mocks contains in its API a class called `MockRepository` that has special methods for creating mocks and stubs. The first one we'll look at is `StrictMock()`. The method is called with a generic parameter matching the type of an interface or class that you'd like to fake, and it *dynamically* creates a fake object that adheres to that interface at runtime. You don't need to implement that new object in real code.

5.2.2 Replacing a handwritten mock object with a dynamic one

As an example, let's look at a handwritten mock object used to check whether a call to the log was performed correctly. Listing 5.2 shows the test class and the handwritten mock.

Listing 5.2 Asserting against a handwritten mock object

```
[TestFixture]
 public class LogAnalyzerTests
 {
     [Test]
      public void Analyze_TooShortFileName_CallsWebService()
     {
         ManualMockService mockService = new ManualMockService ();
          LogAnalyzer log = new LogAnalyzer(mockService);
          string tooShortFileName="abc.ext";
          log.Analyze(tooShortFileName);
         Assert.AreEqual("Filename too short:abc.ext",
             mockService.LastError);
     }
 }
 public class ManualMockService:IWebService
 {
     public string LastError;

     public void LogError(string message)
     {
         LastError = message;
     }
 }
```

The parts of the code in bold are the parts that will change when we start using dynamic mock objects.

We'll now create a dynamic mock object, and eventually replace the earlier test. Listing 5.3 shows a simple piece of code that creates a simulated object based on an interface using the record-and-replay syntax in Rhino Mocks.

Listing 5.3 Creating a dynamic mock object using Rhino Mocks

```
[Test]
 public void Analyze_TooShortFileName_ErrorLoggedToService()
 {
 MockRepository mocks = new MockRepository();        ❶ Creates dynamic
 IWebService simulatedService =                        mock object
 mocks.StrictMock<IWebService>();

   using(mocks.Record())
   {
       simulatedService                              ❷ Sets
 .LogError("Filename too short:abc.ext");            expectation
   }

      LogAnalyzer log =
          new LogAnalyzer(simulatedService);
       string tooShortFileName="abc.ext";          ❸ Invokes
       log.Analyze(tooShortFileName);                 LogAnalyzer

 mocks.Verify(simulatedService);                   ❹ Asserts expectations
 }                                                    have been met
```

A couple of lines rid us of the need to use a handwritten stub or mock, because they generate one dynamically ❶. The `simulatedService` object instance is a dynamically generated object that implements the `IWebService` interface, but there's no implementation inside any of the `IWebService` methods.

Next, we set the simulated service object into a "record" state. This is a special state where each method call on the simulated object is recorded as an *expectation* that something should happen to our simulated object ❷. These *expectations* will later be verified by calling `mockEngine.Verify-`

`All()` or preferably by calling `mockEngine.Verify(mockObject)`. In this case, we only have one expectation—that `LogError()` will be called with the exact input of `"file name was too short"`.

> **Expectations on mocks and stubs**
>
> An *expectation* on a fake object is an ad hoc rule that's set on the object.
>
> - *Expectations on mocks*—The rule will usually tell the object that a specific method call on that object is expected to happen later. It may also define how many times it should be called, whether or not the object should throw an exception when that call arrives, or perhaps that the call to this method should never be expected. Expectations are usually set on mock objects during the recording phase of the object, and they're verified at the end of the test where the mock object lives.
>
>   You set expectations on mocks using the static method of `MockRepository.StrictMock<T>` or `MockRespository.DynamicMock<T>`.
>
> - *Expectations on stubs*—This wording may feel unintuitive at first, but the rule can tell the stub what value to return based on expected method calls, whether to throw exceptions, and so on. These expectations aren't to be verified at the end of the test. They're there so that you can run the test and simulate some alternative reality for your code under test.
>
>   You create stubs and set expectations on them using `MockRepository.GenerateStub<T>` or the instance method of `MockRepository.Stub<T>`.

Then we invoke the object under test—our `LogAnalyzer`—by injecting it with our mock object and sending in a short filename that should make it invoke the logger internally ❸.

The last step in this test is to do some sort of assert. In this case, we'll need to find a way to assert that all the expectations have been met by our mock object (that `LogError` was indeed called with the correct string). We can do this by using `mocks.Verify(simulatedService)` ❹. The `Verify(mock)` method will go through each of the expectations that we've set on our mock object and make sure they're true (called correctly).

What happens if the implementation of `log.Analyze()` contains an unexpected call to the service, either through an unexpected parameter value or an unexpected method call that we never recorded?

```
public void Analyze(string fileName)
{
    if(fileName.Length<8)
    {
// expected "Filename too short:abc.extfile name was too short"
        service.LogError("bad string");
    }
}
```

The test will fail, but it won't fail when calling the `Verify()` method. It will fail *before that*, during the test run when the call to `LogError()` is executed. The test will never get to the `Verify()` line because an exception will be thrown before that. To understand why, we'll review the idea of strict and nonstrict mocks.

5.3 Strict versus nonstrict mock objects

Let's discuss what strict and nonstrict mocks mean, and why I consider nonstrict mocks better for most tests.

5.3.1 Strict mocks

A *strict mock object* can only be called by methods that were explicitly set via expectations. Any call that differs either by the parameter values defined or by the method name will usually be handled by throwing an exception. The test will fail on the first *unexpected* method call to a strict mock object. I say "usually" because whether or not the mock throws an exception depends on the implementation of the isolation framework. Some frameworks allow you to define whether to delay all exceptions until calling `verify()` at the end of the test.

This means that a strict mock can fail in two ways: when an unexpected method is called on it, or when expected methods aren't called on it (which is determined by calling `Verify()`).

In Rhino Mocks, strict mocks are created by calling the `StrictMock<T>` method. Unexpected method call exceptions will always be thrown, even if your test contains a global `try-catch` clause, which you'd think would catch such an exception thrown from the isolation framework.

5.3.2 Nonstrict mocks

Most of the time, nonstrict mocks make for less brittle tests. A *nonstrict mock object* will allow any call to be made to it, even if it was not expected. As long as the call doesn't require a return value, it will do what's necessary for everything in the test to work out.

If a method that needs to return a value is called, and you did not set up a return value when you set up that mock object, a Rhino Mocks nonstrict mock or stub object can return the default value for that method's return type (`0` or `null` usually). Other frameworks may take different approaches and may throw an exception if the method isn't configured to return anything.

A nonstrict mock can only fail a test if an expected method was not called. You have to call the `Verify(mock)` method to find out if such a call is missing from the interaction, or the test will pass.

The example in listing 5.3 uses a strict mock approach, which is why running the test fails mid-test instead of when calling `Verify()`. By calling `MockRepository.DynamicMock<type>()` instead of `MockRepository.StrictMock<Type>()`, you'll get a test that only fails on the last line.

Listing 5.4 shows how the test from listing 5.3 would look if we used a nonstrict mock object with Rhino Mocks.

Listing 5.4 Creating a nonstrict mock

```
[Test]
 public void Analyze_TooShortFileName_ErrorLoggedToService()
 {
 MockRepository mocks = new MockRepository();
 IWebService simulatedService =
   MockRespository.DynamicMock<IWebService>();

   using(mocks.Record())
   {
```

```
    //we expected "Filename too short:abc.ext"
        simulatedService.LogError("bad string");
}

        LogAnalyzer log = new LogAnalyzer(simulatedService);
        string tooShortFileName="abc.ext";
        log.Analyze(tooShortFileName);

mocks.VerifyAll();
}
```

Mocks created with an isolation framework can also be used as stubs. We can tell them to return simulated values and create other interesting effects. The next section shows how to do that.

5.4 Returning values from fake objects

To return values from fake objects, you'll almost always want to create a *stub*, and not a *mock* object. That means you can use either the static `MockRepository.GenerateStub<T>` method or the `Stub<T>` instance method. You'll see this in the next section.

You won't often need to, but you can also return values using mock objects, so let's look at how to do that. You can instruct the mock object to return a value based on a method call by using a special class called `LastCall`.

Listing 5.5 shows how we can return a value from a mock object when the interface method has a nonvoid return value. For this example, we'll add an `IGetResults` interface into the system. During the recording stage, we use the `LastCall` class to set the return value for that method call when that specific input (a, in this case) is sent to the method.

Listing 5.5 Returning a value from a mock object using the `LastCall` class

```
[Test]
 public void ReturnResultsFromMock()
 {
    MockRepository mocks = new MockRepository();
    IGetResults resultGetter = mocks.DynamicMock<IGetResults>();
```

```
using(mocks.Record())                        ◁─────①
{
    resultGetter.GetSomeNumber("a");
    LastCall.Return(1);                      ◁────── Forces method call
                                                     to return value
    resultGetter.GetSomeNumber("a");
    LastCall.Return(2);

    resultGetter.GetSomeNumber("b");
    LastCall.Return(3);
}

int result = resultGetter.GetSomeNumber("b");
Assert.AreEqual(3, result);

int result2 = resultGetter.GetSomeNumber("a");
Assert.AreEqual(1, result2);

int result3 = resultGetter.GetSomeNumber("a");
Assert.AreEqual(2, result3);
}
```

As you can see in listing 5.5, there are three expectations set on the mock object, and after each one we set the result to be returned from these method calls. Our mock object will be smart enough to return the correct value based on the input that was set in the expectation. If the same input is set with different return values, they will be returned in the order the code has added them.

You'll notice that, after the recording stage ①, we call `GetSomeNumber` with the `b` input, but the test will still pass, which means the order of the calls doesn't matter.

> **NOTE** If we wanted the order to matter, we could use a concept called ordered mocks, which are used to define the correct order in which calls and return values should be executed. You can find out more about ordered mocks on the Rhino Mocks website.

If we change the order of the last two asserts in the test (which both input `a`), the test will fail because the recording order matters when the input is the same for the expectations.

You can also use `LastCall` to set the method call to throw a specific exception:

```
LastCall.Throw(Exception)
```

Or you can even execute your own delegate:

```
LastCall.Do(yourdelegatehere)
```

Again, it's usually a bad idea to tell a mock to return a value and also to verify mock expectations. In this case, your test may be overspecified; it checks too many things and can break easily. A fake object should either be used as a mock or as a stub, not both.

Stubs are usually more appropriate for returning fake values than mock objects, and isolation frameworks can also create them.

5.5 Creating smart stubs with an isolation framework

A *stub* returns the appropriate responses when called and is never used to see if a test passes or not. Calling `VerifyAll()` or `Verify(stub)` won't verify anything against stub objects—only against mocks. Most isolation frameworks contain the semantic notion of a stub, and Rhino Mocks is no exception.

5.5.1 Creating a stub in Rhino Mocks

Listing 5.6 shows how you create a stub object in Rhino Mocks.

Listing 5.6 Creating a stub is remarkably similar to creating a mock object

```
[Test]
 public void ReturnResultsFromStub()
 {
    MockRepository mocks = new MockRepository();
    IGetResults resultGetter = mocks.Stub<IGetResults>();
    using(mocks.Record())
    {
        resultGetter.GetSomeNumber("a");
        LastCall.Return(1);

    }
```

```
    int result = resultGetter.GetSomeNumber("a");
    Assert.AreEqual(1, result);
}
```

The syntax for creating a stub is almost the same as for mock objects. But consider what happens if you run a test that doesn't call an expected method on the stub, but still verifies expectations. This is shown in listing 5.7.

Listing 5.7 Verifying expectations on a stub object can't fail a test

```
[Test]
 public void StubNeverFailsTheTest()
    {
        MockRepository mocks = new MockRepository();
        IGetResults resultGetter = mocks.Stub<IGetResults>();
        using(mocks.Record())
        {
            resultGetter.GetSomeNumber("a");       Specifies a rule,
            LastCall.Return(1);                    not an expectation

        }
        resultGetter.GetSomeNumber("b");
        mocks.Verify(resultGetter);           ◁—— Will never fail on stubs
    }
```

The test in listing 5.7 will still pass because the stub, by definition, is incapable of breaking a test. Any expectations set on it are purely to determine the return value or the exceptions they should throw.

Rhino Mocks contains a handy feature that isn't supported by most frameworks (except Typemock Isolator). For simple properties on stub objects, get and set properties are automatically implemented and can be used as if the stub were a real object. You can still set up a return value for a property, but you don't need to do it for each and every property on a stub object. Here's an example:

```
ISomeInterfaceWithProperties stub =
    mocks.Stub<ISomeInterfaceWithProperties>();
```

```
stub.Name = "Itamar";
Assert.AreEqual("Itamar",stub.Name);
```

We can also simulate an exception using expectations on a stub. Listing 5.8 shows how you would simulate an `OutOfMemoryException`.

Listing 5.8 Faking an exception using the `LastCall` class

```
[Test]
 public void StubSimulatingException()
    {
        MockRepository mocks = new MockRepository();
        IGetResults resultGetter = mocks.Stub<IGetResults>();
        using(mocks.Record())
        {
            resultGetter.GetSomeNumber("A");
            LastCall.Throw(
 new OutOfMemoryException("The system is out of memory!")
);
        }
        resultGetter.GetSomeNumber("A");
    }
```

This test will fail due to a nasty out-of-memory exception. That's how easy it is.

In the next section, we'll use this ability to simulate errors when testing a more complex scenario.

5.5.2 Combining dynamic stubs and mocks

We'll use the example from listing 4.2 in chapter 4, where we talked about `LogAnalyzer` using a `MailSender` class and a `WebService` class. This is shown in figure 5.1.

We want to make sure that, if the service throws an exception, `LogAnalyzer` will use `MailSender` to send an email to an administrator.

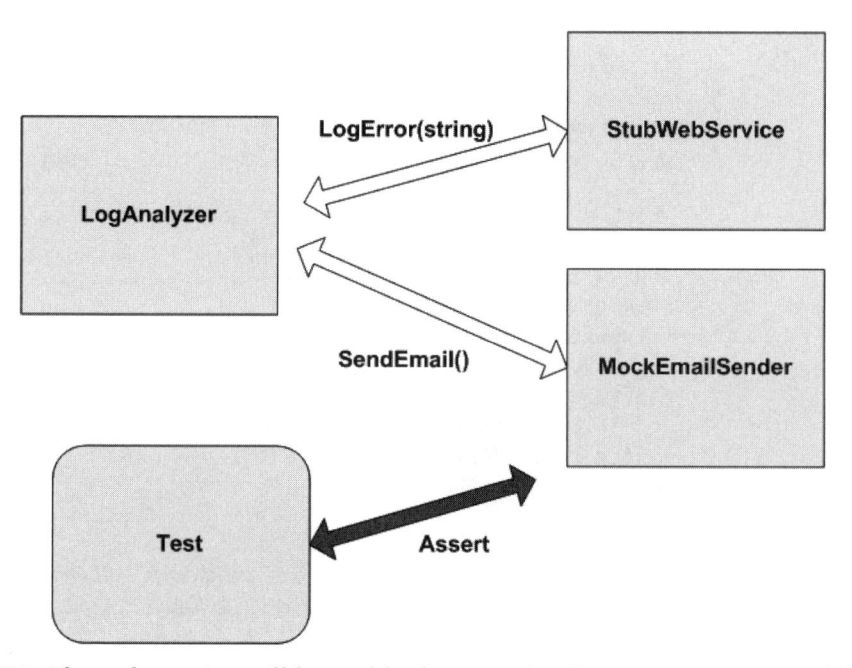

Figure 5.1 The web service will be stubbed out to simulate an exception, and the email sender will be mocked to see if it was called correctly. The whole test will be about how LogAnalyzer interacts with other objects.

Listing 5.9 shows what the logic looks like with all the tests passing.

Listing 5.9 The method under test and a test that uses handwritten mocks and stubs

```
public void Analyze(string fileName)
{
        if(fileName.Length<8)
        {
           try
           {
           service.LogError("Filename too short:" + fileName);
           }
           catch (Exception e)
           {
               email.SendEmail("a","subject",e.Message);
           }
        }
   //..other logic
}
```

```
    [Test]
     public void Analyze_WebServiceThrows_SendsEmail()
     {
         StubService stubService = new StubService();
         stubService.ToThrow=  new Exception("fake exception");

         MockEmailService mockEmail = new MockEmailService();

         LogAnalyzer2 log = new LogAnalyzer2();
    //we use setters instead of
    //constructor parameters for easier coding
         log.Service = stubService;
         log.Email=mockEmail;

         string tooShortFileName="abc.ext";
         log.Analyze(tooShortFileName);

         Assert.AreEqual("a",mockEmail.To);
         Assert.AreEqual("fake exception",mockEmail.Body);
         Assert.AreEqual("subject",mockEmail.Subject);
     }
}
public class StubService:IWebService
{
     ...
}

public class MockEmailService:IEmailService
{
     ...
}
```

Listing 5.10 shows what the test could look like if we used Rhino Mocks.

Listing 5.10 Converting the previous test into one that uses dynamic mocks and stubs

```
[Test]
 public void Analyze_WebServiceThrows_SendsEmail()
 {
     MockRepository mocks = new MockRepository();
     IWebService stubService =
             mocks.Stub<IWebService>();
     IEmailService mockEmail =
```

```
            mocks.StrictMock<IEmailService>();

    using(mocks.Record())
    {
        stubService.LogError("whatever");
        LastCall.Constraints(Is.Anything());        ❶  Ensures
        LastCall.Throw(new Exception("fake exception"));   exception
                                                           is thrown
        mockEmail.SendEmail("a","subject","fake exception");
    }

    LogAnalyzer2 log = new LogAnalyzer2();
    log.Service = stubService;
    log.Email = mockEmail;

    string tooShortFileName = "abc.ext";
    log.Analyze(tooShortFileName);

    mocks.VerifyAll();
}
```

The nice thing about this test is that it requires no handwritten mocks, and it's still readable for the developer.

You might notice a line in listing 5.10 that you haven't come across yet ❶. That's a parameter constraint that makes sure the exception is thrown no matter what we send the stub as a parameter. Parameter constraints are the topic of the next section.

5.6 Parameter constraints for mocks and stubs

Isolation frameworks enable us to easily test the value of parameters being passed into our mock objects. In the coming sections, we'll look at the various ways you can check parameters, such as strings, properties, and full object models, using very little code.

5.6.1 Checking parameters with string constraints

Consider the following scenario. We'd like to test that our `LogAnalyzer` sends a message of this nature to the error log:

"[Some GUID] Error message"

Here's an example:

```
"33DFCC9D-D6C5-45ea-A520-A6018C88E490 Out of memory"
```

In our test, we don't care about the GUID (globally unique identifier) at the beginning, but we care what the error message is. In fact, we don't really have control over the GUID. (We could gain control by creating some sort of `IGuidCreator` interface and stubbing it out in the test, but that might prove a little too much work for what we need.)

Parameter constraints allow us to specify demands or rules to our mocks and stubs for each specific parameter to a method call. Isolation frameworks allow you to create these parameter constraints, and each framework has its own syntax for doing so.

The simplest way to use constraints, as shown in listing 5.11, is by using the `LastCall` class in conjunction with one of the constraints classes. In our case, it would be the `Contains` class, which takes as a constructor the inner string to search for.

Listing 5.11 Using a string constraint in a test

```
[Test]
public void SimpleStringConstraints()
{
    MockRepository mocks = new MockRepository();
    IWebService mockService = mocks.CreateMock<IWebService>();
    using (mocks.Record())
    {
        mockService.LogError("ignored string");
        LastCall.Constraints(new Contains("abc"));
    }

    mockService.LogError(Guid.NewGuid() + " abc");
    mocks.VerifyAll();
}
```

Using the `LastCall.Constraints()` method, we can send in a constraint object (which has to inherit from `AbstractConstraint`, defined as part of Rhino Mocks) for each parameter the method expects. There are four major "helper" classes for constraints in Rhino Mocks, listed in table 5.1. For string-related constraints, we have `Contains`, `EndsWith`, `Like`, and `StartsWith`. All of these classes take a string at the constructor. To help you use these constraints, Rhino Mocks includes a helper class called `Text` that has static methods to return these constraint objects.

Here's the same test using the `Text` class:

```
LastCall.Constraints(Text.Contains("abc"));
```

Table 5.1 The four types of constraints in Rhino Mocks

Helper class	Description	Methods
Text	Checks string-related constraints	Contains(string) EndsWith(string) StartsWith(string) Like(string)
List	Checks collection-related constraints	Count(constraint) Element(int, constraint) Equal(IEnumerable) IsIn(object) OneOf(IEnumerable)
Is	Checks the direct value of parameters passed in	Anything() Equal(object) GreaterThan(IComparable) LessThan(IComparable) Matching<T>(Predicate<T>) NotNull() Same(object) TypeOf(Type)
Property	Checks the value of a specific property on an object that's passed in as a parameter	IsNull() Value(Type, PropertyName, object) ValueConstraint(Type, PropertyName, constraint)
And, Or	Allows combining multiple constraints into a single logical constraint	
Callback	Allows triggering a custom delegate whenever the method is called	

Some of the more interesting constraints are `Property` constraints, `And` and `Or` constraints, and `Callback` constraints. Let's review them one by one.

5.6.2 Checking parameter object properties with constraints

Assume that the `IWebService` interface has a method that expects to take in a `TraceMessage` object, which contains specific rules about its properties. We could easily check the values of the passed-in `TraceMessage` object properties by using the `Property`-related constraints. This is shown in listing 5.12.

Listing 5.12 Using the `Property` constraints by using the `Property` static class

```
[Test]
 public void ConstraintsAgainstObjectPropeties()
 {
     MockRepository mocks = new MockRepository();
     IWebService mockservice = mocks.CreateMock<IWebService>();
     using (mocks.Record())
     {
         mockservice.LogError(new TraceMessage("",0,""));
         LastCall.Constraints(
             Property.Value("Message", "expected msg")
          && Property.Value("Severity", 100)
          && Property.Value("Source", "Some Source"));
     }
     mockservice.LogError(new TraceMessage("",1,"Some Source"));
     mocks.VerifyAll();
 }
```

Checks property values

Notice the use of the `&&` operators here.

Combining constraints with AND and OR

The `&&` operators in listing 5.12 are overloaded to use a special `And` constraint, which requires *all* of these constraints to be `true` for the test to pass. You could also use the `||` overload to set a special `Or` constraint, which only requires *one* of the constraints to be `true`.

The `And` and `Or` constraints both take two `AbstractConstraint` objects in their constructor. The previous example in listing 5.12 combines two `And` constraints and could have been written as in listing 5.13.

Listing 5.13 Combining constraints with And and Or

```
And combined1 =
    new And(
        Property.Value("Message", "expected msg" ),
        Property.Value("Severity", 100));

And combined2 =
    new And(combined1,
        Property.Value("Source", "Some Source"));

LastCall.Constraints(combined2);
```

As you can see, this sort of syntax can get messy pretty fast, and I don't have much use for it. This is where using a manual stub or a callback can make things much clearer, instead of using the And/Or syntax.

Comparing full objects against each other

If we're going to test things in the simplest way, we could compare two objects. We could send the "expected" object with all the expected properties set as part of the recording process (no need for constraints), and then call verify(), as shown in listing 5.14.

Listing 5.14 Comparing full objects

```
[Test]
 public void TestingObjectPropertiesWithObjects()
 {
     MockRepository mocks = new MockRepository();
     IWebService mockservice = mocks.CreateMock<IWebService>();
     using (mocks.Record())
     {
         mockservice.LogError(
 new TraceMessage("Some Message",100,"Some Source"));
     }
     mockservice.LogError(new TraceMessage("",1,"Some Source"));
     mocks.VerifyAll(); //this should fail the test
 }
```

Testing full objects only works for cases where
- it's easy to create the object with the expected properties.
- you want to test all the properties of the object in question.

- you know the exact values of each constraint.
- the `Equals()` method is implemented correctly on the two objects being compared. (It's usually bad practice to rely on the out-of-the-box implementation of `object.Equals()`.)

5.6.3 Executing callbacks for parameter verification

The `Is.Matching<T>(Predicate<T>)` constraint is a powerful feature that allows the developer to test whatever he wants against the passed-in parameter, and return `true` or `false` based on complex rules.

For example, assume that the `IWebService` interface has a method that expects to take in a `TraceMessage` object, which in turn has a property that holds an object you'd like to check. If we had a `ComplexTraceMessage` class with an `InnerMessage` property and a complex verification on it, it might look like listing 5.15.

Listing 5.15 Using an anonymous delegate to verify a parameter

```
LastCall.Constraints(
Is.Matching<ComplexTraceMessage>(
        delegate(ComplexTraceMessage msg)
            {
                if (msg.InnerMessage.Severity < 50
                    && msg.InnerMessage.Message.Contains("a"))
                    {
                       return false;
                    }
                    return true;
            }));
```

In listing 5.15, we're creating a delegate that holds the logic to verify the complex parameter structure.

Instead of using a delegate, we could create a method with the same signature that does the same thing, as shown in listing 5.16.

Listing 5.16 Using a regular method instead of an anonymous delegate

```
[Test]
 public void ComplexConstraintsWithCallbacks()
    {
```

```
    ...
    using (mocks.Record())
    {
        mockservice.LogError(new TraceMessage("", 0, ""));
        LastCall.Constraints(
Is.Matching<ComplexTraceMessage>(verifyComplexMessage));
    }
...
}
private bool verifyComplexMessage(ComplexTraceMessage msg)
{
    if (msg.InnerMessage.Severity < 50
        && msg.InnerMessage.Message.Contains("a"))
    {
        return false;
    }
    return true;
}
```

Rhino Mocks has a simpler syntax if you're only testing a method that accepts a single parameter. Instead of using this syntax,

```
LastCall.Constraints(
    Is.Matching<ComplexTraceMessage>(verifyComplexMessage));
```

you can write this:

```
LastCall.Callback(verifyComplexMessage);
```

Next, we'll see how to test whether objects raise events properly, or whether other objects have registered for an event properly.

5.7 Testing for event-related activities

Testing event-related actions has always been one of the gaping holes in isolation frameworks and has required manual workarounds to test things such as whether an object registered to get an event from another object, or whether an object triggered an event when it should have. Rhino Mocks has facilities to help in these areas as well.

The first scenario we'll tackle is checking whether an object registered to receive an event from another object.

5.7.1 Testing that an event has been subscribed to

Let's assume we have a `Presenter` class that needs to register to the `Load` event of a view class it receives. The code for presenter might look like listing 5.17.

Listing 5.17 Testing that an event was registered properly

```
public class Presenter
{
    IView view;
    public Presenter(IView view)
    {
        this.view = view;
        this.view.Load += new EventHandler(view_Load);    ◄─── ❶ Registers for real event
    }
    void view_Load(object sender, EventArgs e)
    {
        throw new Exception("Not implemented.");
    }
}

  [Test]
    public void VerifyAttachesToViewEvents()
    {
        MockRepository mocks = new MockRepository();
        IView viewMock = (IView)mocks.CreateMock(typeof(IView));
        using (mocks.Record())
        {
            viewMock.Load += null;              ◄─── ❷ Records expected
            LastCall.IgnoreArguments();              event registration
        }
        new Presenter(viewMock);
        mocks.VerifyAll();
    }
```

During the recording stage, we overload the `Load` event ❶. Then we make sure we ignore the arguments in the call, and make sure the call happened ❷.

Some people find that testing whether an event was subscribed to is helpful, but knowing that someone has registered to an event doesn't mean she did something meaningful with it. It's not a real functional requirement that's tested here. If I were doing a test review, I'd say that this was not needed. Instead, you should test that something happened in response to the event being triggered.

To test this scenario as part of a functional requirement, we could say that, upon getting the `Load` event, the presenter's production code will do something that we can see from our test (write to a log, for example). To get that something to happen, we need to find a way to trigger the event from within the stub object and see if the presenter does that action in response. That's what the next section is about.

5.7.2 Triggering events from mocks and stubs

Listing 5.18 shows a test that makes sure `Presenter` writes to a log upon getting an event from our stub. It also uses a class called `EventRaiser`, which triggers the event from the interface.

Listing 5.18 Triggering an event via the `EventRaiser` class in Rhino Mocks

```
[Test]
public void TriggerAndVerifyRespondingToEvents()
{
    MockRepository mocks = new MockRepository();         ◁──①  Uses stub
    IView viewStub = mocks.Stub<IView>();                       for event
    IWebService serviceMock =                                    triggering
        mocks.CreateMock<IWebService>();             ◁──②  Uses mock to
    using (mocks.Record())                                  check log call
    {
        serviceMock.LogInfo("view loaded");
    }
    new Presenter(viewStub,serviceMock);             Creates
                                                     event
                                                     raiser
    IEventRaiser eventer =
        EventRaiser.Create(viewStub, "Load");        ◁──┘
    eventer.Raise(null,EventArgs.Empty);             ◁──── Triggers event

    mocks.Verify(serviceMock);
}
```

Another way of getting an `EventRaiser` object is by using the recording mechanism:

```
IEventRaiser eventer;
using (mocks.Record())
    {
        viewStub.Load += null;
        eventer = LastCall.GetEventRaiser();
    }
```

Notice in listing 5.18 that we're using a stub ❶ to trigger the event, and a mock ❷ to check that the service was written to. The `EventRaiser` takes a stub or a mock and the name of the event to raise from that stub or mock. The `Raise()` method of `EventRaiser` takes a `params object[]` array that requires you to send the number of parameters that the event signature requires. The verification of whether the message was received happened against the mock service.

Now, let's take a look at the opposite end of the testing scenario. Instead of testing the subscriber, we'd like to make sure that the event source triggers the event at the right time. The next section shows how we can do that.

5.7.3 Testing whether an event was triggered

There are two basic approaches to testing that an event was triggered. One is simple, but only works in C#, and the other takes a bit more work, but will work in VB.NET. First, let's look at the simplest way—using a handwritten anonymous method.

Testing event firing inline

A simple way to test the event is by manually registering to it inside the test method using an anonymous delegate. Listing 5.19 shows a simple example.

Listing 5.19 Using an anonymous delegate to register to an event

```
[Test]
public void EventFiringManual()
{
    bool loadFired = false;
```

```
        SomeView view = new SomeView();
        view.Load+=delegate
                    {
                            loadFired = true;
                    };
             view.TriggerLoad(null, EventArgs.Empty);
        Assert.IsTrue(loadFired);
    }
```

The delegate simply records whether the event was fired or not. You could also have it record the values, and they could later be asserted as well. That code could become quite cumbersome, but most of the time it's quite a workable solution, and I recommend it if you use C#. Unfortunately, this won't work in VB.NET because VB.NET currently doesn't support inline anonymous delegates that don't return a value. (It does support nonvoid anonymous delegates and will support the void ones in version 10.)

With VB.NET, the solution requires a bit more work. You need to send in the address of a full method in the class, and have that method set a class scope variable flag telling our test whether the event was fired or not. It's not as clean as I'd like, but it works.

The next section shows a less cumbersome way to test the event triggering and the values that are passed in if we can't use anonymous delegates.

Using EventsVerifier for event testing

Another approach is to use a class called EventsVerifier (not part of Rhino Mocks), which will dynamically register against the required delegate and verify the values that are passed in by the fired event. EventsVerifier can be downloaded from http://weblogs.asp.net/rosherove/archive/2005/06/13/EventsVerifier.aspx. Listing 5.20 shows an example of its use.

Listing 5.20 Using the EventsVerifier class to test for event values

```
[Test]
 public void EventFiringWithEventsVerifier()
 {
```

```
    EventsVerifier verifier = new EventsVerifier();
    SomeView view = new SomeView();
    verifier.Expect(view, "Load",null,EventArgs.Empty);

    view.TriggerLoad(null, EventArgs.Empty);

    verifier.Verify();
}
```

This test assumes we have a class that implements `IView`, and that the class has a method that triggers the event. The verifier takes the object to test against, the name of the event, and any parameter values that are passed in as part of the event signature. Rhino Mocks currently doesn't have a decent enough API to test event verification the way `EventsVerifier` does.

We've covered the basic techniques with Rhino Mocks, so let's look at a different syntax that it supports: arrange-act-assert.

5.8 Arrange-act-assert syntax for isolation

The record-and-replay model for setting expectations on stubs and mocks has always been a polarizing feature. Some people found it easy to grasp, and some people found it unnatural and cumbersome to write. It also makes tests less readable if you have lots of stubs and expectations in a single test.

The Moq framework changed the landscape in the .NET isolation arena by offering a simplified and concise syntax for setting expectations. Rhino Mocks and Typemock Isolator soon followed.

The idea is based on the way we structure our unit tests today: we arrange objects, act on them, and assert that something is true or false (arrange-act-assert, or AAA). It would be nice if we could use isolation frameworks similarly—to arrange mocks and stubs, set their default behavior, and, only at the end of the test, verify whether a call to the mock object took place.

Listing 5.21 shows a simple test with the record-and-replay syntax, followed by the same test in AAA-style syntax using Typemock Isolator and Rhino Mocks.

Listing 5.21 Record-and-replay versus AAA-style isolation

```
[Test]
public void CreateMock_WithReplayAll()
{
    MockRepository mockEngine = new MockRepository();
    IWebService simulatedService =
  mockEngine.DynamicMock<IWebService>();
    using (mockEngine.Record())
    {
       simulatedService.LogError("Filename too short:abc.ext");
    }
    LogAnalyzer log = new LogAnalyzer(simulatedService);
    string tooShortFileName = "abc.ext";
    log.Analyze(tooShortFileName);

    mockEngine.Verify(simulatedService);
}

//the same test using AAA syntax
[Test]
public void CreateMock_WithReplayAll_AAA()
{
    MockRepository mockEngine = new MockRepository();
    IWebService simulatedService =
  mockEngine.DynamicMock<IWebService>();
    LogAnalyzer log = new LogAnalyzer(simulatedService);

    mockEngine.ReplayAll();                    ◁──── Moves to act mode
    log.Analyze("abc.ext");

    simulatedService.AssertWasCalled(                Asserts using
       svc => svc.LogError("name too short:abc.ext"));   Rhino Mocks
}
  //the same test using Typemock Isolator AAA syntax
[Test]
public void CreateMock_Isolator()
{
    IWebService simulatedService =
  Isolate.Fake.Instance<IWebService>();
    LogAnalyzer log = new LogAnalyzer(simulatedService);
    log.Analyze("abc.ext");
```

```
Isolate.Verify.WasCalledWithExactArguments(()=>
    simulatedService
        .LogError("name too short:abs.ext"));
}
```
Asserts using Typemock Isolator

> **Setting up Typemock Isolator**
>
> To use Typemock Isolator, you'll need to first download it from Typemock.com and install it. It's a commercial product with a 21-day (extendable) evaluation period. Unlike the other frameworks, you can't just reference a DLL and start using it. It requires a Visual Studio plugin to work, and a special runner to run tests in command-line mode.
>
> To add a reference to Typemock, right-click on the test project in Solution Explorer, and select Add Reference. From there, go to the .NET tab and select both "Typemock Isolator" and "Typemock Isolator—C#" or "Typemock Isolator—VB". (The product has a special VB-friendly API that solves some VB-specific issues with regard to anonymous delegate usage.)

The main difference between the record-and-replay model and the AAA model is that in AAA we don't need to record what we expect will happen. We just need to check at the end of the test that something did happen correctly. This makes the test more readable, but you'll also notice the use of .NET 3.5 lambda syntax in the AAA-style tests. This is an essential part of these new APIs and what makes these syntax changes technically possible.

If you're not comfortable using lambdas yet, you might be better off using the record-and-replay style until you get used to lambdas, and they're not an obstacle to understanding the code.

Listing 5.22 shows how you'd use AAA-style stubs with Rhino Mocks and Typemock Isolator.

Listing 5.22 Stubs in AAA-style isolation

```
[Test]
 public void StubThatThrowsException_RhinoMocks()
 {
```

```
    IWebService simulatedService =
  MockRepository.GenerateStub<IWebService>();        ❶ Uses
    simulatedService                                    extension
        .Expect(t => t.LogError(""))                    methods
        .Throw(new Exception("fake exception"))
        .Constraints(Is.Anything());                 ❷ Throws fake
                                                       exception
    LogAnalyzer log = new LogAnalyzer(simulatedService);
    log.Analyze("abc.ext");
}

[Test]
 public void StubThatThrowsException_Isolator()
 {
     IWebService simulatedService =
   Isolate.Fake.Instance<IWebService>();            ❸ Provides
     Isolate                                           single point
 .WhenCalled(()=>simulatedService.LogError(""))        of entry to API
 .WillThrow(new Exception("fake exception"));     ❷ Throws fake
                                                     exception
    LogAnalyzer log = new LogAnalyzer(simulatedService);
    log.Analyze("abc.ext");
 }
```

These tests will fail because we're throwing a fake exception ❷ from the web service stub. The `Expect()` method that magically appears on the `IWebService` interface ❶ when using Rhino Mocks is due to extension methods that are used in .NET 3.5. With Typemock Isolator, there's a single point of entry to the API ❸, so no extension methods are necessary.

Personally, I find that the AAA syntax for Typemock Isolator is more readable than in Rhino Mocks. There are many other facets to the new AAA syntax. You can learn more about it at the websites for the various frameworks.

It's now time to compare Rhino Mocks to other isolation frameworks in the .NET world.

5.9 Current isolation frameworks for .NET

Rhino Mocks is certainly not the only isolation framework around. But in an informal poll held March 2009, I asked my blog readers, "Which isolation framework do you use?" Close to 46 percent of the more than 600 people who responded reported using Rhino Mocks, 20 percent were using Moq, and 7 percent were using Typemock. (See figure 5.2.)

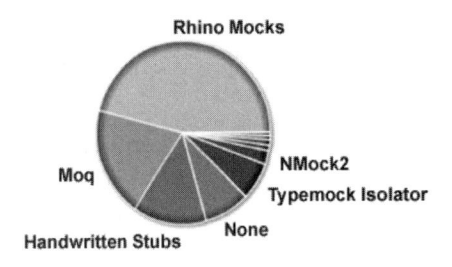

Answer Text	Votes	%
Rhino Mocks	343	46%
Moq	147	20%
Handwritten Stubs	101	14%
None	64	9%
Typemock Isolator	50	7%
NMock2	18	2%

Figure 5.2 Usage of isolation frameworks among my blog readers

What follows is a short review of the current isolation frameworks in .NET. It's usually a good idea to pick one and stick with it as much as possible, for the sake of readability and to lower the learning curve for team members. The information that follows should help you make a choice, but note that each of the frameworks mentioned (especially the top three) can add new features at an alarming pace, so the choice of what's best for your team will seem to be in a constant state of flux.

5.9.1 NUnit.Mocks

NUnit.Mocks is an internal side project of the NUnit framework. It was originally created to provide a simple, lightweight isolation framework that could be used to test NUnit itself, without having to rely on external libraries and version dependencies. Part of NUnit is open source, but it was never regarded as public, so there's little or no documentation about using it on the web today. Charlie Poole, the current maintainer of NUnit, has said that he is considering either removing it completely from the distribution of NUnit or making it public in version 3.0 of NUnit.

Here are a few of the limitations of NUnit.Mocks:

- It doesn't support stub syntax.
- It requires strings to expect calls on method names.
- It has no support for testing or firing events.
- It doesn't support parameter constraints (expected parameter values that are hardcoded in the test).

5.9.2 NMock

NMock is a port of the jMock framework from the Java language. As such, it has been around quite a long time and has many users. It has been largely unmaintained since early 2008 because the developers have gone to work on something bigger and better: NMock2. NMock is open source.

NMock supports the stub syntax but still requires strings for method name expectations. It has no event-raise or test support, but it does support parameter constraints.

5.9.3 NMock2

NMock2 is a large leap forward from NMock. The APIs have changed greatly to accommodate a more fluent calling interface. NMock2, unfortunately, at the time of this writing, has been largely unmaintained since early 2008 and has only come back into some sort of update cycle in 2009, which has driven many people away from using it. NMock2 is open source.

NMock2 supports most, if not all, of the features that Rhino Mocks has, with the main difference being that method expectations are string-based in NMock2, whereas in Rhino Mocks they're call-based. (You call the method as part of the recording process.) NMock2 also features parameter constraints, event-related assertions, and callback abilities.

5.9.4 Typemock Isolator

Typemock Isolator is a commercial isolation framework, although there's a free edition with the same features for use in open source project development. Because it's commercial, it also has good documentation that's always up to date, a support program, and continually updated versions. Isolator is a perfect fit for testing not only new code but also legacy code (untested, existing code) where testing can be impossible in many situations.

Typemock Isolator builds on top of the abilities of the other frameworks, and it also allows mock (called "fake" in the Isolator API) classes that have private constructors, static methods, and much more. It does this by attaching to the .NET profiler APIs—a set of APIs that allow you to intercept a call to anything, anywhere, including private members, statics, and events. Anything that goes on in the .NET runtime can be intercepted. Typemock Isolator has raised quite a stir in the unit-testing and isolation world of .NET. Some people claim that it may be *too powerful*, because it makes it easy to simulate and break the dependencies of any object in your existing code. In that way, it doesn't force you to think about how your design might need to change.

Others feel that it provides a sort of bridge for getting started with testing even if the design is untestable, allowing you to learn better design as you go, instead of having to refactor and learn better design skills before testing. If you can't mock an object in your code, it can mean that the design could be improved to be more decoupled. That's why many people like to use their tests to flush out design problems. Appendix A discusses this issue.

5.9.5 Rhino Mocks

Rhino Mocks was first released in June 2005, and has gained a massive user base already. It's open source, is continuously being worked upon, and has frequent releases. Currently, it's maintained by a single developer (who seems to have no life whatsoever). It has powerful APIs, and one of the things it's most noted for is avoiding the use of strings inside tests. To understand why strings in tests are bad, see the sidebar.

> **Why method strings are bad inside tests**
>
> The best way to explain this is to look at an example of using NUnit.Mocks and Rhino Mocks to do the same thing. We'll see the differences in using strings for method names and using the isolation framework syntax.
>
> We'll mock the following interface:
>
> ```
> interface ILogger
> {
>     void LogError(string msg, int level, string location);
> }
> ```
>
> First, we'll look at how we'd mock this interface using NUnit.Mocks:
>
> ```
> //Using NUnit.Mocks
> DynamicMock mock = new DynamicMock(typeof(ILogger));
> mock.Expect("LogError",
> "param value 1 is string",
> 2,
> "param value 3 is a string as well");
> ILogger myMockInterface = mock.MockInstance as ILogger;
> MytestedClass.SetLogger(myMockInterface);
> ```
> ❶ Uses a string
>
> The Rhino Mocks code looks different:
>
> ```
> //Using Rhino.Mocks
> MockRepository mocks = new MockRepository();
> ILogger simulatedLogger = mocks.StrictMock<ILogger>();
>
> simulatedLogger.LogError("param value 1 is a string", 2,
> "param value 3 is a string");
> mocks.ReplayAll();
>
>  MyTestedClass.SetLogger(simulatedLogger);
> MyTestedClass.DoSomething();
> mocks.VerifyAll();
> ```
> ❷ Uses a strongly typed call
>
> Notice how lines ❶ and ❷ are different in these two versions. If we were to change the name of the `LogError` method on the `ILogger` interface, any tests using NUnit would still compile and would only break at runtime, throwing an exception indicating that a method named `LogError` could not be found.

> With Rhino Mocks, changing the name would not be a problem, because we're invoking the method API as part of our recording stage. Any method changes would keep the test from compiling, and we'd know immediately that there was a problem with the test.
>
> With automated refactoring tools like those in Visual Studio 2005 and 2008, renaming a method is easier, but most refactorings will still ignore strings in the source code. (ReSharper for .NET is an exception. It also corrects strings, but that's only a partial solution that may prove problematic in some scenarios.)

5.9.6 Moq

Moq is a relatively new framework. It requires using .NET 3.5 because it uses lambda constructs to work its magic. It's simple to use if you're comfortable with lambda syntax, but it will only work on interface types and classes that are nonsealed with virtual methods. Unlike Rhino Mocks, it does allow you to fake protected methods.

Let's recap the advantages of using isolation frameworks over handwritten mocks. Then we'll discuss things to watch out for when using isolation frameworks.

5.10 Advantages of isolation frameworks

From what we've covered in this chapter, we can see some distinct advantages to using isolation frameworks:

- *Easier parameter verification*—Using handwritten mocks to test that a method was given the correct parameter values can be a tedious process, requiring time and patience. Most isolation frameworks make checking the values of parameters passed into methods a trivial process even if there are many parameters.
- *Easier verification of multiple method calls*—With manually written mocks, it can be difficult to check that multiple method calls on the same method were made correctly with each having appropriate different parameter values. As we'll see later, this is a trivial process with isolation frameworks.

- *Easier fakes creation*—Isolation frameworks can be used for creating both mocks and stubs more easily.

NOTE When we create mock objects, we establish *expectations* as to what calls will be made against our mock object, and we define any return values necessary. With isolation frameworks, an *expectation* is an essential part of the work process, and it's an integral part of the isolation syntax. This makes it far easier to write multiple expectations on a mock instance while keeping the test readable.

5.11 Traps to avoid when using isolation frameworks

Although there are many advantages to using isolation frameworks, there are some possible dangers too. Some examples are overusing an isolation framework when a manual mock object would suffice, making tests unreadable because of overusing mocks in a test, or not separating tests well enough.

Here's a simple list of things to watch out for:

- Unreadable test code
- Verifying the wrong things
- Having more than one mock per test
- Overspecifying the tests

Let's look at each of these in more depth.

5.11.1 Unreadable test code

Using a mock in a test already makes the test a little less readable, but still readable enough that an outsider can look at it and understand what's going on. Having many mocks, or many expectations, in a single test can ruin the readability of the test so it's hard to maintain or even to understand what's being tested.

If you find that your test becomes unreadable or hard to follow, consider removing some mocks or some mock expectations, or separating the test into several smaller tests that are more readable.

5.11.2 Verifying the wrong things

Mock objects allow us to verify that methods were called on our interfaces, but that doesn't necessarily mean that we're testing the right thing. Testing that an object subscribed to an event doesn't tell us anything about the functionality of that object. Testing that when the event is raised something meaningful happens is a better way to test that object.

5.11.3 Having more than one mock per test

It's considered good practice to only test one thing per test. Testing more than one thing can lead to confusion and problems maintaining the test. Having two mocks in a test is the same as testing several things. If you can't name your test because it does too many things, it's time to separate it into more than one test.

5.11.4 Overspecifying the tests

If your test has too many expectations, you may create a test that breaks down with even the lightest of code changes, even though the overall functionality still works. Consider this a more technical way of not verifying the right things. Testing interactions is a double-edged sword: test it too much, and you start to lose sight of the big picture—the overall functionality; test it too little, and you'll miss the important interactions between objects.

Here are some ways to balance this effect:

- *Use nonstrict mocks when you can.*

    The test will break less often because of unexpected method calls. This helps when the private methods in the production code keep changing.

- *Use stubs instead of mocks when you can.*

    You only need to test one scenario at a time. The more mocks you have, the more verifications will take place at the end of the test, but only one of them will usually be the important one. The rest will be noise against the current test scenario.

- *Avoid using stubs as mocks.*

Use a stub only for faking return values into the program under test, or to throw exceptions. Don't verify that methods were called on stubs. Use a mock only for verifying that some method was called on it, but don't use it to return values into your program under test. If you can't avoid this situation, you should probably be using a stub and testing something other than what the mock object receives.

- *Don't repeat logic in your tests.*

  If you're asserting that some calculation is correct in your code, make sure your test doesn't repeat the calculation in the test code, or the bug might be duplicated and the test will magically pass.

- *Don't use "magic" values.*

  Try to always use hardcoded, known return values to assert against production code, and don't create expected values dynamically. That would significantly increase the chances for an unreadable test or a bug in the test.

Overspecification is a common form of test abuse. Make sure you keep your eyes on this by doing frequent test reviews with your peers.

5.12 Summary

Dynamic mock objects are pretty cool, and you should learn to use them at will. But it's important to lean toward state-based testing (as opposed to interaction testing) whenever you can, so that your tests assume as little as possible about internal implementation details. Mocks should be used only when there's no other way to test the implementation, because they eventually lead to tests that are harder to maintain if you're not careful.

Learn how to use the advanced features of an isolation framework such as Rhino Mocks or Typemock Isolator, and you can pretty much make sure that anything happens or doesn't happen in your tests. All you need is for your code to be testable.

You can also shoot yourself in the foot by creating overspecified tests that aren't readable or will likely break. The art lies in knowing when to use dynamic versus handwritten mocks. My guideline is that, when the code using the isolation framework starts to look ugly, it's a sign that you may want to simplify things. Use a handwritten mock, or change your test to test a different result that proves your point but is easier to test.

When all else fails and your code is hard to test, you have three choices: use a "super" framework like Typemock Isolator, change the design, or quit your job.

Isolation frameworks can help make your testing life much easier and your tests more readable and maintainable. But it's also important to know when they might hinder your development more than they help. In legacy situations, for example, you might want to consider using a different framework based on its abilities. It's all about picking the right tool for the job, so be sure to look at the big picture when considering how to approach a specific problem in testing.

That's it! We've covered the core techniques for writing unit tests. The next part of the book deals with managing test code, arranging tests, and patterns for tests that you can rely on, maintain easily, and understand clearly.

Part 3

The test code

This part of the book covers techniques for managing and organizing unit tests and for ensuring that the quality of unit tests in real-world projects is high.

Chapter 6 first covers the role of unit testing as part of an automated build process, and follows with several techniques for organizing the different kinds of tests according to categories (speed, type) with a goal of reaching what I call the "safe green zone." It also explains how to "grow" a test API or test infrastructure for your application.

In chapter 7, we'll take a look at the three basic pillars of good unit tests—readability, maintainability, and trustworthiness—and look at techniques to support them. If you only read one chapter in the book, this should be it.

Test hierarchies and organization

This chapter covers
- *Running unit tests during automated nightly builds*
- *Using continuous integration for automated builds*
- *Organizing tests in a solution*
- *Exploring test class inheritance patterns*

Unit tests are as important to an application as the production source code. As with the regular code, you need to give careful thought to where the tests reside, both physically and logically, in relation to the code under test. If you put the tests in the wrong place, the tests you've written so carefully may not be run.

Similarly, if you don't devise ways to reuse parts of your tests, create utility methods for testing, or use test hierarchies, you'll end up with test code that's either unmaintainable or hard to understand.

This chapter addresses these issues with patterns and guidelines that will help you shape the way your tests look, feel, and run, and will affect how well they play with the rest of your code and with other tests.

Where the tests are located depends on where they will be used and who will run them. There are two common scenarios: tests run as part of the automated build process, and tests run locally by developers on their own machines. The automated build process is very important, and that's what we'll focus on.

6.1 Having automated builds run automated tests

The power of the automated build cannot and should not be ignored. If you plan to make your team more agile and equipped to handle requirement changes as they come into your shop, you need to be able to do the following:

1 Make a small change to your code.
2 Run all the tests to make sure you haven't broken any existing functionality.
3 Make sure your code can still integrate well and not break any other projects you depend upon.

Running those tests lets you know whether you've broken any existing or new functionality. *Integrating* your code with the other projects will indicate whether or not you broke the compilation of the code or things that are logically dependent on your code.

Integrating your code usually means doing the following:

1 Getting the latest version of everyone's source code from the source control repository
2 Trying to compile it all locally
3 Running all tests locally
4 Fixing anything that has been broken
5 Checking in your source code

An automated build process combines all these steps under a special build script that will make sure all these things are done without human interaction. If anything breaks in the process, the build server will notify the relevant parties of a *build break*.

6.1.1 Anatomy of an automated build

An automated build process should perform *at least* the bold points in the following list, but it may include many other things:

- **Get the latest version of all projects in question.**

- **Compile all the projects in their latest version.**
- Deploy build output to a test server.
- Run tests locally or on the test server.
- Create an archive of build outputs based on date and build number.
- Deploy outputs to staging or even production server.
- Configure and install components on target server.
- **Notify relevant people (by email) if any of the steps failed.**
- Merge databases.
- Create reports on build quality, history, and test statuses.
- Create tasks or work items automatically (such as adding a Team System work item) if specific tasks have failed.

The easiest way to get an automated build going is by creating a build process and scripts as soon as the project is started. It's much easier to create an automated build for a small project and keep adding to it as the project grows than it is to start later in the game.

There are many tools that can help you create an automated build system. Some are free or open source, and some are commercial. Here are a few tools you can look at:

- CruiseControl.NET (cruisecontrol.sourceforge.net)
- TeamCity (JetBrains.com)
- NAnt (nant.sourceforge.net)
- MSBuild (http://msdn.microsoft.com/en-us/library/wea2sca5(VS.80).aspx)
- FinalBuilder (www.FinalBuilder.com)
- Visual Build Pro (www.kinook.com)
- Visual Studio Team Foundation Server (http://msdn.microsoft.com/en-us/teamsystem/default.aspx)

These are all configuration-based programs that allow you to create a series of steps that will be run in a hierarchy structure. You can create custom commands to be run, and you can schedule these builds to run automatically.

6.1.2 Triggering builds and continuous integration

The term *continuous integration* is literally about making the automated build and integration process run continuously. For example, you could have the build run every time someone checks in source code to the system, or every 45 minutes.

One popular continuous integration tool is CruiseControl.NET. It's fully open source and supports both the idea of *tasks*, which are individual commands that are run during a build, and the concept of *triggers*, which can start a build automatically when certain events occur, such as source control updates.

Among the commercial tools, Visual Studio Team System 2008 supports automated builds and continuous integration out of the box. If that's a bit beyond your budget, look at FinalBuilder and Visual Build Pro. These two commercial and highly successful build tools allow visual editing and maintenance of automated build projects. That means easier maintenance of the build file, which can get pretty scary for larger projects.

6.1.3 Automated build types

You can configure many types of automated builds to produce different results or builds that run in specific amounts of time (all of which compile the code first, though). Here are a few examples:

- A nightly build
  - runs all the long-running tests.
  - runs system tests.
- A release build
  - runs the nightly build.
  - deploys to server and archives.
- A CI (continuous integration) build
  - runs all the fast-running tests.
  - finishes in less than 10 minutes.

When you start writing tests, you should categorize them by their running times:

- Fast-running tests
- Slow-running tests

Integration tests generally run slower than unit tests, which usually happen in memory, so the fast-running tests are usually unit tests and the slow-running tests are usually integration tests.

Automated builds usually fall into two categories: those that are too long to run every 15 minutes, and those that can be run every 15 minutes or less. Once you've categorized the tests, you can set the short and quick builds that run continuously to run a subset of the tests—the quick ones. If you can afford it, it's much better to run *all* the tests. But if your tests really slow down a build, running a subset of quick tests is the next best thing.

6.2 Mapping out tests based on speed and type

It's easy to run the tests to check their run times and to determine which are integration tests and which are unit tests. Once you do, put them in separate places. They don't need to be in separate test projects; a separate folder and namespace should be enough.

Figure 6.1 shows a simple folder structure you can use inside your Visual Studio projects.

Some companies, based on the build software and unit-testing framework they use, find it easier to use separate test projects for unit and integration tests. This makes it easier to use command-line tools that

Figure 6.1 Integration tests and unit tests can reside in different folders and namespaces but remain under the same project. Base classes have their own folders.

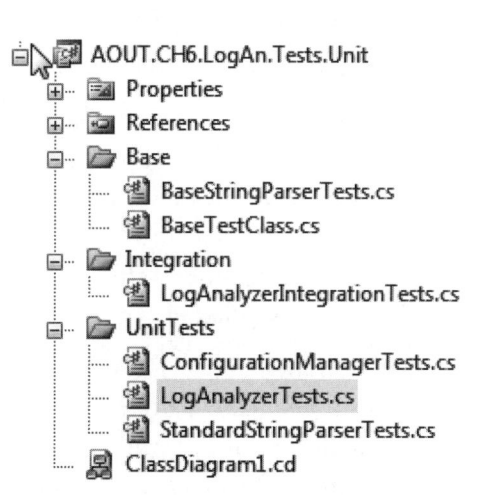

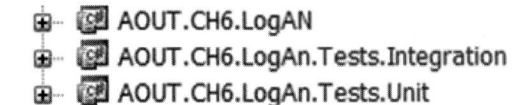

- AOUT.CH6.LogAN
- AOUT.CH6.LogAn.Tests.Integration
- AOUT.CH6.LogAn.Tests.Unit

Figure 6.2 The unit-testing and integration projects are unique for the LogAn project and have different namespaces.

accept and run a full test assembly containing only specific kinds of tests. Figure 6.2 shows how you'd set up two separate kinds of test projects under a single solution.

Even if you haven't already implemented an automated build system, separating unit from integration tests is a good idea. Mixing up the two tests can lead to severe consequences, such as people not running your tests, as we'll see next.

6.2.1 The human factor of separating unit from integration tests

I recommend separating unit from integration tests. If you don't, there's a big risk people won't run the tests often enough. If the tests exist, why wouldn't people run them as often as needed? One reason is that developers can be lazy.

If a developer gets the latest version of the source code and finds that some unit tests fail, there are several possible causes:

- There's a bug in the code under test.
- The test has a problem in the way it's written.
- The test is no longer relevant.
- The test requires some configuration to run.

All but the last point are valid reasons for a developer to stop and investigate the code. The last one isn't a development issue; it's a configuration problem, which is often considered less important because it gets in the way of running the tests. If such a test fails, the developer will often ignore the test failure and go on to other things. (He has "more important" things to do.)

In many ways, having such "hidden" integration tests mixed in with unit tests and scattered around your test project with unknown or unexpected configuration requirements (like a database connection) is bad form. These tests are less approachable, they waste time and money on finding problems that aren't there, and they generally discourage the developer from trusting the set of tests again. Like bad apples in a bunch, they make all the others look bad. The next time something similar happens, the developer may not even look for a cause for the failure, and may simply say, "Oh, that test sometimes fails; it's OK."

To make sure this doesn't happen, you can create a safe green zone.

6.2.2 The safe green zone

Separate your integration and unit tests into separate places. By doing that, you give the developers on your team a *safe green test area* that only contains unit tests, where they know that they can get the latest code version, they can run all tests in that namespace or folder, and they should all be *green*. If some tests in the safe green zone don't pass, there's a real problem, not a (false positive) configuration problem in the test.

This doesn't mean that the integration tests shouldn't all be passing. But because integration tests inherently take longer to execute, it's more likely that developers will run the unit tests more times a day and run the integration tests fewer, but still hopefully at least during the nightly build. Developers can focus on being productive and getting at least a partial sense of confidence when all their unit tests are passing. The nightly build should have all the configuration needed to make the integration tests pass.

In addition, creating a separate *integration zone* (the opposite of a safe green zone) for the integration tests gives you not only a place to quarantine tests that may run slowly, but also a place to put documents detailing what configuration needs to take place to make all these tests work.

An automated build system will do all that configuration work for you. However, if you want to run locally, you should have in your solution or project an *integration zone* that has all the information you need to make things run but that you can also skip if you want to just run the quick tests (in the safe green zone).

But none of this matters if you don't have your tests inside the source control tree, as we'll see next.

6.3 Ensuring tests are part of source control

Tests *must be* part of source control. The test code that you write needs to reside in a source control repository, just like your real production code. In fact, you should treat your test code as thoughtfully as you treat your production code. It should be part of the branch for each version of the product, and it should be part of the code that developers get automatically when they get the latest version.

Because unit tests are so connected to the code and API, they should always stay attached to the version of the code they're testing. Getting version 1.0.1 of your product will also get version 1.0.1 of the tests for your product; version 1.0.2 of your product and its tests will be different.

Also, having your tests as part of the source control tree is what allows your automated build processes to make sure they run the correct version of the tests against your software.

6.4 Mapping test classes to code under test

When you create test classes, the way they're structured and placed should allow you to easily do the following:

- Look at a *project* and find all the tests that relate to it.
- Look at a *class* and find all the tests that relate to it.
- Look at a *method* and find all the tests that relate to it.

There are several patterns that can help you do this. We'll go through these points one by one.

6.4.1 Mapping tests to projects

Create a project to contain the tests, and give it the same name as the project under test, adding [.Tests] to the end of the name. For example, if I had a project named Osherove.MyLibrary, I would also have a test project named Osherove.MyLibrary.Tests.Unit as well as Osherove.MyLibrary.Tests.Integration. (See figure 6.2, earlier in this chapter, for an example.) This may sound crude, but it's easy, and it allows a developer to find all the tests for a specific project.

You may also want to use Visual Studio's ability to create folders under the solution, and group this threesome into its own folder, but that's a matter of taste.

6.4.2 Mapping tests to classes

There are several ways to go about mapping the tests for a class you're testing. We'll look at two main scenarios: having one test class for each class under test and having separate test classes for complex methods being tested.

> **TIP** These are the two test class patterns I use most, but others exist. I suggest you look at Gerard Meszaros' *xUnit Test Patterns* book for more.

One test class per class under test

You want to be able to quickly locate all tests for a specific class, and the solution is much like the previous pattern for projects: take the name of the class you want to write tests for and, in the test project, create a test class with the same name postfixed with "Tests". For a class called LogAnalyzer, you'd create a test class in your test project named LogAnalyzerTests.

Note the plural; this is a class that holds multiple tests for the class under test, not just one test. It's important to be accurate. Readability and language matter a lot when it comes to test code, and once you start cutting corners in one place, you'll be doing so in others, which can lead to problems.

The one-test-class-per-class pattern (also mentioned in Meszaros' *xUnit Test Patterns* book) is the simplest and most common pattern for organizing tests. You put all the tests for all methods of the class under test in one big test class. When using this pattern, some methods in the class under test may have so many tests that the test class becomes much less readable or browsable. Sometimes the tests for one method drown out the other tests for other methods. That in itself could indicate that maybe the method is doing too much.

> **TIP** Test readability is important. You're writing tests as much for the person who will read them as for the computer that will run them.

If the person reading the test has to spend more time browsing the test code than understanding it, the test will cause maintenance headaches as the code gets bigger and bigger. That's why you might think about doing it differently.

One test class per feature

An alternative is creating a separate test class for a particular feature (which could be as small as a method). The *one-test-class-per-feature* pattern is also mentioned in Meszaros' *xUnit Test Patterns* book. If you seem to have lots of test methods that make your test class difficult to read, find the method or group of methods whose tests are drowning out the other tests for that class, and create a separate test class for it, with the name relating to the feature.

For example, suppose a class named `LoginManager` has a `ChangePassword` method you'd like to test, but it has so many test cases that you want to put it in a separate test class. You might end up with two test classes: `LoginManagerTests`, which contains all the other tests; and `LoginManagerTestsChangePassword`, which contains only the tests for the `ChangePassword` method.

6.4.3 Mapping tests to specific methods

Beyond making test names readable and understandable, our main goal is to be able to easily find all test methods for a specific method under test, so we should give our test methods meaningful names. We can use the method name as part of the test name.

We could name a test `ChangePassword_scenario_expectedbehavior`. This naming convention is discussed in chapter 2 (section 2.3.2).

6.5 Building a test API for your application

Sooner or later, as you start writing tests for your applications, you're bound to refactor them, and create utility methods, utility classes, and many other constructs (either in the test projects or in the code under test) solely for the purpose of testability or test readability and maintenance.

Here are some things you may find you want to do:

- Use inheritance in your test classes for code reuse, guidance, and more.
- Create test utility classes and methods.
- Make your API known to developers.

Let's look at these in turn.

6.5.1 Using test class inheritance patterns

One of the most powerful arguments for object-oriented code is that you can reuse existing functionality instead of recreating it over and over again in other classes—what Andy Hunt and Dave Thomas called the DRY ("don't repeat yourself") principle in *The Pragmatic Programmer*. Because the unit tests you write in .NET and most object-oriented languages are in an object-oriented paradigm, it's not a crime to use inheritance in the test classes themselves. In fact, I urge you to do this if you have a good reason to. Implementing a base class can help alleviate standard problems in test code by

- reusing utility and factory methods.
- running the same set of tests over different classes. (We'll look at this one in more detail.)
- using common setup or teardown code (also useful for integration testing).
- creating testing guidance for programmers who will derive from the base class.

I'll introduce you to three patterns based on test class inheritance, each one building on the previous pattern. I'll also explain when you might want to use each of them and what the pros and cons are for each of them.

These are the basic three patterns:

- Abstract test infrastructure class
- Template test class
- Abstract test driver class

We'll also take a look at the following refactoring techniques that you can apply when using the preceding patterns:

- Refactoring into a class hierarchy
- Using generics

Abstract test infrastructure class pattern

The *abstract test infrastructure class pattern* creates an abstract test class that contains essential common infrastructure for test classes deriving from it. Scenarios where you'd want to create such a base class can range from having common setup and teardown code to having special custom asserts that are used throughout multiple test classes.

We'll look at an example that will allow us to reuse a setup method in two test classes. Here's the scenario: all tests need to override the default logger implementation in the application so that logging is done in memory instead of in a file (that is, all tests need to break the logger dependency in order to run correctly).

Listing 6.1 shows these classes:

- *The* `LogAnalyzer` *class and method*—The class and method we'd like to test
- *The* `LoggingFacility` *class*—The class that holds the logger implementation we'd like to override in our tests
- *The* `ConfigurationManager` *class*—Another user of `LoggingFacility`, which we'll test later
- *The* `LogAnalyzerTests` *class and method*—The initial test class and method we're going to write
- *The* `StubLogger` *class*—An internal class that will replace the real logger implementation
- *The* `ConfigurationManagerTests` *class*—A class that holds tests for `ConfigurationManager`

Listing 6.1 An example of not following the DRY principle in test classes

```
//This class uses the LoggingFacility Internally
public class LogAnalyzer
    {
        public void Analyze(string fileName)
        {
            if (fileName.Length < 8)
```

Building a test API for your application   153

```
            {
                LoggingFacility.Log("Filename too short:" + fileName);
            }
            //rest of the method here
        }
    }

//another class that uses the LoggingFacility internally
public class ConfigurationManager
    {
        public bool IsConfigured(string configName)
        {
            LoggingFacility.Log("checking " + configName);
            //return result;
        }
    }

public static class LoggingFacility
    {
        public static void Log(string text)
        {
            logger.Log(text);
        }
        private static ILogger logger;

        public static ILogger Logger
        {
            get { return logger; }
            set { logger = value; }
        }
    }

    [TestFixture]
    public class LogAnalyzerTests
    {
        [SetUp]
        public void Setup()                          ◁──① Uses Setup() method
        {
            LoggingFacility.Logger = new StubLogger();
        }

        [Test]
        public void Analyze_EmptyFile_ThrowsException()
        {
            LogAnalyzer la = new LogAnalyzer();
```

```
            la.Analyze("myemptyfile.txt");
            //rest of test
        }
    }

    internal class StubLogger : ILogger
    {
        public void Log(string text)
        {
            //do nothing
        }
    }

[TestFixture]
public class ConfigurationManagerTests
{
    [SetUp]
    public void Setup()                       ◁─────① Uses Setup() method
    {
        LoggingFacility.Logger = new StubLogger();
    }

    [Test]
    public void Analyze_EmptyFile_ThrowsException()
    {
        ConfigurationManager cm = new ConfigurationManager();
        bool configured = cm.IsConfigured("something");
        //rest of test
    }
}
```

The `LoggingFacility` class is probably going to be used by many classes. It's designed so that the code using it is testable by allowing the implementation of the logger to be replaced using the property setter (which is static).

There are two classes that use the `LoggingFacility` class internally, and we'd like to test both of them: the `LogAnalyzer` and `ConfigurationManager` classes.

One possible way to refactor this code into a better state is to find a way to reuse the setup method ①, which is essentially the same for both test classes. They both replace the default logger implementation.

We could refactor the test classes and create a base test class that contains the setup method. The full code for the test classes is shown in listing 6.2.

Listing 6.2 A refactored solution

```
public class BaseTestClass
    {
      [SetUp]
       public void Setup()
       {
           Console.WriteLine("in setup");                    Refactors into
           LoggingFacility.Logger = new StubLogger();        a common
       }                                                     setup method
    }

    [TestFixture]
     public class LogAnalyzerTests : BaseTestClass   |#2
    {
      [Test]
       public void Analyze_EmptyFile_ThrowsException()
       {
           LogAnalyzer la = new LogAnalyzer();
           la.Analyze("myemptyfile.txt");
           //rest of test
       }
    }
    [TestFixture]                                              Inherits Setup()
     public class ConfigurationManagerTests :BaseTestClass     method
    {                                                          implementation
      [Test]
       public void Analyze_EmptyFile_ThrowsException()
       {
           ConfigurationManager cm = new ConfigurationManager();
           bool configured = cm.IsConfigured("something");
           //rest of test
       }
    }
```

Figure 6.3 shows this pattern more clearly.

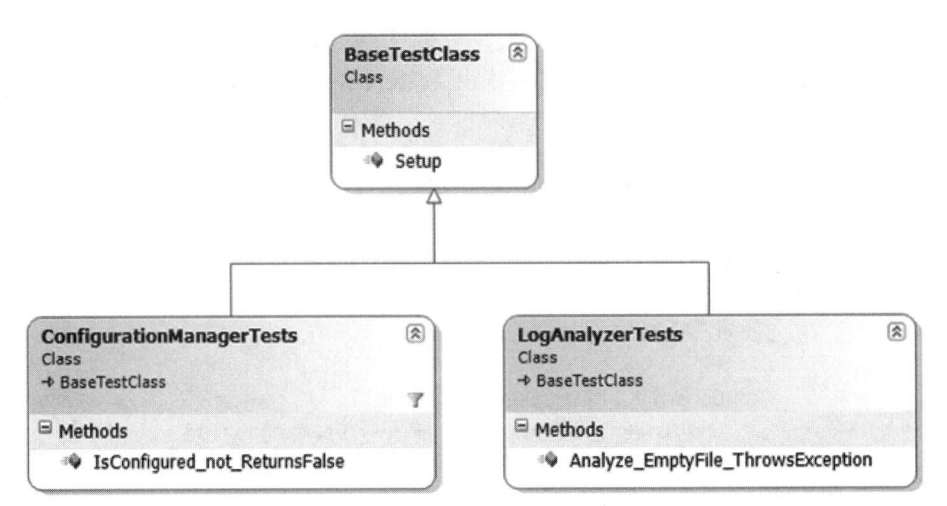

Figure 6.3 One base class with a common setup method, and two test classes that reuse that setup method

The Setup method from the base class is now automatically run before each test in either of the derived classes. We've definitely reused some code, but there are pros and cons in every technique. The main problem we've introduced into the derived test classes is that anyone reading the code can no longer easily understand what happens when setup is called. They will have to look up the setup method in the base class to see what the derived classes get by default. This leads to less readable tests, but it also leads to more code reuse.

What if you wanted to have your own derived setup in one of the derived classes? Most of the unit-testing frameworks (including NUnit) will allow you to make the setup method virtual and then override it in the derived class. Listing 6.3 shows how a derived class can have its own setup method but still keep the original setup method (making them work one after the other).

Listing 6.3 A derived test class with its own setup method

```
public class BaseTestClass
{
    [SetUp]
    public virtual void Setup()    ◁─── Makes Setup() virtual to allow overriding
    {
```

```
        Console.WriteLine("in setup");
        LoggingFacility.Logger = new StubLogger();
    }
}

[TestFixture]
 public class ConfigurationManagerTests :BaseTestClass
 {
    [SetUp]
     public override void Setup()                    ◁──┐  Overrides and
     {                                                   │  calls base
        base.Setup();
        Console.WriteLine("in derived");
        LoggingFacility.Logger = new StubLogger();
     }

    //...
 }
```

This style of inheritance is easier for the reader of the test class, because it specifically indicates that there's a base setup method that's called each time. You may be helping your team by requiring them to always override base methods and call their base class's implementation in the tests for the sake of readability. This approach is shown in listing 6.4.

Listing 6.4 Overriding a setup method purely for clarity

```
[TestFixture]
 public class ConfigurationManagerTests :BaseTestClass
 {
   [SetUp]
    public override void Setup()
    {
       base.Setup();                                 ◁──┐  Overrides and
    }                                                   │  calls base

    //...
 }
```

This type of coding may feel a bit weird at first, but anyone reading the tests will thank you for making it clear what's going on.

Template test class pattern

The *template test class pattern* creates an abstract class that contains abstract test methods that derived classes will have to implement. The driving force behind this pattern is the need to be able to dictate to deriving classes which tests they should always implement. It's commonly used when there's a need to create one or more test classes for a set of classes that implement the same interface.

Think of an interface as a "behavior contract" where the same end behavior is expected from all who have the contract, but they can achieve the end result in different ways. An example of such a behavior contract could be a set of parsers all implementing parse methods that act the same way but on different input types.

Developers often neglect or forget to write all the required tests for a specific case. Having a base class for each set of identically interfaced classes can help create a basic test contract that all developers must implement in derived test classes.

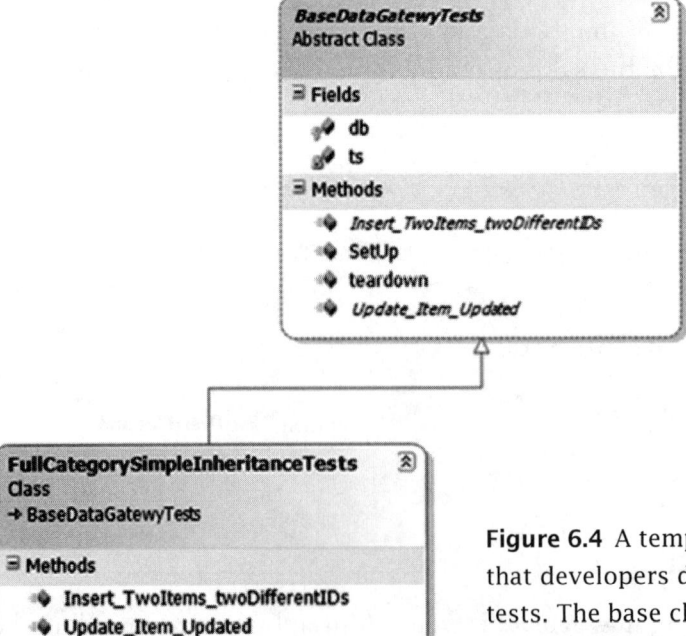

Figure 6.4 A template test pattern ensures that developers don't forget important tests. The base class contains abstract tests that derived classes must implement.

Figure 6.4 shows an example base class that helps to test data-layer CRUD (create, retrieve, update, and delete) classes.

I've found this technique useful in many situations, not only as a developer, but also as an architect. As an architect, I was able to supply a list of essential test classes for developers to implement, and to provide guidance on what kinds of tests they'd want to write next. It's essential in this situation that the naming of the tests is understandable.

But what if you were to inherit real tests from the base class, and not abstract ones?

Abstract test driver class pattern

The *abstract test driver class pattern* creates an abstract test class that contains test method implementations that all derived classes inherit by default, without needing to reimplement them. Instead of having abstract test methods, you implement real tests on the abstract class that your derived classes will inherit. It's essential that your tests don't explicitly test one class type, but instead test against an interface or base class in your production code under test.

Let's see a real scenario. Suppose you have the object model shown in figure 6.5 to test.

The `BaseStringParser` is an abstract class that other classes derive from to implement some functionality over different string content types. From each string type (XML strings, IIS log strings, standard strings), we can get some sort of versioning info (metadata on the string that was put there earlier). We can get the version info from a custom header (the first few lines of the string) and check whether that header is valid for the purposes of our application. The `XMLStringParser`, `IISLogStringParser`, and `StandardStringParser` classes derive from this base class and implement the methods with logic for their specific string types.

The first step in testing such a hierarchy is to write a set of tests for one of the derived classes (assuming the abstract class has no logic to test in it). Then you'd have to write the same kinds of tests for the other classes that have the same functionality.

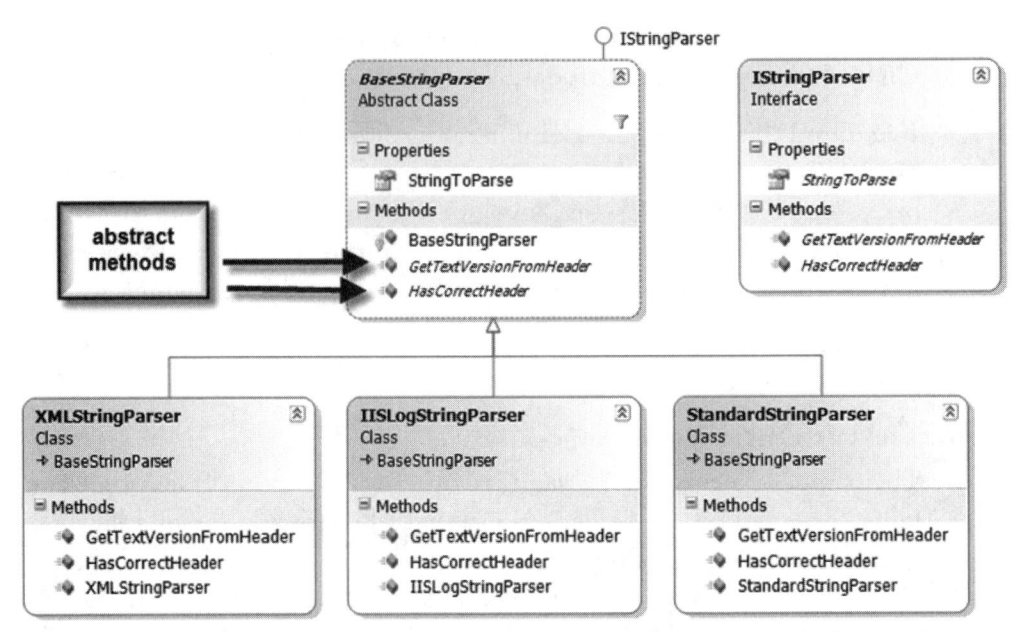

Figure 6.5 A typical inheritance hierarchy that we'd like to test includes an abstract class and classes that derive from it.

Listing 6.5 shows tests for the `StandardStringParser` that we might start out with before we refactor our test classes.

Listing 6.5 An outline of a test class for `StandardStringParser`

```
[TestFixture]
 public class StandardStringParserTests
 {
    private StandardStringParser GetParser(string input)     ◁─❶  Defines the parser factory method
    {
        return new StandardStringParser(input);
    }

    [Test]
    public void GetStringVersionFromHeader_SingleDigit_Found()
    {
        string input = "header;version=1;\n";
        StandardStringParser parser = GetParser(input);     ◁─❷  Uses factory method

        string versionFromHeader = parser.GetTextVersionFromHeader();
        Assert.AreEqual("1",versionFromHeader);
    }
```

```
[Test]
 public void GetStringVersionFromHeader_WithMinorVersion_Found()
 {
     string input = "header;version=1.1;\n";
     StandardStringParser parser = GetParser(input);         ❷ Uses
                                                               factory
     //rest of the test                                        method
 }

[Test]
 public void GetStringVersionFromHeader_WithRevision_Found()
 {
     string input = "header;version=1.1.1;\n";
     StandardStringParser parser = GetParser(input);
     //rest of the test
 }

[Test]
 public void HasCorrectHeader_NoSpaces_ReturnsTrue()
 {
     string input = "header;version=1.1.1;\n";
     StandardStringParser parser = GetParser(input);

     bool result = parser.HasCorrectHeader();
     Assert.IsTrue(result);
 }

[Test]
 public void HasCorrectHeader_WithSpaces_ReturnsTrue()
 {
     string input = "header ; version=1.1.1 ; \n";
     StandardStringParser parser = GetParser(input);

     //rest of the test
 }

[Test]
 public void HasCorrectHeader_MissingVersion_ReturnsFalse()
 {
     string input = "header; \n";
     StandardStringParser parser = GetParser(input);

     //rest of the test
 }
}
```

Note how we use the `GetParser()` helper method ❶ to refactor away ❷ the creation of the parser object, which we use in all the tests. We use the helper method, and not a setup method, because the constructor takes the input string to parse, so each test needs to be able to create a version of the parser to test with its own specific inputs.

When you start writing tests for the other classes in the hierarchy, you'll want to repeat the same tests that are in this specific parser class. All the other parsers should have the same outward behavior: getting the header version and validating that the header is valid. How they do this differs, but the behavior semantics are the same. This means that, for each class that derives from `BaseStringParser`, we'd write the same basic tests, and only the type of class under test would change.

Instead of repeating all those tests manually, we can create a `ParserTestsBase` class that contains all the basic tests we'd like to perform on any class that implements the `IStringParser` interface (or any class that derives from `BaseStringParser`). Listing 6.6 shows an example of this base class.

Listing 6.6 An abstract test base class with test logic for `IStringParser` interface

```
public abstract class BaseStringParserTests          Turns GetParser()
{                                                    into an abstract method
    protected abstract IStringParser
                        GetParser(string input);    ⬅❶

    [Test]
    public void GetStringVersionFromHeader_SingleDigit_Found()
    {
        string input = "header;version=1;\n";                 ❷ Calls abstract
        IStringParser parser = GetParser(input);    ⬅          factory method

        string versionFromHeader = parser.GetTextVersionFromHeader();
        Assert.AreEqual("1",versionFromHeader);
    }

    [Test]
    public void GetStringVersionFromHeader_WithMinorVersion_Found()
    {
        string input = "header;version=1.1;\n";               ❷ Calls abstract
        IStringParser parser = GetParser(input);    ⬅          factory method
        //...
```

```
    }

    [Test]
    public void GetStringVersionFromHeader_WithRevision_Found()
    {
        string input = "header;version=1.1.1;\n";
        IStringParser parser = GetParser(input);
        //...
    }

    [Test]
    public void HasCorrectHeader_NoSpaces_ReturnsTrue()
    {
        string input = "header;version=1.1.1;\n";
        IStringParser parser = GetParser(input);

        bool result = parser.HasCorrectHeader();
        Assert.IsTrue(result);
    }

    [Test]
    public void HasCorrectHeader_WithSpaces_ReturnsTrue()
    {
        string input = "header ; version=1.1.1 ; \n";
        IStringParser parser = GetParser(input);
        //...
    }

    [Test]
    public void HasCorrectHeader_MissingVersion_ReturnsFalse()
    {
        string input = "header; \n";
        IStringParser parser = GetParser(input);
        //...
    }
}
```

Several things are different from listing 6.5 and are important in the implementation of the base class:

- The `GetParser()` method is abstract ❶, and its return type is now `IStringParser`. This means we can override this factory method in derived test classes and return the type of the parser we'd like to test.

- The test methods only get an `IStringParser` interface ❷ and don't know the actual class they're running against.
- A derived class can choose to add tests against a specific subclass of `IStringParser` by adding another test method in its own test class (as we'll see next).

Once we have the base class in order, we can easily add tests to the various subclasses. Listing 6.7 shows how we can write tests for the `StandardStringParser` by deriving from `BaseStringParserTests`.

Listing 6.7 A derived test class that overrides a small number of factory methods

```
[TestFixture]
 public class StandardStringParserTests : BaseStringParserTests
 {
    protected override IStringParser GetParser(string input)
    {
        return new StandardStringParser(input);      ❶ Overrides
    }                                                   abstract factory
                                                        method
[Test]
    public void                                      ❷ Adds
        GetStringVersionFromHeader_DoubleDigit_Found()    new test
    {
        //this test is specific to the StandardStringParser type
        string input = "header;version=11;\n";
        IStringParser parser = GetParser(input);

        string versionFromHeader = parser.GetTextVersionFromHeader();
        Assert.AreEqual("11", versionFromHeader);
    }

}
```

Note that in listing 6.7 we only have two methods in the derived class:

- The factory method ❶ that tells the base class what instance of the class to run tests on
- A new test ❷ that may not belong in the base class, or that may be specific to the current type under test

```
BaseStringParserTests
Abstract Class

Methods
    GetParser
    GetStringVersionFromHeader_SingleDigit_Found
    GetStringVersionFromHeader_WithMinorVersion_Found
    GetStringVersionFromHeader_WithRevision_Found
    HasCorrectHeader_MissingVersion_ReturnsFalse
    HasCorrectHeader_NoSpaces_ReturnsTrue
    HasCorrectHeader_WithSpaces_ReturnsTrue
```

```
IISLogParserTests              StandardStringParserTests       XMLStringParserTests
Class                          Class                           Class
 → BaseStringParserTests         → BaseStringParserTests         → BaseStringParserTests
Methods                        Methods                         Methods
    GetParser                     GetParser                       GetParser
```

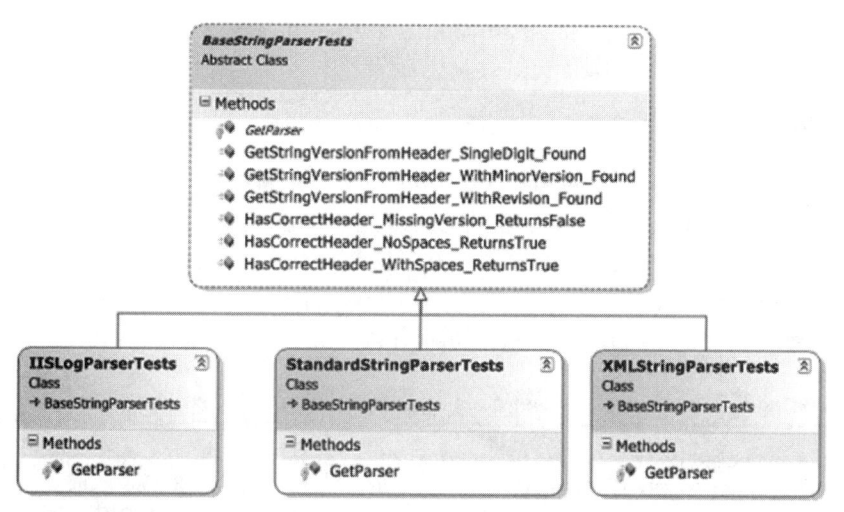

Figure 6.6 A standard test class hierarchy implementation. Most of the tests are in the base class, but derived classes can add their own specific tests.

Figure 6.6 shows the visual inheritance chain that we've just created.

How do we modify existing code to use this pattern? That's our next topic.

Refactoring your test class into a test class hierarchy

Most developers don't start writing their tests with these inheritance patterns in mind. Instead, they write the tests normally, as was shown in listing 6.5. The steps to convert your tests into a base class are fairly easy, particularly if you have IDE refactoring tools available, like the ones found in Eclipse, IntelliJ IDEA, or Visual Studio 2008 (Jet-Brains' ReSharper or Refactor! from DevExpress).

Here is a list of possible steps for refactoring your test class:

1 Refactor: extract the superclass.
   - Create a base class (`BaseXXXTests`).
   - Move the factory methods (like `GetParser`) into the base class.
   - Move all the tests to the base class.
2 Refactor: make factory methods abstract, and return interfaces.
3 Refactor: find all the places in the test methods where explicit class types are used, and change them to use the interfaces of those types instead.

4 In the derived class, implement the abstract factory methods and return the explicit types.

You can also use .NET generics to create the inheritance patterns.

A variation using .NET generics to implement test hierarchy

You can use generics as part of the base test class. This way, you don't even need to override any methods in derived classes; just declare the type you're testing against. Listing 6.8 shows both the generic version of the test base class and a class derived from it.

Listing 6.8 Implementing test case inheritance with .NET generics

```
public abstract class StringParserTests<T>            Defines generic
    where T:IStringParser                        ① constraint
{                                                     on parameter

    protected T GetParser(string input)          ② Returns generic type
    {
        return (T) Activator.CreateInstance(typeof (T), input);
    }

    [Test]
    public void GetStringVersionFromHeader_SingleDigit_Found()
    {                                              ③ Gets generic type
        string input = "header; \n";                 variable instead
        T parser = GetParser(input);                 of an interface

        bool result = parser.HasCorrectHeader();
        Assert.IsFalse(result);
    }

    //more tests
    //...
}

// this is the derived test class:
[TestFixture]
public class StandardStringParserGenericTests
           :StringParserTests<StandardStringParser>    Inherits
{                                                      from generic
}                                                      base class
```

There are several things that change in the generic implementation of the hierarchy:

- The `GetParser` factory method ❷ no longer needs to be overridden. Create the object using `Activator.CreateInstance` (which allows creating objects without knowing their type) and send the input string arguments to the constructor.
- The tests themselves don't use the `IStringParser` interface, but instead use the T generic type ❸.
- The generic class declaration contains the `where` clause that specifies that the T type of the class must implement the `IStringParser` interface ❶.

Overall, I don't find more benefit in using generic base classes. Any performance gain that would result is insignificant to these tests, but I leave it to you to see what makes sense for your projects. It's more a matter of taste than anything else.

Let's move on to something completely different: infrastructure API in your test projects.

6.5.2 Creating test utility classes and methods

As you write your tests, you'll also create many simple utility methods that may or may not end up inside your test classes. These utility classes become a big part of your test API, and they may turn out to be a simple object model you could use as you develop your tests.

You might end up with the following types of utility methods:

- Factory methods for objects that are complex to create or that routinely get created by your tests.
- System initialization methods (such as methods for setting up the system state before testing, or changing logging facilities to use stub loggers).
- Object configuration methods (for example, methods that set the internal state of an object, such as setting a customer to be invalid for a transaction).

- Methods that set up or read from external resources such as databases, configuration files, and test input files (for example, a method that loads a text file with all the permutations you'd like to use when sending in inputs for a specific method, and the expected results). This is more commonly used in integration or system testing.
- Special assert utility methods, which may assert something that's complex or that's repeatedly tested inside the system's state. (If something was written to the system log, the method might assert that X, Y, and Z are `true`, but not G.)

You may end up refactoring your utility methods into these types of utility classes:

- Special assert utility classes that contain all the custom assert methods
- Special factory classes that hold the factory methods
- Special configuration classes or database configuration classes that hold integration style actions

Having those utility methods around doesn't guarantee anyone will use them. I've been to plenty of projects where developers kept reinventing the wheel, recreating utility methods they didn't know already existed. That's why making your API known is an important next step.

6.5.3 Making your API known to developers

It's imperative that the people who write tests know about the various APIs that have been developed while writing the application and its tests. There are several ways to make sure your APIs are used:

- Have teams of two people write tests together (at least once in a while), where one of the people is familiar with the existing APIs and can teach the other person, as they write new tests, about the existing benefits and code that could be used.
- Have a short document (no more than a couple of pages) or a cheat sheet that details the types of APIs out there and where to find them. You can create short documents for specific parts of your testing framework (APIs specific to the data layer, for example) or a global one for the whole application. If it's not short, no one will maintain it.

One possible way to make sure it's up to date is by automating the generation process:

- Have a known set of prefixes or postfixes on the API helpers' names (helperXX for example).
- Have a special tool that parses out the names and their locations and generates a document that lists them and where to find them, or have some simple directives that the special tool can parse from comments you put on them.
- Automate the generation of this document as part of the automated build process.

- Discuss changes to the APIs during team meetings—one or two sentences outlining the main changes and where to look for the significant parts. That way the team knows that this is important and it's always on people's minds.
- Go over this document with new employees during their orientation.
- Perform test reviews (as opposed to code reviews) that make sure tests are up to standards of readability, maintainability, and correctness, and ensure that the right APIs are used when needed.

Following one or more of these recommendations can help keep your team productive and will create a shared language the team can use when writing their tests.

6.6 Summary

Let's look back and see what we can draw out from the chapter we've been through.

- Whatever testing you do—however you do it—automate it, and use an automated build procedure to run it as many times as possible during day or night.
- Separate the integration tests from the unit tests (the slow tests from the fast ones) so that your team can have a safe green zone where all the tests must pass.
- Map out tests by project and by type (unit versus integration tests, slow versus fast tests), and separate them into different directories,

folders, or namespaces (or all of the above). I usually use all three types of separation.

- Use a test class hierarchy to apply the same set of tests to multiple related types under test in a hierarchy, or to types that share a common interface or base class.
- Use helper classes and utility classes instead of hierarchies if the test class hierarchy makes tests less readable, especially if there's a shared setup method in the base class. Different people have different opinions on when to use which, but readability is usually the key reason for not using hierarchies.
- Make your API known to your team. If you don't, you'll lose time and money as team members unknowingly reinvent many of the APIs over and over again.

The next three chapters will deal with practices you can use to make your tests more maintainable, readable, and correct (in the sense that they test the right things).

7
The pillars of good tests

This chapter covers

- *Writing trustworthy tests*
- *Writing maintainable tests*
- *Writing readable tests*
- *Exploring naming conventions for unit tests*

No matter how you organize your tests, or how many you have, they're worth very little if you can't trust them, maintain them, or read them. The tests that you write should have three properties that together make them *good*:

- *Trustworthiness*—Developers will *want* to run trustworthy tests, and they'll accept the test results with confidence. Trustworthy tests don't have bugs, and they test the right things.
- *Maintainability*—Nonmaintainable tests are nightmares because they can ruin project schedules, or you risk losing the tests when the project is put on a more aggressive schedule. Developers will simply stop maintaining and fixing tests that take too long to change.
- *Readability*—This means not just being able to read a test but also figuring out the problem if the test seems to be wrong. Without readability, the other two pillars fall pretty quickly. Maintaining tests becomes harder, and you can't trust them anymore.

This chapter presents a series of practices related to each of these three pillars that you can use when doing test reviews. Together, the three pillars ensure your time is well used. Drop one of them, and you run the risk of wasting everyone's time.

7.1 Writing trustworthy tests

There are several indications that a test is trustworthy. If it passes, you don't say, "I'll step through the code in the debugger to make sure." You trust that it passes and that the code it tests works for that specific scenario. If the test fails, you don't tell yourself, "Oh, it's supposed to fail," or "That doesn't mean the code isn't working." You believe that there's a problem in your code and not in your test. In short, a trustworthy test is one that makes you feel you know what's going on and that you can do something about it.

In this chapter, I'll introduce guidelines and techniques to help you do the following:

- Decide when to remove or change tests
- Avoid test logic
- Test only one thing
- Make tests easy to run
- Assure code coverage

I've found that tests that follow these guidelines tend to be tests that I can trust more than others, and that I feel confident will continue to find errors in my code.

7.1.1 Deciding when to remove or change tests

Once you have tests in place, you should generally not change or remove them. They are there as your safety net, to let you know if anything breaks when you change your code. That said, there are times you might feel compelled to change or remove existing tests. To understand when this might cause a problem and when it's reasonable to do so, let's look at the reasons for each.

The main reason for removing a test is when it fails. A test can "suddenly" fail for several reasons:

- *Production bugs*—There's a bug in the production code under test.
- *Test bugs*—There's a bug in the test.
- *Semantics or API changes*—The semantics of the code under test changed, but not the functionality.
- *Conflicting or invalid tests*—The production code was changed to reflect a conflicting requirement.

There are also reasons for changing or removing tests when nothing is wrong with the tests or code:

- To rename or refactor the test
- To eliminate duplicate tests

Let's see how you might deal with each of these cases.

Production bugs

A production bug occurs when you change the production code and an existing test breaks. If indeed this is a bug in the code under test, your test is fine, and you shouldn't need to touch the test. This is the best and most desired outcome of having tests.

Because the occurrence of production bugs is one of the main reasons we have unit tests in the first place, the only thing left to do is to fix the bug in the production code. Don't touch the test.

Test bugs

If there's a bug in the test, you need to change the test. Bugs in tests are notoriously hard to detect in the first place, because the test is assumed to be correct. I've detected several stages developers go through when a test bug is encountered:

1 *Denial*—The developer will keep looking for a problem in the code itself, changing it, causing all the other tests to start failing. The developer introduces *new* bugs into production code while hunting for the bug that's actually in the test.
2 *Amusement*—The developer will call another developer, if possible, and they will hunt for the non-existent bug together.

3 *Debuggerment*—The developer will patiently debug the test and discover that there's a problem in the test. This can take anywhere from an hour to a couple of days.

4 *Acceptance and slappage*—The developer will eventually realize where the bug is, and will slap herself on the forehead.

When you finally find and start fixing the bug, it's important to make sure that the bug gets fixed, and that the test doesn't magically pass by testing the wrong thing. You need to do the following:

1 Fix the bug in your test.
2 Make sure the test fails when it should.
3 Make sure the test passes when it should.

The first step, fixing the test, is quite straightforward. The next two steps make sure you're still testing the correct thing, and that your test can still be trusted.

Once you have fixed your test, go to the production code under test and change it so that it manifests the bug that the test is supposed to catch. Then run the test. If the test fails, that means it's half working. The other half will be completed in step 3. If the test doesn't fail, you're most likely testing the wrong thing. (I've seen developers accidentally delete the asserts from their tests when fixing bugs in tests. You'd be surprised how often that happens and how effective step 2 is at catching these cases.)

Once you see the test fail, change your production code so that the bug no longer exists. The test should now pass. If it doesn't, you either still have a bug in your test, or you're testing the wrong thing. You want to see the test fail and then pass again after you fix it so that you can be sure that it fails and passes when it should.

Semantics or API changes

A test can fail when the production code under test changes so that an object being tested now needs to be *used* differently, even though it may still have the same end functionality.

Consider the simple test in listing 7.1.

Listing 7.1 A simple test against the `LogAnalyzer` class

```
[Test]
public void SemanticsChange()
{
    LogAnalyzer logan = new LogAnalyzer();
    Assert.IsFalse(logan.IsValid("abc"));      ◁——①
}
```

Let's say that a semantics change has been made to the `LogAnalyzer` class, in the form of an `Initialize` method. You now have to call `Initialize` on the `LogAnalyzer` class before calling any of the other methods on it.

If you introduce this change in the production code, the assert line ① of the test in listing 7.1 will throw an exception because `Initialize` was not called. The test will be broken, but it's still a valid test. The functionality it tests still works, but the semantics of using the object under test has changed.

In this case, we need to change the test to match the new semantics, as shown in listing 7.2.

Listing 7.2 The changed test using the new semantics of `LogAnalyzer`

```
[Test]
public void SemanticsChange()
{
    LogAnalyzer logan = new LogAnalyzer();
logan.Initialize();
    Assert.IsFalse(logan.IsValid("abc"));
}
```

Changing semantics accounts for most of the bad experiences developers have with writing and maintaining unit tests, because the burden of changing tests while the API of the code under test keeps changing gets bigger and bigger. Listing 7.3 shows a more maintainable version of the test in listing 7.2.

Listing 7.3 A refactored test using a factory method

```
[Test]
public void SemanticsChange()
{
    LogAnalyzer logan = MakeDefaultAnalyzer();
    Assert.IsFalse(logan.IsValid("abc"));
}

public static LogAnalyzer MakeDefaultAnalyzer()
{
    LogAnalyzer analyzer = new LogAnalyzer();
    analyzer.Initialize();
    return analyzer;
}
```

① Uses factory method

In this case, the refactored test uses a utility factory method ①. We can do the same for other tests and have them use the same utility method. Then, if the semantics of creating and initializing the object should change again, we don't need to change all the tests that create this object; we just need to change one little utility method. We'll see other maintainability techniques later in this chapter.

Conflicting or invalid tests

A conflict problem arises when the production code introduces a new feature that's in direct conflict with a test. This means that, instead of the test discovering a bug, it discovers conflicting requirements.

Let's look at a short example. Suppose the customer requests `LogAnalyzer` to not allow filenames shorter than three letters. The analyzer should throw an exception in that case. The feature is implemented and tests are written.

Much later on, the customer realizes that three-letter filenames do have a use and requests that they be handled in a special way. The feature is added and the production code changed. Then we write new tests so that the production code no longer throws an exception. Suddenly, an old test (the one with a three-letter filename) breaks because it expects an exception. Fixing the production code to make that test pass would break the new test that expects three-letter filenames to be handled in a special way.

This either-or scenario, where only one of two tests can pass, serves as a warning that these may be conflicting tests. In this case, you first need to make sure that the tests are in conflict. Once that's confirmed, you need to decide which requirement to keep. You should then remove (not comment out) the invalid requirement and its tests.

Conflicting tests can sometimes point out problems in customer requirements, and the customer may need to decide on the validity of each requirement.

Renaming or refactoring tests

An unreadable test is more of a problem than a solution. It can hinder your code's readability and your understanding of any problems it finds.

If you encounter a test that has a bad name or that can be made more maintainable, change the test code (but don't change the basic functionality of the test). Listing 7.3 showed one such example of refactoring a test for maintainability, which also makes it a lot more readable.

Eliminating duplicate tests

When dealing with a team of developers, it's common to come across multiple tests written by different developers for the same functionality. I'm not crazy about removing duplicate tests for a couple of reasons:

- The more (good) tests you have, the more certain you are to catch bugs.
- You can read the tests and see different ways or semantics of testing the same thing.

Here are some of the cons of having duplicate tests:

- It may be harder to maintain several different tests that provide the same functionality.
- Some tests may be higher quality than others, and you need to review them all for correctness.
- Multiple tests may break when a single thing doesn't work. (This may not really be a con.)
- Similar tests must be named differently, or the tests can be spread across different classes.
- Multiple tests may create more maintainability issues.

Here are some pros:

- Tests may have little differences, and so can be thought of as testing the same things slightly differently. They may make for a larger and better picture of the object being tested.
- Some tests may be more expressive than others, so more tests may improve the chances of test readability.

Although, as I said, I am not crazy about removing duplicate tests, I usually do so; the cons usually outweigh the pros.

7.1.2 Avoiding logic in tests

The chances of having bugs in your tests increase almost exponentially as you include more and more logic in them. I've seen plenty of tests that should have been simple turned into dynamically changing logic, random-number generating, thread-creating, file-writing monsters that are little test engines in their own right. Sadly, because they had a `[Test]` attribute on them, the writer didn't consider that they might have bugs or didn't write them in a maintainable manner. Those test monsters take more time to debug and verify than they save.

But all monsters start out small. Often, a guru in the company will look at a test and start thinking, "What if we made the method loop and create random numbers as input? We'd surely find lots more bugs that way!" And you will, especially in your tests. Test bugs are one of the most annoying things for developers, because you'll almost never search for the cause of a failing test in the test itself.

If you have any of the following inside a test method, your test contains logic that should not be there:

- `switch`, `if`, or `else` statements
- `foreach`, `for`, or `while` loops

A test that contains logic is usually testing more than one thing at a time, which isn't recommended, because the test is less readable and more fragile. But test logic also adds complexity that may contain a hidden bug.

Tests should, as a general rule, be a series of method calls with no control flows, not even `try-catch`, and with assert calls. Anything more complex causes the following problems:

- The test is harder to read and understand.
- The test is hard to re-create. (Imagine a multithreaded test, or a test with random numbers that suddenly fail.)
- The test is more likely to have a bug or to test the wrong thing.
- Naming the test may be harder because it does multiple things.

Generally, monster tests replace original simpler tests, and that makes it harder to find bugs in the production code. If you must create a monster test, it should be *added to* and not *replace* existing tests.

7.1.3 Testing only one thing

If your test contains more than a single assert, it may be testing more than one thing. That doesn't sound so bad until you go to name your test or consider what happens if the first assert fails.

Naming a test may seem like a simple task, but if you're testing more than one thing, giving the test a good name that indicates what is being tested becomes almost impossible. When you test just one thing, naming the test is easy.

A failed assert message in most test frameworks (NUnit included) throws a special type of exception that's caught by the test framework runner. When the test framework catches that exception, it means the test has failed. Unfortunately, exceptions, by design, don't let the code continue. The method exits on the same line the exception is thrown. Listing 7.4 shows an example. If the first assert (`IsFalse()`) fails, it will throw an exception, which means the second assert will never run.

Listing 7.4 A test with multiple asserts

```
[Test]
 public void TestWithMultipleAsserts()
{
    LogAnalyzer logan = MakeDefaultAnalyzer();

    Assert.IsFalse(logan.IsValid("abc"));
    Assert.IsTrue(logan.IsValid("abcde.txt"));
}
```

Consider assert failures as symptoms of a disease. The more symptoms you can find, the easier the disease will be to diagnose. After a failure, subsequent asserts aren't executed, and you miss seeing other possible symptoms that could provide valuable data (symptoms) that would help you narrow your focus and discover the underlying problem.

Running multiple asserts in a single test adds complexity with little value. You should run additional asserts in separate, self-contained unit tests so that you can see what really fails.

7.1.4 Making tests easy to run

In chapter 6, I discussed the safe green zone for tests. If developers don't trust your tests to run out of the box easily and consistently, they won't run them. Refactoring your tests so they're easy to run and provide consistent results will make them feel more trustworthy. Having a safe green zone in your tests can lead to more confidence in your tests.

7.1.5 Assuring code coverage

To ensure good coverage for your new code, use one of the automated tools (for example, NCover or Visual Studio Team System Test Edition). Find a good tool and stick with it, making sure you never have low coverage; less than 20 percent means you're missing a whole bunch of tests. You never know if the next developer will try to play with your code. He may try to optimize it or wrongly delete some essential line, and if you don't have a test that will fail, the mistake may go unnoticed.

When doing code and test reviews, you can also do a manual check, which is great for ad hoc testing of a test: try *commenting out* a line or a constraint check. If all tests still pass, you might be missing some tests, or the current tests may not be testing the right thing.

When you add a new test that was missing, check whether you've added the correct test with these steps:

1 Comment out the production code you think isn't being covered.
2 Run all the tests.

3 If all the tests pass, you're missing a test or are testing the wrong thing. Otherwise there would have been a test somewhere that was expecting that line to be called, or some resulting consequence of that line of code to be true, and that missing test would now fail.

4 Once you've found a missing test, you'll need to add it. Keep the code commented out and write a new test that fails, proving that the code you've commented is missing.

5 Uncomment the code you commented before.

6 The test you wrote should now pass. You've detected and added a missing test!

7 If the test still fails, it means the test may have a bug or is testing the wrong thing. Modify the test until it passes. Now you'll want to see that the test is OK, making sure it fails when it should, and doesn't just pass when it should. To make sure the test fails when it should, reintroduce the bug into your code (commenting out the line of production code) and see if the test indeed fails.

As an added confidence booster, you might also try replacing various parameters or internal variables in your method under test with constants (making a `bool` always `true` to see what happens, for example).

The trick to all this testing is making sure it doesn't take up too much time to make it worth your while. That's what the next section is about: maintainability.

7.2 Writing maintainable tests

Maintainability is one of the core issues most developers face when writing unit tests. Eventually the tests seem to become harder and harder to maintain and understand, and every little change to the system seems to break one test or another, even if bugs don't exist. With all pieces of code, time adds a layer of "indirection" between what you think the code does and what it really does.

This chapter will cover some techniques I've learned the hard way, writing unit tests in various teams. They include testing only against public contracts, removing duplication in tests, and enforcing test isolation, among others.

7.2.1 Testing private or protected methods

Private or protected methods are usually private for a good reason in the developer's mind. Sometimes it's to hide implementation details, so that the implementation can change later without the end functionality changing. It could also be for security-related or IP-related reasons (obfuscation, for example).

When you test a private method, you're testing against a contract internal to the system, which may well change. Internal contracts are dynamic, and they can change when you refactor the system. When they change, your test could fail because some internal work is being done differently, even though the overall functionality of the system remains the same.

For testing purposes, the public contract (the overall functionality) is all that you need to care about. Testing the functionality of private methods may lead to breaking tests, even though the overall functionality is correct.

If a method is worth testing, it might be worth making it public, static, or at least internal, and defining a public contract against any user of it. In some cases, the design may be cleaner if you put the method in a different class altogether. We'll look at these approaches in a moment.

Does this mean there should eventually be no private methods in the code base? No. With test-driven development, we usually write tests against methods that are public, and those public methods are later refactored into calling smaller, private methods. All the while, the tests against the public methods continue to pass.

Making methods public

Making a method public isn't necessarily a bad thing. It may seem to go against the object-oriented principles you were raised on, but wanting to test a method means that the method has a known *behavior* or *contract* against the calling code. By making it public, you're making this official. By keeping the method private, you tell all the developers who come after you that they can change the implementation of the method without worrying about unknown code that uses it, because it only serves as part of a larger group of things that together make up a contract to the calling code.

Extracting methods to new classes

If your method contains a lot of logic that can stand on its own, or it uses state in the class that's only relevant to the method in question, it may be a good idea to extract the method into a new class, with a specific role in the system. You can then test that class separately. Michael Feathers' book, *Working Effectively with Legacy Code*, has some good examples of this technique.

Making methods static

If your method doesn't use any of its class's variables, you might want to refactor the method by making it static. That makes it much more testable, but also states that this method is a sort of utility method that has a known public contract specified by its name.

Making methods internal

When all else fails, and you can't afford to expose the method in an "official" way, you might want to make it internal, and then use the `[InternalsVisibleTo("TestAssembly")]` attribute on the production code assembly so that tests can still call that method. This is my least favorite approach, but sometimes there's no choice (perhaps because of security reasons, lack of control over the code's design, and so on).

Making the method internal isn't a great way to make sure your tests are more maintainable, because a coder can still feel it's easier to change the method. But by exposing a method as an explicit public contract, the coder who may change it knows that the method has a real usage contract he can't break.

Removing the method isn't a good option because the production code uses the method too. Otherwise, there would be no reason to write the tests in the first place.

Another way to make code more maintainable is to remove duplication in tests.

7.2.2 Removing duplication

Duplication in our unit tests can hurt us as developers just as much as (if not more than) duplication in production code. The "don't repeat yourself" (DRY) principle should be in effect in test code as in production code. Duplicated code means more code to change when one aspect we test against changes. Changing a constructor or changing the semantics of using a class can have a large effect on tests that have a lot of duplicated code.

To understand why, let's begin with a simple example of a test, seen in listing 7.5.

Listing 7.5 A class under test, and a test that uses it

```
public class LogAnalyzer
    {
        public bool IsValid(string fileName)
        {
            if (fileName.Length < 8)
            {
                return true;
            }
            return false;
        }
    }

    [TestFixture]
     public class LogAnalyzerTestsMaintainable
     {
         [Test]
          public void IsValid_LengthBiggerThan8_IsFalse()
          {
              LogAnalyzer logan = new LogAnalyzer();
              bool valid = logan.IsValid("123456789");
              Assert.IsFalse(valid);
          }
     }
```

The test at the bottom of listing 7.5 seems reasonable, until you introduce another test for the same class and end up with two tests, as in listing 7.6.

Listing 7.6 Two tests with duplication

```
[Test]
   public void IsValid_LengthBiggerThan8_IsFalse()
   {
       LogAnalyzer logan = new LogAnalyzer();
       bool valid = logan.IsValid("123456789");
       Assert.IsFalse(valid);
   }

   [Test]
   public void IsValid_LengthSmallerThan8_IsTrue()
   {
       LogAnalyzer logan = new LogAnalyzer();
       bool valid = logan.IsValid("1234567");
       Assert.IsTrue(valid);
   }
```

What's wrong with the tests in listing 7.6? The main problem is that, if the way you use `LogAnalyzer` changes (its semantics), the tests will have to be maintained independently of each other, leading to more maintenance work. Listing 7.7 shows an example of such a change.

Listing 7.7 `LogAnalyzer` with changed semantics that now requires initialization

```
public class LogAnalyzer
    {
    private bool initialized=false;

       public bool IsValid(string fileName)
       {
           if(!initialized)
           {
                throw new NotInitializedException(
               "The analyzer.Initialize() method should be" +
               " called before any other operation!");
           }
```

```
            if (fileName.Length < 8)
            {
                return true;
            }
            return false;
        }
        public void Initialize()
        {
        //initialization logic here
        ...
        initialized=true;
        }
    }
```

Now, the two tests in listing 7.6 will both break because they both neglect to call `Initialize()` against the `LogAnalyzer` class. Because we have code duplication (both of the tests create the class within the test), we need to go into each one and change it to call `Initialize()`.

We can refactor the tests to remove the duplication by creating the `LogAnalyzer` in a `CreateDefaultAnalyzer()` method that both tests can call. We could also push the creation and initialization up into a new setup method in our test class.

Removing duplication using a helper method

Listing 7.8 shows how you could refactor the tests into a more maintainable state by introducing a shared factory method that creates a default instance of `LogAnalyzer`. Assuming all the tests were written to use this factory method, we could then add a call to `Initialize()` within that factory method instead of changing all the tests to call `Initialize()`.

Listing 7.8 Adding the `Initialize()` call in the factory method

```
[Test]
public void IsValid_LengthBiggerThan8_IsFalse()
{
    LogAnalyzer logan = GetNewAnalyzer();
    bool valid = logan.IsValid("123456789");
    Assert.IsFalse(valid);
}
```

```
[Test]
 public void IsValid_LengthSmallerThan8_IsTrue()
 {
     LogAnalyzer logan = GetNewAnalyzer();
     bool valid = logan.IsValid("1234567");
     Assert.IsTrue(valid);
 }

 private LogAnalyzer GetNewAnalyzer()
 {
     LogAnalyzer analyzer = new LogAnalyzer();
     analyzer.Initialize();
     return analyzer;
 }
```

Factory methods aren't the only way to remove duplication in tests, as the next section shows.

Removing duplication using [SetUp]

We could also easily initialize `LogAnalyzer` within the `Setup` method, as shown in listing 7.9.

Listing 7.9 Using a setup method to remove duplication

```
[SetUp]
 public void Setup()
 {
     logan=new LogAnalyzer();
     logan.Initialize();
 }

 private LogAnalyzer logan= null;

[Test]
 public void IsValid_LengthBiggerThan8_IsFalse()
 {
     bool valid = logan.IsValid("123456789");
     Assert.IsFalse(valid);
 }

[Test]
 public void IsValid_LengthSmallerThan8_IsTrue()
 {
```

```
        bool valid = logan.IsValid("1234567");
        Assert.IsTrue(valid);
}
```

In this case, we don't even need a line that creates the analyzer object in each test: a shared class instance is initialized before each test with a new instance of `LogAnalyzer`, and then `Initialize()` is called on that instance. But beware: using a setup method to remove duplication isn't always a good idea, as I explain in the next section.

7.2.3 Using setup methods in a maintainable manner

The `Setup()` method is easy to use. In fact, it's almost too easy to use—enough so that developers tend to use it for things it was not meant for, and tests become less readable and maintainable.

Nevertheless, setup methods have several limitations, which you can get around using simple helper methods:

- Setup methods can only help when you need to initialize things.
- Setup methods aren't always the best candidate for duplication removal. Removing duplication isn't always about creating and initializing new instances of objects. Sometimes it's about removing duplication in assertion logic, calling out code in a specific way.
- Setup methods can't have parameters or return values.
- Setup methods can't be used as factory methods that return values. They're run before the test executes, so they must be more generic in the way they work. Tests sometimes need to request specific things or call shared code with a parameter for the specific test (for example, retrieve an object and set its property to a specific value).
- Setup methods should only contain code that applies to all the tests in the current test class, or the method will be harder to read and understand.

Now that we know the basic limitations of setup methods, let's see how developers try to get around them in their quest to use setup methods no matter what, instead of using helper methods. Developers abuse setup methods in several ways:

- Initializing objects in the setup method that are only used in some of the tests in the class
- Having setup code that's long and hard to understand
- Setting up mocks and fake objects within the setup method

Let's take a closer look at these.

Initializing objects that are only used by some of the tests

This sin is a deadly one. Once you commit it, it becomes difficult to maintain the tests or even read them, because the setup method quickly becomes loaded with objects that are specific only to some of the tests. Listing 7.10 shows what our test class would look like if we initialized a `FileInfo` object setup method but only used it in one test ❶.

Listing 7.10 A poorly implemented `Setup()` method

```
[SetUp]
 public void Setup()
 {
    logan=new LogAnalyzer();
    logan.Initialize();

    fileInfo=new FileInfo("c:\\someFile.txt");     ❶ Used only in one test
 }

 private FileInfo fileInfo = null;
 private LogAnalyzer logan= null;

[Test]
 public void IsValid_LengthBiggerThan8_IsFalse()
 {
    bool valid = logan.IsValid("123456789");
    Assert.IsFalse(valid);
 }

[Test]
 public void IsValid_BadFileInfoInput_returnsFalse()
 {
    bool valid = logan.IsValid(fileInfo);
    Assert.IsFalse(valid);
 }
```

```
[Test]
public void IsValid_LengthSmallerThan8_IsTrue()
{
   bool valid = logan.IsValid("1234567");
   Assert.IsTrue(valid);
}

private LogAnalyzer GetNewAnalyzer()
{
...
}
```

Why is the setup method in listing 7.10 less maintainable? Because, to read the tests for the first time and understand why they break, you need to do the following:

1. Go through the setup method to understand what is being initialized.
2. Assume that objects in the setup method are used in all tests.
3. Find out later you were wrong, and read the tests again more carefully to see which test uses the objects that may be causing the problems.
4. Dive deeper into the test code for no good reason, taking more time and effort to understand what the code does.

Always consider the readers of your tests when writing the tests. Imagine this is the first time they read them. Make sure they don't get angry.

Having setup code that's long and hard to understand

Because the setup method provides only one place in the test to initialize things, developers tend to initialize many things, which inevitably is cumbersome to read and understand. One solution is to refactor the calls to initialize specific things into helper methods that are called from the setup method. This means that refactoring the setup method is usually a good idea; the more readable it is, the more readable your test class will be.

But there's a fine line between over-refactoring and readability. Over-refactoring can lead to less readable code. This is a matter of personal preference. You need to watch for when your code is becoming less readable. I recommend getting feedback from a partner during the refactoring. We all can become too enamored with code we've written, and having a second pair of eyes involved in refactoring can lead to good and objective results. Having a peer do a code review (a test review) after the fact is also good, but not as productive as doing it as it happens.

Setting up mocks and fakes in the setup method

It's not always a bad idea to use the setup method to create mocks and fake objects, but it's important that only those mocks and fakes that are used in *all the tests* in the class are initialized in the setup method, or it will become hard to read and maintain.

My preference is to have each test create its own mocks and stubs by calling helper methods within the test, so that the reader of the test knows exactly what is going on, without needing to jump from test to setup to understand the full picture.

7.2.4 Enforcing test isolation

The lack of test isolation is the biggest single cause of test blockage I've seen while consulting and working on unit tests. The basic concept is that a test should always run in its own little world, isolated from even the *knowledge* that other tests out there may do similar or different things.

> **The test that cried "fail"**
>
> One project I was involved in had unit tests behaving strangely, and they got even stranger as time went on. A test would fail and then suddenly pass for a couple of days straight. A day later, it would fail, seemingly randomly, and other times it would pass even if code was changed to remove or change its behavior. It got to the point where developers would tell each other, "Ah, it's OK. If it sometimes passes, that means it passes."
>
> It turned out that the test was calling out a different test as part of its code, and when the other test failed, it would break the first test.
>
> It only took us three days to figure this out, after spending a month living with the situation. When we finally had the test working correctly, we discovered that we had a bunch of *real* bugs in our code that we were ignoring because we were getting what we thought were false positives from the failing test. The story of the boy who cried "wolf" holds true even in development.

When tests aren't isolated well, they can step on each other's toes enough to make you miserable, making you regret deciding to try unit testing on the project, and promising yourself never again. I've seen this happen. We don't bother looking for problems in the tests, so when there's a problem with the tests, it can take a lot of time to find it.

There are several test "smells" that can hint at broken test isolation:

- *Constrained test order*—Tests expecting to be run in a specific order or expecting information from other test results
- *Hidden test call*—Tests calling other tests
- *Shared-state corruption*—Tests sharing in-memory state without rolling back
- *External-shared-state corruption*—Integration tests with shared resources and no rollback

Let's look at these simple *anti-patterns*.

Anti-pattern: constrained test order

This problem arises when tests are coded to expect a specific state in memory, in an external resource, or in the current test class—a state that was created by running other tests in the same class before the current test. The problem is that most test platforms (including NUnit, JUnit, and MbUnit) don't guarantee that tests will run in a specific order, so what passes today may fail tomorrow.

For example, listing 7.11 shows a test against `LogAnalyzer` that expects that an earlier test had already called `Initialize()`.

Listing 7.11 Constrained test order: the second test will fail if it runs first

```
[TestFixture]
 public class IsolationsAntiPatterns
 {
    private LogAnalyzer logan;
    [Test]
    public void CreateAnalyzer_BadFileName_ReturnsFalse()
    {
        logan = new LogAnalyzer();
        logan.Initialize();
```

```
        bool valid = logan.IsValid("abc");
        Assert.That(valid, Is.False);
    }

    [Test]
     public void CreateAnalyzer_GoodFileName_ReturnsTrue()
    {
        bool valid = logan.IsValid("abcdefg");
        Assert.That(valid, Is.True);
    }
}
```

A myriad of problems can occur when tests don't enforce isolation. Here's a short list:

- A test may suddenly start breaking when a new version of the test framework is introduced that runs the tests in a different order.
- Running a subset of the tests may produce different results than running all the tests or a different subset of the tests.
- Maintaining the tests is more cumbersome, because you need to worry about how other tests relate to particular tests and how each one affects state.
- Your tests may fail or pass for the wrong reasons; for example, a different test may have failed or passed before it, leaving the resources in an unknown state.
- Removing or changing some tests may affect the outcomes of other tests.
- It's difficult to name your tests appropriately because they test more than a single thing.

There are a couple of common patterns that lead to poor test isolation:

- *Flow testing*—A developer writes tests that must run in a specific order so that they can test flow execution, a big use case composed of many actions, or a full integration test where each test is one step in that full test.
- *Laziness in cleanup*—A developer is lazy and doesn't return any state her test may have changed back to its original form, and other devel-

opers write tests that depend on this symptom, knowingly or unknowingly.

These problems can be solved in various manners:

- *Flow testing*—Instead of writing flow-related tests in unit tests (long-running use cases, for example), consider using some sort of integration testing framework like FIT or FitNesse, or QA-related products such as AutomatedQA, WinRunner, and the like.
- *Laziness in cleanup*—If you're too lazy to clean up your database after testing, your filesystem after testing, or your memory-based objects, consider moving to a different profession. This isn't a job for you.

Anti-pattern: hidden test call

In this anti-pattern, tests contain one or more direct calls to other tests in the same class or other test classes, which causes tests to depend on one another. For example, listing 7.12 shows the `CreateAnalyzer_GoodNameAndBadNameUsage` test calling a different test at the end, creating a dependency between the tests and breaking both of them as isolated units.

Listing 7.12 One test calling another breaks isolation and introduces a dependency

```
    [TestFixture]
public class HiddenTestCall
{
    private LogAnalyzer logan;
    [Test]
    public void CreateAnalyzer_GoodNameAndBadNameUsage()
    {
        logan = new LogAnalyzer();
        logan.Initialize();
        bool valid = logan.IsValid("abc");
        Assert.That(valid, Is.False);

        CreateAnalyzer_GoodFileName_ReturnsTrue();
    }

    [Test]
    public void CreateAnalyzer_GoodFileName_ReturnsTrue()
    {
```

```
        bool valid = logan.IsValid("abcdefg");
        Assert.That(valid, Is.True);
    }
}
```

This type of dependency can cause several problems:

- Running a subset of the tests may produce different results than running all the tests or a different subset of the tests.
- Maintaining the tests is more cumbersome, because you need to worry about how other tests relate to particular tests and how and when they call each other.
- Tests may fail or pass for the wrong reasons. For example, a different test may have failed, thus failing your test or not calling it at all. Or a different test may have left some shared variables in an unknown state.
- Changing some tests may affect the outcome of other tests.
- It's difficult to clearly name tests that call other tests.

Here are a few causes for this problem:

- *Flow testing*—A developer writes tests that need to run in a specific order so that they can test flow execution, a big use case composed of many actions, or a full integration test where each test is one step in that full test.
- *Trying to remove duplication*—A developer tries to remove duplication in the tests by calling other tests (which have code they don't want the current test to repeat).
- *Laziness in separating the tests*—A developer is lazy and doesn't take the time to create a separate test and refactor the code appropriately, instead taking a shortcut and calling a different test.

Here are some solutions for those problems:

- *Flow testing*—Instead of writing flow-related tests in unit tests (long-running use cases, for example), consider using some sort of integration testing framework like FIT or FitNesse, or QA-related products such as AutomatedQA, WinRunner, and the like.

- *Trying to remove duplication*—Don't ever remove duplication by calling another test from a test. You're preventing that test from relying on the setup and teardown methods in the class and are essentially running two tests in one (because the calling test has an assertion as well as the test being called). Instead, refactor the code you don't want to write twice into a third method that both your test and the other test call.
- *Laziness in separating the tests*—If you're too lazy to separate your tests, think of all the extra work you'll have to do if you don't separate them. Try to imagine a world where the current test you're writing is the only test in the system, so it can't rely on any other test.

Anti-pattern: shared-state corruption

This anti-pattern manifests in two major ways, independent of each other:

- Tests touch shared resources (either in memory or in external resources, such as databases, filesystems, and so on) without cleaning up or rolling back any changes they make to those resources.
- Tests don't set up the initial state they need before they start running, relying on the state to be there.

Either of these situations will cause the symptoms we'll look at shortly.

The problem is that tests rely on specific state to have consistent pass/fail behavior. If a test doesn't control the state it expects, or other tests corrupt that state for whatever reason, the test can't run properly or report the correct result consistently.

For example, assume we have a `Person` class with simple features: it has a list of phone numbers and the ability to search for a number by specifying the beginning of the number. Listing 7.13 shows a couple of tests that don't clean up or set up a `Person` object instance correctly.

Listing 7.13 Shared-state corruption by a test

```
[TestFixture]
 public class SharedStateCorruption
    {
        Person person = new Person();         ◁──── Defines shared Person state
```

```
[Test]
public void CreateAnalyzer_GoodFileName_ReturnsTrue()
{
    person.AddNumber("055-4556684(34)");          ◄────┐ ❶ Changes
    string found =                                     │   shared state
        person.FindPhoneStartingWith("055");
    Assert.AreEqual("055-4556684(34)", found);
}

[Test]
public void FindPhoneStartingWith_NoNumbers_ReturnsNull()
{
    string found =
        person.FindPhoneStartingWith("0");       ◄────┐ Reads
    Assert.IsNull(found);                              │ shared state
}
}
```

In this example, the second test (expecting a `null` return value) will fail because the previous test has already added a number ❶ to the `Person` instance.

This type of problem causes a number of symptoms:

- Running a subset of the tests may produce different results than running all the tests or a different subset of the tests.
- Maintaining the test is more cumbersome, because you may break the state for other tests, breaking those tests without realizing it.
- Your test may fail or pass for the wrong reason; for example, a different test may have failed or passed before it, leaving the shared state in a problematic condition, or it may not have cleaned up after it ran.
- Changing some tests may affect the outcomes of other tests, seemingly randomly.

Here are a few causes of this problem:

- *Not setting up state before each test*—A developer doesn't set up the state required for the test, or assumes the state was already correct.
- *Using shared state*—A developer uses shared memory or external resources for more than one test without taking precautions.

- *Using static instances in tests*—A developer sets static state that's used in other tests.

Here are some solutions:

- *Not setting up state before each test*—This is a mandatory practice when writing unit tests. Use either a setup method or call specific helper methods at the beginning of the test to ensure the state is what you expect it to be.
- *Using shared state*—In many cases, you don't need to share state at all. Having separate instances of an object for each test is the safest way to go.
- *Using static instances in tests*—You need to be careful how your tests manage static state. Be sure to clean up the static state using setup or teardown methods. Sometimes it's effective to use direct helper method calls to clearly reset the static state from within the test. If you're testing singletons, it's worth adding public or internal setters so your tests can reset them to a clean object instance.

Anti-pattern: external-shared-state corruption

This anti-pattern is similar to the in-memory state corruption pattern, but it happens in integration-style testing:

- Tests touch shared resources (either in memory or in external resources, such as databases, filesystems, and so on) without cleaning up or rolling back any changes they make to those resources.
- Tests don't set up the initial state they need before they start running, relying on the state to be there.

Now that we've looked at isolating tests, let's manage our *assert*s to make sure we get the full story when a test fails.

7.2.5 Avoiding multiple asserts

To understand the problem of multiple asserts, let's take a look at the example in listing 7.14.

Listing 7.14 A test that contains multiple asserts

```
[Test]
 public void CheckVariousSumResults()
  {
```

```
    Assert.AreEqual(3, Sum(1001, 1, 2));
    Assert.AreEqual(3, Sum(1, 1001, 2));
    Assert.AreEqual(3, Sum(1, 2, 1001));
}
```

There's more than one test in this test method. The author of the test method tried to save some time by including three tests as three simple asserts. What's the problem here? When asserts fail, they throw exceptions. (In NUnit's case, they throw a special `AssertException` that's caught by the NUnit test runner, which understands this exception as a signal that the current test method has failed.) Once an assert clause throws an exception, no other line executes in the test method. That means that, if the first assert in listing 7.14 failed, the other two assert clauses would never execute.

There are several ways to achieve the same goal:

- Create a separate test for each assert.
- Use parameterized tests.
- Wrap the assert call with `try-catch`.

> **Why does it matter if some asserts aren't executed?**
>
> If only one assert fails, you never know if the other asserts in that same test method would have failed or not. You may *think* you know, but it's an assumption until you can prove it with a failing or passing assert. When people see only part of the picture, they tend to make a judgment call about the state of the system, which can turn out wrong. The more information you have about all the asserts that have failed or passed, the better equipped you are to understand where in the system a bug may lie, and where it doesn't.
>
> I've gone on wild goose chases hunting for bugs that weren't there because only one assert out of several failed. Had I bothered to check whether the other asserts failed or passed, I might have realized that the bug was in a different location.
>
> Sometimes people go and find bugs that they think are real, but when they "fix" them, the assert that previously failed passes and the *other* asserts in that test fail (or continue to fail). Sometimes you can't see the

> full problem, so fixing part of it can introduce new bugs into the system, which will only be discovered after you've uncovered each assert's result.
>
> That's why it's important that all the asserts have a chance to run, even if other asserts have failed before. In most cases, that means putting single asserts in tests.

Refactoring into multiple tests

Multiple asserts are really multiple tests without the benefit of test isolation; a failing test causes the other asserts (tests) to not execute. Instead, we can create separate test methods with meaningful names that represent each test case. Listing 7.15 shows an example of refactoring from the code from listing 7.14.

Listing 7.15 A refactored test class with three different tests

```
[Test]
 public void Sum_1001AsFirstParam_Returns3()
 {
     Assert.AreEqual(3, Sum(1001, 1, 2));
 }

[Test]
 public void Sum_1001AsMiddleParam_Returns3()
 {
     Assert.AreEqual(3, Sum(1, 1001, 2));
 }

[Test]
 public void Sum_1001AsThirdParam_Returns3()
 {
     Assert.AreEqual(3, Sum(1, 2, 1001));
 }
```

As you can see, the refactoring in listing 7.15 gives us three separate tests, each with a slightly different name indicating how we're testing the unit. The benefit is that, if one of those tests fails, the others will still run. Unfortunately, this is too verbose, and most developers would feel this refactoring is overkill for the benefit. Although I disagree that it's overkill (it took about 20 seconds of work to get the benefit), I agree that the verbosity is an issue. It's an issue because developers won't do it, and we end up with our original problem.

That's why many unit-testing frameworks, including MbUnit and NUnit, have a custom attribute you can use that achieves the same goal with much more concise syntax.

Using parameterized tests

Both MbUnit and NUnit support the notion of parameterized tests using a special attribute called [RowTest]. Listing 7.16 shows how you can use the [RowTest] and [Row] attributes (found in NUnit.Extensions.dll under the NUnit bin directory) to run the same test with different parameters in a single test method. Notice that, when you use the [RowTest] attribute, it replaces the [Test] attribute in NUnit.

Listing 7.16 A refactored test class using parameterized tests

```
[RowTest]
[Row(1001,1,2,3)]
[Row(1,1001,2,3)]
[Row(1,2,1001,3)]
 public void SumTests(int x,int y, int z,int expected)
 {
    Assert.AreEqual(expected, Sum(x, y, z));
 }
```

NOTE   To use [RowTest] in NUnit, you'll need to add a reference to NUnit.Extensions.dll, which is found in the bin directory of NUnit's installation folder.

Parameterized test methods in NUnit and MbUnit are different from regular tests in that they can take parameters. They also expect at least one [RowTest] attribute to be placed on top of the current method instead of a regular [Test] attribute. The attribute takes any number of parameters, which are then mapped at runtime to the parameters that the test method expects in its signature.

The example in listing 7.16 expects four arguments. We call an assert method with the first three parameters, and use the last one as the expected value. This gives us a declarative way of creating a single test with different inputs.

The best thing about this is that, if one of the `[RowTest]` attributes fails, the other attributes are still executed by the test runner, so we see the full picture of pass/fail states in all tests.

Wrapping with try-catch

Some people think it's a good idea to use a `try-catch` block for each assert to catch and write its exception to the console, and then continue to the next statement, bypassing the problematic nature of exceptions in tests. I think using parameterized tests is a far better way of achieving the same thing. Use parameterized tests instead of `try-catch` around multiple asserts.

Now that we know how to avoid multiple asserts acting as multiple tests, let's look at multiple asserts being used to test multiple aspects of a single object.

7.2.6 Avoiding testing multiple aspects of the same object

Let's look at another example of a test with multiple asserts, but this time it's not trying to act as multiple tests in one test, it's trying to check multiple aspects of the same state. If even one aspect fails, we need to know about it. Listing 7.17 shows such a test.

Listing 7.17 Testing multiple aspects of the same object in one test

```
[Test]
 public void
   Analyze_SimpleStringLine_UsesDefaulTabDelimiterToParseFields()
{
    LogAnalyzer log = new LogAnalyzer();
    AnalyzedOutput output =
        log.Analyze("10:05\tOpen\tRoy");

    Assert.AreEqual(1,output.LineCount);
    Assert.AreEqual("10:05",output.GetLine(1)[0]);
    Assert.AreEqual("Open",output.GetLine(1)[1]);
    Assert.AreEqual("Roy",output.GetLine(1)[2]);
}
```

This example is testing that the parse output from the `LogAnalyzer` worked by testing each field in the result object separately. They should all work, or the test should fail.

Making tests more maintainable

Listing 7.18 shows a way to refactor the test from listing 7.17 so that it's easier to read and maintain.

Listing 7.18 Comparing objects instead of using multiple asserts

```
[Test]
 public void
   Analyze_SimpleStringLine_UsesDefaulTabDelimiterToParseFields2()
 {
    LogAnalyzer log = new LogAnalyzer();
    AnalyzedOutput expected = new AnalyzedOutput();          ◁── Sets up an expected object
    expected.AddLine("10:05", "Open", "Roy");

    AnalyzedOutput output =
        log.Analyze("10:05\tOpen\tRoy");
                                                             ◁── Compares expected and actual objects
    Assert.AreEqual(expected,output);
 }
```

Instead of adding multiple asserts, we can create a full object to compare against, set all the properties that should be on that object, and compare the result and the expected object in one assert. The advantage of this approach is that it's much easier to understand what we're testing and to recognize that this is one logical block that should be passing, not many separate tests.

Note that, for this kind of testing, the objects being compared must override the `Equals()` method, or the comparison between the objects won't work. Some people find this an unacceptable compromise. I use it from time to time, but am happy to go either way. Use your own discretion.

Overriding ToString()

Another approach you might try is to override the `ToString()` method of compared objects so that, if tests fail, you'll get more meaningful error messages. For example, here's the output of the test in listing 7.18 when it fails.

```
TestCase 'AOUT.CH7.LogAn.Tests.MultipleAsserts
.Analyze_SimpleStringLine_UsesDefaulTabDelimiterToParseFields2'
failed:
  Expected: <AOUT.CH789.LogAn.AnalyzedOutput>
  But was:  <AOUT.CH789.LogAn.AnalyzedOutput>
    C:\GlobalShare\InSync\Book\Code\ARtOfUniTesting
            \LogAn.Tests\MultipleAsserts.cs(41,0):
at AOUT.CH7.LogAn.Tests.MultipleAsserts
.Analyze_SimpleStringLine_UsesDefaulTabDelimiterToParseFields2()
```

Not very helpful, is it?

By implementing `ToString()` in both the `AnalyzedOutput` class and the `LineInfo` class (which are part of the object model being compared), we can get more readable output from the tests. Listing 7.19 shows the two implementations of the `ToString()` methods in the classes under test, followed by the resulting test output.

Listing 7.19 Implementing `ToString()` in compared classes for cleaner output

```
///Overriding ToString inside The AnalyzedOutput Object/////////////
        public override string ToString()
        {
            StringBuilder sb = new StringBuilder();
            foreach (LineInfo line in lines)
            {
                sb.Append(line.ToString());
            }
            return sb.ToString();
        }
///Overriding ToString inside each LineInfo Object/////////////
        public override string ToString()
        {
            StringBuilder sb = new StringBuilder();
            for (int i = 0; i < this.fields.Length; i++)
            {
                sb.Append(this[i]);
                sb.Append(",");
            }
```

```
            return sb.ToString();
        }

///TEST OUTPUT//////////////
------ Test started: Assembly: er.dll ------

TestCase 'AOUT.CH7.LogAn.Tests.MultipleAsserts
.Analyze_SimpleStringLine_UsesDefaulTabDelimiterToParseFields2'
failed:
  Expected: <10:05,Open,Roy,>
  But was:  <>
    C:\GlobalShare\InSync\Book\Code\ARtOfUniTesting
\LogAn.Tests\MultipleAsserts.cs(41,0):
at AOUT.CH7.LogAn.Tests.MultipleAsserts
.Analyze_SimpleStringLine_UsesDefaulTabDelimiterToParseFields2()
```

Now the test output is much clearer, and we can understand that we got very different objects. Clearer output makes it easier to understand why the test fails and makes for easier maintenance.

Another way tests can become hard to maintain is when we make them too fragile by overspecification.

7.2.7 Avoiding overspecification in tests

An overspecified test is one that contains assumptions about how a specific unit under test should implement its behavior, instead of only checking that the end behavior is correct.

Here are some ways unit tests are often overspecified:

- A test specifies purely internal behavior for an object under test.
- A test uses mocks when using stubs would be enough.
- A test assumes specific order or exact string matches when it isn't required.

TIP   This topic is also discussed in *xUnit Test Patterns* by Gerard Meszaros.

Let's look at some examples of overspecified tests.

Specifying purely internal behavior

Listing 7.20 shows a test against `LogAnalyzer`'s `Initialize()` method that tests internal state, and no outside functionality.

Listing 7.20 An overspecified test that tests a purely internal behavior

```
[Test]
 public void Initialize_WhenCalled_SetsDefaultDelimiterIsTabDelimiter()
 {
    LogAnalyzer log = new LogAnalyzer();

    Assert.AreEqual(null,log.GetInternalDefaultDelimiter());
    log.Initialize();
    Assert.AreEqual('\t', log.GetInternalDefaultDelimiter());
 }
```

This test is overspecified because it only tests the internal state of the `LogAnalyzer` object. Because this state is internal, it could change later on.

Unit tests should be testing the public contract and public functionality of an object. In this example, the tested code isn't part of any public contract or interface.

Using mocks instead of stubs

Using mocks instead of stubs is a common mistake. Let's look at an example.

Listing 7.21 shows a test that uses mocks to assert the interaction between `LogAnalyzer` and a provider it uses to read a text file. The test wrongly checks that `LogAnalyzer` calls the provider correctly to read the file's text (an implementation detail that could change later and break our test). Instead, the test could use a stub to return the fake results from the text file, and assert against the public output of the `LogAnalyzer`'s method, which makes for a more robust, less brittle test.

Listing 7.21 shows the method we want to test, followed by an overspecified test for that code.

Listing 7.21 An overspecified test that uses mocks when stubs would do fine

```
public AnalyzeResults AnalyzeFile(string fileName)
    {
        int lineCount = logReader.GetLineCount();
        string text = "";
```

```
        for (int i = 0; i < lineCount; i++)
        {
            text += logReader.GetText(fileName, i, i);
        }
        return new AnalyzeResults(text);
    }
//////////////////////////the test/////////////////
    [Test]
    public void AnalyzeFile_FileWith3Lines_CallsLogProvider3Times()
    {
        MockRepository mocks = new MockRepository();
        ILogProvider mockLog = mocks.CreateMock<ILogProvider>();
        LogAnalyzer log = new LogAnalyzer(mockLog);
        using(mocks.Record())
        {
            mockLog.GetLineCount();
            LastCall.Return(3);

            mockLog.GetText("someFile.txt", 1, 1);
            LastCall.Return("a");

            mockLog.GetText("someFile.txt", 2, 2);
            LastCall.Return("b");

            mockLog.GetText("someFile.txt", 3, 3);
            LastCall.Return("c");
        }
        AnalyzeResults results = log.AnalyzeFile("someFile.txt");
        mocks.VerifyAll();
    }
```

The test in listing 7.21 is overspecified because it tests the interaction between the interface of some `LogReader` (which reads text files) and the `LogAnalzyer` object. This means it's testing the underlying reading algorithm inside the method under test, instead of testing for an expected result from the method under test. The test should let the method under test run its own internal algorithms, and test the results. By doing that, we make the test less brittle.

Listing 7.22 shows a modified test that only checks the outcome of the operation.

Listing 7.22 Replacing mocks with stubs and checking outputs instead of interactions

```
[Test]
 public void
   AnalyzeFile_With3Lines_CallsLog3TimesLessBrittle()
{
    MockRepository mocks = new MockRepository();
    ILogProvider stubLog = mocks.Stub<ILogProvider>();
    using(mocks.Record())
    {
        SetupResult.For(stubLog.GetText("", 1, 1))
            .IgnoreArguments()              ◁───┐  Stubs unknown
            .Repeat.Any()                        │  number of calls
            .Return("a");

        SetupResult.For(stubLog.GetLineCount()).Return(3);
    }
    using(mocks.Playback())
    {
        LogAnalyzer log = new LogAnalyzer(stubLog);
        AnalyzeResults results = log.AnalyzeFile("someFile.txt");

        Assert.That(results.Text,Is.EqualTo("aaa"));   ◁──❶ Asserts on
    }                                                       end result
}
```

The important thing about this test is that the end assert ❶ is against the end result, and it doesn't care how many times the internal `Get-Text()` method is called. We also use a stub that doesn't care how many times it gets called, and it always returns the same result. This test is much less fragile, and it tests the right thing.

NOTE   When you refactor internal state to be visible to an outside test, could it be considered a code smell (a sign that something might be wrong in the code's design or logic)? It's not a code smell when you're refactoring to expose collaborators. It's a code smell if you're refactoring and there are no collaborators (so you don't need to stub or mock anything).

I am using NUnit's `Assert.That` syntax instead of `Assert.AreEqual` because the fluent nature of the new syntax is much cleaner and nicer to work with.

TIP Also notice that this test has no mock objects, only stubs. The assert is done against a return value, and a stub is used internally to simulate some scenario. This is often the way I like to write my tests. In fact, less than 10 percent of the tests I write have any mock objects. Most tests will have stubs, and nothing more.

One more way developers tend to overspecify their tests is the overuse of assumptions.

Assuming an order or exact match when it's not needed

Another common pattern people tend to repeat is to have asserts against hardcoded strings in the unit's return value or properties, when only a specific part of a string is necessary. Ask yourself, "Can I use `string.Contains()` rather than `string.Equals()`?"

The same goes for collections and lists. It's much better to make sure a collection contains an expected item than to assert that the item is in a specific place in a collection (unless that's specifically what is expected).

By making these kinds of small adjustments, you can guarantee that, as long as the string or collection contains what is expected, the test will pass. Even if the implementation or order of the string or collection changes, you won't have to go back and change every little character you add to a string.

Now let's cover the third and final pillar of good unit tests: readability.

7.3 Writing readable tests

Readability is so important that, without it, the tests we write are almost meaningless. From giving good names to the tests to having good assert messages, readability is the connecting thread between the person who wrote the test and the poor soul who has to read it a few months later. Tests are stories we tell the next generation of programmers on a project. They allow a developer to see exactly what an application is made of and where it started.

This section is all about making sure the developers who come after you will be able to maintain the production code and the tests that you write, while understanding what they're doing and where they should be doing it.

There are several facets to readability:

- Naming unit tests
- Naming variables
- Creating good assert messages
- Separating asserts from actions

Let's go through these one by one.

7.3.1 Naming unit tests

Naming standards are important because they give us comfortable rules and templates that outline what we should explain about the test. The test name has three parts:

The name of the method being tested—This is essential, so that you can easily see where the tested logic is. Having this as the first part of the test name allows easy navigation and as-you-type intellisense (if your IDE supports it) in the test class.

The scenario under which it's being tested—This part gives us the "with" part of the name: "When I call method X *with a null value*, then it should do Y."

- *The expected behavior when the scenario is invoked*—This part specifies in plain English what the method should do or return, or how it should behave, based on the current scenario: "When I call method X with a null value, *then it should do Y.*"

Removing even one of these parts from a test name can cause the reader of the test to wonder what is going on, and to start reading the test code. Our main goal is to release the next developer from the burden of reading the test code in order to understand what the test is testing.

A common way to write these three parts of the test name is to separate them with underscores, like this: `MethodUnderTest_Scenario_Behavior()`. Listing 7.23 shows a test that uses this naming convention.

Listing 7.23 A test with three parts in its name

```
[Test]
public void
    AnalyzeFile_FileWith3LinesAndFileProvider_ReadsFileUsingProvider()
{
//...
}
```

The method in listing 7.23 tests the `AnalyzeFile` method, giving it a file with three lines and a file-reading provider, and expects it to use the provider to read the file.

If developers stick to this naming convention, it will be easy for other developers to jump in and understand tests.

7.3.2 Naming variables

How you name variables in unit tests is as important as, or even more important than, variable-naming conventions in production code. Apart from their chief function of testing, tests also serve as a form of documentation for an API. By giving variables good names, we can make sure that people reading our tests understand what we're trying to *prove* as quickly as possible (as opposed to understanding what we're trying to *accomplish* when writing production code).

Listing 7.24 shows an example of a poorly named and poorly written test. I call this "unreadable" in the sense that I can't figure out what this test is about.

Listing 7.24 An unreadable test name

```
[Test]
public void BadlyNamedTest()
{
    LogAnalyzer log = new LogAnalyzer();
    int result= log.GetLineCount("abc.txt");
    Assert.AreEqual(-100,result);
}
```

In this instance, the assert is using some magic number (-100) (a number that represents some value the developer needs to know). Because we don't have a descriptive name for what the number is expected to be, we can only *assume* what it's supposed to mean. The test name should have helped us a little bit here, but the test name needs more work, to put it mildly.

Is -100 some sort of exception? Is it a valid return value? This is where we have a choice:

- We can change the design of the API to throw an exception instead of returning -100 (assuming -100 is some sort of illegal result value).
- We can compare the result to some sort of constant or aptly named variable, as shown in listing 7.25.

Listing 7.25 A more readable version of the test

```
[Test]
 public void BadlyNamedTest()
 {
    LogAnalyzer log = new LogAnalyzer();
    int result= log.GetLineCount("abc.txt");
    const int COULD_NOT_READ_FILE = –100;
    Assert.AreEqual(COULD_NOT_READ_FILE,result);
 }
```

The code in listing 7.25 is much better, because we can easily understand the intent of the return value.

The last part of a test is usually the assert, and we need to make the most out of the assert message. If the assert fails, the first thing the user will see is that message.

7.3.3 Asserting yourself with meaning

Writing a good assert message is much like writing a good exception message. It's easy to get it wrong without realizing it, and it makes a world of difference (and time) to the people who have to read it.

There are several key points to remember when writing a message for an assert clause:

- Don't repeat what the built-in test framework outputs to the console.
- Don't repeat what the test name explains.
- If you don't have anything good to say, don't say anything.
- Write what should have happened or what failed to happen, and possibly mention when it should have happened.

Listing 7.26 shows a bad example of an assert message and the output it produces.

Listing 7.26 A bad assert message that repeats what the test framework outputs

```
[Test]
public void BadAssertMessage()
{
    LogAnalyzer log = new LogAnalyzer();
    int result= log.GetLineCount("abc.txt");
    const int COULD_NOT_READ_FILE = -100;
    Assert.AreEqual(COULD_NOT_READ_FILE,result,
            "result was {0} instead of {1}",
            result,COULD_NOT_READ_FILE);
}

//Running this would produce:
TestCase 'AOUT.CH7.LogAn.Tests.Readable.BadAssertMessage'
failed:
  result was -1 instead of -100
  Expected: -100
  But was:  -1
    C:\GlobalShare\InSync\Book\Code
\ARtOfUniTesting\LogAn.Tests\Readable.cs(23,0)
: at AOUT.CH7.LogAn.Tests.Readable.BadAssertMessage()
```

As you can see, there's a message that repeats. Our assert message didn't add anything except more words to read. It would have been better to not output anything but instead have a better-named test. A clearer assert message would be something like this:

```
Calling GetLineCount() for a non-existing file should have returned
    a COULD_NOT_READ_FILE.
```

Now that your assert messages are understandable, it's time to make sure that the assert happens on a different line than the method call.

7.3.4 Separating asserts from actions

This is a short section, but an important one nonetheless. For the sake of readability, avoid writing the assert line and the method call in the same statement.

Listing 7.27 shows a good example, and listing 7.28 shows a bad example.

Listing 7.27 Separating the assert from the thing asserted improves readability

```
[Test]
 public void BadAssertMessage()
{
//some code here
    int result= log.GetLineCount("abc.txt");
    Assert.AreEqual(COULD_NOT_READ_FILE,result);
}
```

Listing 7.28 Not separating the assert from the thing asserted makes reading difficult

```
[Test]
 public void BadAssertMessage()
{
    //some code here

Assert.AreEqual(COULD_NOT_READ_FILE,log.GetLineCount("abc.txt"));
}
```

See the difference between the two examples? Listing 7.28 is much harder to read and understand in the context of a real test, because the call to the `GetLineCount()` method is inside the call to the assert message.

7.3.5 Setting up and tearing down

Setup and teardown methods in unit tests can be abused to the point where the tests or the setup and teardown methods are unreadable. Usually the situation is worse in the setup method than the teardown method.

Let's look at one possible abuse. If you have mocks and stubs being set up in a setup method, that means they don't get set up in the actual test. That, in turn, means that whoever is reading your test may not even realize that there are mock objects in use, or what the expectations are from them in the test.

It's much more readable to initialize mock objects directly in the test itself, with all their expectations. If you're worried about readability, you can refactor the creation of the mocks into a helper method, which each test calls. That way, whoever is reading the test will know exactly what is being set up instead of having to look in multiple places.

> **TIP** I've several times written full test classes that didn't have a setup method, only helper methods being called from each test, for the sake of maintainability. The class was still readable and maintainable.

7.4 Summary

Few developers write tests that they can trust when they first start out writing unit tests. It takes some discipline and some imagination to make sure you're doing things right. A test that you can trust is an elusive beast at first, but when you get it right, you'll feel the difference immediately.

Some ways of achieving this kind of trustworthiness involve keeping good tests alive and removing or refactoring away bad tests, and we discussed several such methods in this chapter. The rest of the chapter was about problems that can arise inside tests, such as logic, testing multiple things, ease of running, and so on. Putting all these things together can be quite an art form.

If there's one thing to take away from this chapter, it's this: tests grow and change with the system under tests. The topic of writing *maintainable* tests has not been covered much in the unit-testing and TDD literature, but as I write, it's starting to appear online in blogs and forums. I believe that this is the next step in the evolution of unit-testing techniques. The first step of acquiring the initial knowledge (what a unit test is, and how you write one) has been covered in many places. The second step involves refining the techniques to improve all aspects of the code we write, and looking into other factors, such as maintainability and readability. It's this critical step that this chapter (and most of this book) focuses on.

In the end, it's simple: readability goes hand in hand with maintainability and trustworthiness. People who can read your tests can understand them and maintain them, and they will also trust the tests when they pass. When this point is achieved, you're ready to handle change, and to change the code when it needs changing, because you'll know when things break.

In the next chapters, we'll take a broader look at what makes code testable, how to design for testability, and how to refactor existing code into a testable state.

Part 4

Design and process

This part of the book covers the problems and techniques that you'll need when introducing unit testing to an existing organization or code.

In chapter 8, we'll deal with the tough issue of implementing unit testing in an organization, and cover techniques that can make your job easier. This chapter provides answers to some tough questions that are common when first implementing unit testing.

In chapter 9, we'll look common problems associated with legacy code and examine some tools for working with it.

8

Integrating unit testing into the organization

This chapter covers

- *Becoming an agent of change*
- *Implementing change from the top down or from the bottom up*
- *Preparing to answer the tough questions about unit testing*

As a consultant, I have helped several companies, big and small, integrate test-driven development and unit testing into their organizational culture. Sometimes this has failed, but those companies that succeeded had several things in common. This chapter draws on stories from both camps as it looks at the following topics:

- *Becoming the agent of change*—The initial steps you should take before introducing any changes
- *Ways to succeed*—Things that contributed to successful changes in a process, based on my experience
- *Ways to fail*—Things that can destroy what you're trying to do, also based on my experience
- *Tough questions and answers*—The most frequently asked questions when introducing unit testing to a team

In any type of organization, changing people's habits is more psychological than technical. People don't like change, and change is usually accompanied with plenty of FUD (fear, uncertainty, and doubt) to go around. It won't be a walk in the park for most people, as you'll see in this chapter.

8.1 Steps to becoming an agent of change

If you're going to be the agent of change in your organization, you should first accept that role. People will view you as the person responsible for what's happening, whether you want them to or not, and there's no use in hiding. In fact, hiding can cause things to go awfully wrong.

As you start to implement changes, people will start asking the tough questions that they care about. How much time will this "waste"? What does this mean for me as a QA engineer? How do we know it works? Be prepared to answer these questions. The answers to the most common questions are discussed in section 8.4. You'll find that convincing other people inside the organization before you start making changes will help you immensely when you need to make tough decisions and answer those questions.

Finally, someone will have to stay at the helm, making sure the changes don't die for lack of momentum. That's you. There are ways to keep things alive, as you'll see in the next sections.

8.1.1 Be prepared for the tough questions

Do your research. Read the answers at the end of this chapter, and look at the related resources. Read forums, mailing lists, and blogs, and consult with your peers. If you can answer your own tough questions, there's a better chance you can answer someone else's.

8.1.2 Convince insiders: champions and blockers

Loneliness is a terrible thing, and not many things make you feel more alone in an organization than going against the current. If you're the only one who thinks what you're doing is a good idea, there's little reason for anyone to make an effort to implement what you're advocating. Consider who can help and hurt your efforts: the champions and blockers.

Champions

As you start pushing for change, identify the people you think are most likely to help in your quest. They will be your *champions*. They're usually early adopters, or people who have open enough minds to try the things you're advocating. They may already be half convinced but are looking for an impetus to start the change. They may have even tried it and failed on their own.

Approach them before anyone else and ask for their opinions on what you're about to do. They may tell you some things that you hadn't considered: teams that might be good candidates to start with, or places where people are more accepting of such changes. They may even tell you what to watch out for from their own personal experience.

By approaching them, you're helping to ensure that they're part of the process. People who feel part of the process usually try to help make it work. Make them your champions: ask them if they can help you and be the ones people can come to with questions. Prepare them for such events.

Blockers

Next, identify the *blockers*. These are the people in the organization who are most likely to resist the changes you're making. For example, a manager might object to adding unit tests, claiming that they will add too much time to the development effort and increase the amount of code that needs to be maintained. Make them part of the process instead of resistors of it by giving them (at least, those who are willing and able) an active role in the process.

The reasons why people might resist particular changes vary, and answers to some of the possible objections are covered in section 8.4. Some people will be afraid for their jobs, and some will feel comfortable with the way things are and object to any changes.

Going to these people and detailing all the things they could have done better is often nonconstructive, as I've found out the hard way. People don't like to be told what they don't do well. Instead, ask those people to help you in the process by being in charge of defining coding standards for unit tests, for example, or by doing code and test reviews with peers every other day. Or make them part of the team that chooses the course materials or outside consultants. You'll have given them a new responsibility that will help them feel relied upon and relevant in the organization. They need to be part of the change or they will almost certainly take part in a mini-rebellion against it.

8.1.3 Identify possible entry points

Identify where in the organization you can start implementing the changes. Most successful implementations take a steady route. Start with a pilot project in a small team, and see what happens. If all goes well, move on to other teams and other projects.

Here are some tips that will help you along the way:

- Choose smaller teams
- Create subteams
- Consider project feasibility

These tips can get you a long way in a mostly hostile environment.

Choose smaller teams

Identifying possible teams to start with is usually easy. You'll generally want a smaller team working on a lower profile project with low risks. If the risk is minimal, it's easier to convince people to try your proposed changes.

One caveat is that the team needs to have members who are open to changing the way they work and to learning new skills. Ironically, the people with less experience on a team are usually most likely to be open to change, and people with more experience tend to be more entrenched in their way of doing things. If you can find a team with an experienced leader who's open to change, but that also includes less-experienced developers, it's likely that team will offer less resistance. Go to the team and ask them their opinion on holding a pilot such as this. They will tell you if this is the right place to start or not.

Create subteams

Another possible candidate for a pilot test is to form a subteam within an existing team. Almost every team will have a "black hole" component that needs to be maintained, and while it does many things right, it also has many bugs. Adding features for such a component is a tough task, and this kind of pain can drive people to experiment with a pilot project.

Consider project feasibility

For a pilot project, make sure you're not biting off more than you can chew. It takes more experience to run more difficult projects, so you might want to have at least two options—a complicated project and an easier project—so that you can choose between them.

Now that you're mentally prepared for the task at hand, it's time to look at some things you can do to make sure it all goes smoothly (or that it goes at all).

8.2 Ways to succeed

There are two main ways an organization or team can start changing a process: bottom-up or top-down (and sometimes both). The two ways are very different, as you'll see, and either could be the right approach for your team or company. There's no one right way.

As you proceed, you'll need to learn how to convince management that your efforts should also be their efforts, or when it would be wise to bring in someone from outside to help. Making progress visible is important, as is setting clear goals that can be measured. Identifying and going around obstacles should also be high on your list. There are many battles that can be fought, and you need to choose the right ones.

8.2.1 Guerrilla implementation (bottom-up)

Guerrilla-style implementation is all about starting out with a team, getting results, and only then convincing other people that the practices are worthwhile. Usually the drivers for guerrilla implementation are the team that's tired of doing things the prescribed way. They set out to do things differently; they study things on their own and make changes happen. When the team shows results, other people in the organization may decide to start implementing similar changes in their own teams.

In some cases, guerrilla-style implementation is a process *adopted* first by developers and then by management. At other times, it's a process *advocated* first by developers and then by management. The difference is that you can accomplish the first covertly, without the higher powers knowing about it. The latter is done in conjunction with management.

It's up to you to figure out which approach will work best. Sometimes the only way to change things is by covert operations. Avoid this if you can, but if there's no other way and you're sure the change is needed, you can just do it.

Don't take this as a recommendation to make a career-limiting move. Developers do things they didn't ask permission for all the time: debugging code, reading email, writing code comments, creating flow diagrams, and so on. These are all tasks developers do as a regular part of the job. The same goes for unit testing. Most developers already write tests of some sort (automated or not). The idea is to redirect that time spent on tests into something that will provide benefits in the long term.

8.2.2 Convincing management (top-down)

The top-down move usually starts in one of two ways. A manager or a developer will start the process and start the rest of the organization moving in that direction, piece by piece. Or a midlevel manager may see a presentation, read a book (such as this one), or talk to a colleague about the benefits of specific changes to the way they work. Such a manager will usually initiate the process by giving a presentation to people in other teams, or even using his authority to make the change happen.

8.2.3 Getting an outside champion

I highly recommend getting an outside person to help with the change. An outside consultant coming in to help with unit testing and related matters has advantages over someone who works in the company:

- *Freedom to speak*—A consultant can say things that people inside the company may not be willing to hear from someone who works there: ("The code integrity is bad," "Your tests are unreadable," and so on).
- *Experience*—A consultant will have more experience dealing with resistance from the inside, coming up with good answers to tough questions, and knowing which buttons to push to get things going.

- *Dedicated time*—For a consultant, this is her job. Unlike other employees in the company who have better things to do than push for change (like writing software), the consultant does this full time and is dedicated to this purpose.

> **Code integrity**
>
> *Code integrity* is a term I use to describe the purpose behind a team's development activities, in terms of code stability, maintainability, and feedback. Mostly, it means that the code does what it's meant to do, and the team knows when it doesn't.
>
> These practices are all part of code integrity:
> - Automated builds
> - Continuous integration
> - Unit testing and test-driven development
> - Code consistency and agreed standards for quality
> - Achieving shortest time possible to fix bugs (or make failing tests pass)
>
> Some consider these to be "values" of development, and you can find them in methodologies such as Extreme Programming, but I like to say, "We have good code integrity," instead of saying that I think we're doing all these things well.

I've often seen a change break down because an overworked champion doesn't have the time to dedicate to the process.

8.2.4 Making progress visible

It's important to keep the progress and status of the change visible. Hang whiteboards or posters up on walls in corridors or in the food-related areas where people congregate. The data displayed should be related to the goals you're trying to achieve.

For example, show the number of passing or failing tests in the last nightly build. Keep a chart showing which teams are already running an automated build process. Put up a Scrum burndown chart of iteration progress or a test-code-coverage report (as seen in figure 8.1) if that's what you have your goals set to. (You can learn more about

Scrum at www.controlchaos.com.) Put up contact details for yourself and all the champions so you can answer any questions that arise.

You're aiming to talk to two groups with these charts:

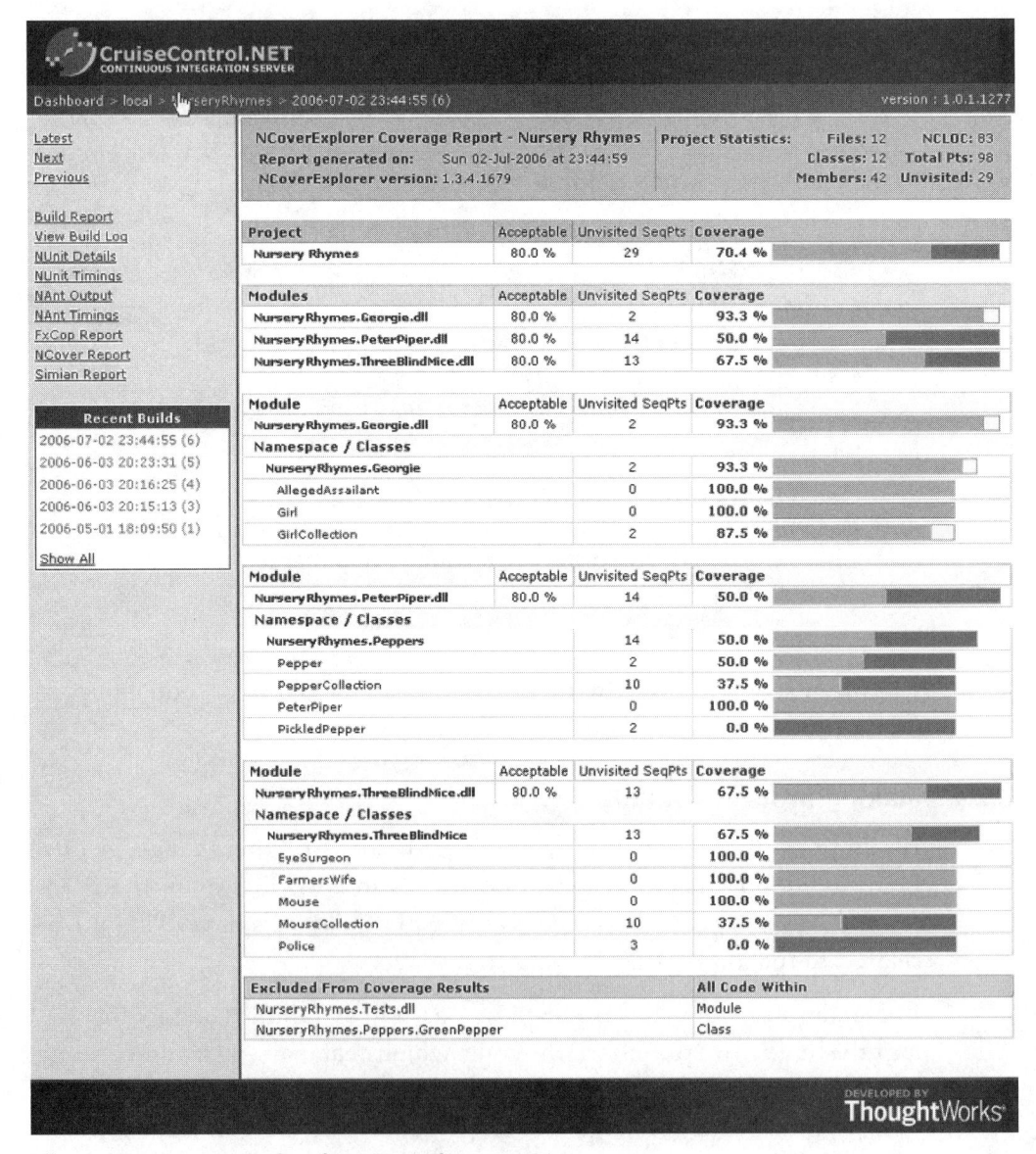

Figure 8.1 An example of a test-code-coverage report

- *The group undergoing the change*—People in this group will gain a greater feeling of accomplishment and pride as the charts (which are open to everyone) are updated, and they will feel more compelled to complete the process because it's visible to others. They will also be able to keep track of how they're doing compared to other groups. They may push harder knowing that another group implemented specific practices more quickly.

- *Those in the organization who aren't part of the process*—You're raising interest and curiosity among these people, triggering conversations and buzz, and creating a current that they can join if they choose.

8.2.5 Aiming for specific goals

Without goals, the change will be hard to measure and to communicate to others. It will be a vague "something" that can easily be shut down at the first sight of trouble.

Here are some goals you might want to consider:

- *Increase the amount of test code coverage.*

  A study by Boris Beizer showed that developers who write tests and don't use code-coverage tools or other techniques to test code coverage will be naively optimistic about the coverage they gained from the tests. Another study, from the book *Peer Reviews in Software: A Practical Guide*, suggests that testing without code-coverage tools may only result in coverage of about 50 to 60 percent of the code. (There's much anecdotal evidence that, by using TDD, one can get up to 95 to 100 percent code coverage for logical code.)

  A simple goal to measure is the percentage of the code covered by the tests. The more coverage, the better chance of finding bugs. It's not a silver bullet, though. One could easily have close to 100 percent code coverage with bad tests that don't mean anything. Low coverage is a bad sign; high coverage is a possible sign that things are better.

  NOTE The study by Boris Beizer is discussed in Mark Johnson's article, "Dr. Boris Beizer on software testing: an interview, part 1," in *The Software QA Quarterly* (summer 1994). The other study is discussed in Karl Wiegers book, *Peer Reviews in Software: A Practical Guide* (Addison-Wesley, 2002).

- *Increase the amount of test code coverage relative to the amount of code churn.*

  Some production systems will allow you to measure the amount of *code churn*—how many lines of code were changed between builds. The fewer lines of code changed, the fewer bugs you're likely to have introduced into a system. Calculating this isn't always practical, particularly in systems where you do a lot of code generation as part of the build process, but this can be solved by ignoring generated code. One system that allows you to measure code churn is Microsoft's Team System. (See Microsoft's "Code Churn Perspective" article at http://msdn.microsoft.com/en-us/library/ms244698(VS.80).aspx.)

- *Reduce the amount of bug reopening.*

  It's easy to fix one thing and mistakenly break something else. If this doesn't happen often, it's a sign that you're able to fix things and maintain the system without breaking previous assumptions.

- *Reduce the average bug-fixing time (the time from bug opened to bug closed).*

  A system with good tests and coverage will usually allow you to fix things more quickly (assuming the tests are written in a maintainable manner). That, in turn, means better turnaround times, and release cycles that are less stressful.

In his book *Code Complete* (Microsoft Press), Steve McConnell outlines several metrics you can use to test progress. They include the following, among others:

- The number of defects found per class by priority
- The number of defects per routine number of testing hours per bug found
- The average number of defects per test case

I highly recommend reading chapter 22 of that book, which deals with developer testing.

8.2.6 Realizing that there will be hurdles

There are always hurdles. Most will come from within the organizational structure, and some will be technical. The technical ones are easier to fix, because it's just a matter of finding the right solution. The organizational ones need care and attention and a psychological approach.

It's important not to surrender to a feeling of temporary failure when an iteration goes bad, tests go slower than expected, and so on. It's sometimes hard to get going, and you'll need to persist for at least a couple of months to start feeling comfortable with the new process and to iron out all the kinks. Have management commit to continuing for at least three months even if things don't go as planned. It's important to get their agreement up front. You don't want to be running around trying to convince people in the middle of a stressful first month.

Now that we've looked at ways of ensuring things go right, let's look at some things that can lead to failure.

8.3 Ways to fail

In the preface to this book, I talked about one project I was involved with that failed, partly because unit testing was not implemented correctly. That's one way you can fail a project. I've listed several others here, along with one that cost me that project, and some things that can be done about them.

8.3.1 Lack of a driving force

In all the places where I've seen change fail, the lack of a driving force was the most powerful factor in play. Being a consistent driving force of change has its price. It will take time away from your normal job to teach others, help them, and wage internal political wars for change. You need to be willing to surrender the time you have for these tasks, or the change won't happen. Bringing in an outside person, as mentioned in section 8.2.3, will help you in your quest for a consistent driving force.

8.3.2 Lack of political support

If your boss explicitly tells you not to make the change, there isn't a whole lot you can do, besides trying to convince management to see what you see. But sometimes the lack of support is much more subtle than that, and the trick is to realize that you are facing opposition.

For example, you may be told, "Sure, go ahead and implement those tests. We're adding 10 percent to your time to do this." Anything below

30 percent isn't realistic for beginning a unit-testing effort. This is one way a manager may try to stop a trend—by choking it out of existence.

First, you need to recognize that you're facing opposition, but once you do, it's easy to identify. When you tell them that their limitations aren't realistic, you'll be told, "So don't do it."

8.3.3 Bad implementations and first impressions

If you're planning to implement unit testing without prior knowledge of how to write good unit tests, do yourself one big favor: involve someone who has experience, and follow some best practices (such as those outlined in this book).

I've seen developers jump into the deep water without a proper understanding of what to do or where to start, and it's not a good place to be. Not only will it take a huge amount of time to learn how to make changes that are acceptable for your situation, but you'll also lose a lot of credibility along the way for starting out with a bad implementation. This can lead to the pilot project being shut down.

If you read the preface of this book, you'll know that this is what happened to me. You only have a couple of months to get things up to speed and convince the higher-ups that you're achieving results. Make that time count, and remove any risks that you can. If you don't know how to write good tests, read a book or get a consultant. If you don't know how to make your code testable, do the same. Don't waste time reinventing testing methods you don't have to.

8.3.4 Lack of team support

If your team doesn't support your efforts, it will be nearly impossible to succeed, because you'll have a hard time consolidating your extra work on the new process with your regular work. You should strive to have your team be part of the new process, or at least not stop it.

Talk to your team members about the changes. Getting their support one by one is sometimes a good way to start, but talking to them as a group about your efforts—and answering their hard questions—can also prove valuable. Whatever you do, don't take the team's support for granted. Make sure you know what you're getting into; these are the people you have to work with on a daily basis.

Regardless of how you proceed, you're going to be asked some tough questions about unit testing. The following questions and answers will help prepare you for your discussions with people who can make or break your agenda for change.

8.4 Tough questions and answers

This section covers some questions I've come across in various places. They usually arise from the premise that implementing unit testing can hurt someone personally—a manager looking out for his deadlines or a QA employee looking out for her relevancy. Once you understand where a question is coming from, it's important to address the issue, directly or indirectly. Otherwise, there will always be subtle resistance.

8.4.1 How much time will this add to the current process?

Team leads, project managers, and clients are the ones who usually ask how much time unit testing will add to the process. They're the people in the front lines in terms of timing.

Let's begin with some facts. Studies have shown that raising the overall code quality in a project can increase productivity and shorten schedules. How does this match up with the fact that writing tests makes coding slower? Through maintainability and the ease of fixing bugs, mostly.

> **NOTE** For studies on code quality and productivity, see Capers Jones, *Programming Productivity* (McGraw-Hill, 1986) and his *Software Assessments, Benchmarks, and Best Practices* (Addison-Wesley, 2000).

When asking about time, team leads may really be asking, "What should I tell my project manager when we go way past our due date?" They may actually think the process is useful but are looking for ammunition for the upcoming battle. They may also be asking the question not in terms of the whole product, but in terms of specific feature sets or functionality.

A project manager or customer who asks about timing, on the other hand, will usually be talking in terms of full product releases.

Because different people care about different scopes, the answers you give them may vary. For example, unit testing can double the time it takes to implement a specific feature, but the overall release date for the product may actually be reduced. To understand this, let's look at a real example I was involved with.

A tale of two features

A large company I consulted with wanted to implement unit testing into their process, beginning with a pilot project. The pilot consisted of a group of developers adding a new feature to a large existing application. The company's main livelihood was in creating this large billing application and customizing parts of it for various clients. The company had thousands of developers around the world.

The following measures were taken to test the pilot's success:

- The time the team took for each of the development stages
- The overall time for the project to be released to the client
- The number of bugs found by the client after the release

The same statistics were collected for a similar feature created by a different team for a different client. The two features were nearly the same size, and the teams were roughly at the same skill and experience level. Both tasks were customization efforts—one with unit tests, the other without. Table 8.1 shows the differences in time.

Table 8.1 Team progress and output measured with and without tests

Stage	Team without tests	Team with tests
Implementation (coding)	7 days	14 days
Integration	7 days	2 days
Testing and bug fixing	Testing, 3 days Fixing, 3 days Testing, 3 days Fixing, 2 days Testing, 1 day Total: 12 days	Testing, 3 days Fixing, 1 day Testing, 1 day Fixing, 1 day Testing, 1 day Total: 8 days

| Overall release time | 26 days | 24 days |
| Bugs found in production | 71 | 11 |

Overall, the time to release with tests was less than without tests. Still, the managers on the team with the unit tests didn't initially believe the pilot would be a success because they only looked at the implementation (coding) statistic (the first row in table 8.1) as the criteria for success, instead of the bottom line. It took twice the amount of time to code the feature (because unit tests cause you to write more code). Despite this, the time "wasted" more than made up for itself when the QA team found fewer bugs to deal with.

That's why it's important to emphasize that, although unit testing can increase the amount of time it takes to implement a feature, the time balances out over the product's release cycle because of increased quality and maintainability.

8.4.2 Will my QA job be at risk because of this?

Unit testing doesn't eliminate QA-related jobs. QA engineers will receive the application with full unit-test suites, which means they can make sure all the unit tests pass before they start their own testing process. Having unit tests in place will actually make their job more interesting. Instead of doing UI debugging (where every second button click results in an exception of some sort), they will be able to focus on finding more logical (applicative) bugs in real-world scenarios. Unit tests provide the first layer of defense against bugs, and QA work provides the second layer—the user's acceptance layer. As with security, the application always needs to have more than one layer of protection. Allowing the QA process to focus on the larger issues can produce better applications.

In some places, QA engineers write code, and they can help write unit tests for the application. That happens in conjunction with the work of the application developers and not instead of it. Both developers and QA engineers can write unit tests.

8.4.3 How do we know this is actually working?

To determine whether your unit testing is working, create a metric of some sort, as discussed in section 8.2.5. If you can measure it, you'll have a way to know; plus, you'll feel it.

Figure 8.2 shows a sample test-code-coverage report (coverage per build). Creating a report like this, by running a tool like NCover for .NET automatically during the build process, can demonstrate progress in one aspect of development.

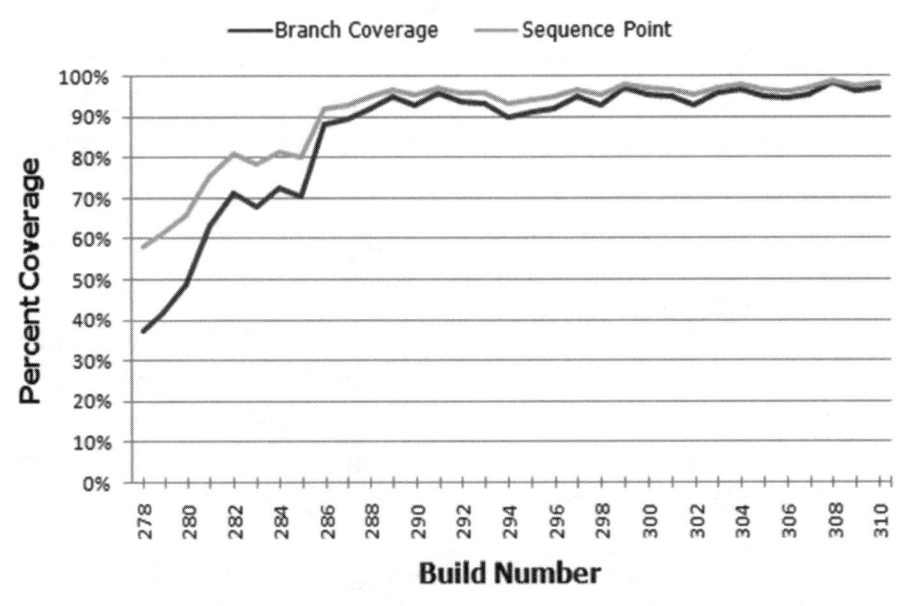

Figure 8.2 An example test-code-coverage trend report

Code coverage is a good starting point if you're wondering whether you're missing unit tests.

8.4.4 Is there proof that unit testing helps?

There aren't any specific studies I can point to on whether unit testing helps achieve better code quality. Most related studies talk about adopting specific agile methods, with unit testing being just one of them. Some empirical evidence can be gleaned from the web, of companies and colleagues having great results and never wanting to go back to a code base without tests.

A few studies on TDD can be found at http://biblio.gdinwiddie.com/biblio/StudiesOfTestDrivenDevelopment.

8.4.5 Why is the QA department still finding bugs?

The job of a QA engineer is to find bugs at many different levels, attacking the application from many different approaches. Usually a QA engineer will perform integration-style testing, which can find problems that unit tests can't. For example, the way different components work together in production may point out bugs even though the individual components pass unit tests (which work well in isolation). In addition, a QA engineer may test things in terms of use cases or full scenarios that unit tests usually won't cover. That approach can discover logical bugs or acceptance-related bugs and is a great help to ensuring better project quality.

A study by Glenford Myre showed that developers writing tests were not really looking for bugs, and so found only half to two-thirds of the bugs in an application. Broadly, that means there will always be jobs for QA engineers, no matter what. Although that study is 30 years old, I think the same mentality holds today, which makes the results still relevant today, at least for me.

> NOTE Glenford Myre's study is discussed in "A controlled experiment in program testing and code walkthroughs/inspections," in *Communications of the ACM* 21, no. 9 (September 1978), 760–68.

8.4.6 We have lots of code without tests: where do we start?

Studies conducted in the 1970s and 1980s showed that, typically, 80 percent of the bugs are found in 20 percent of the code. The trick is to find the code that has the most problems. More often than not, any team can tell you which components are the most problematic. Start there. You can always add some metrics, as discussed in section 8.2.5, relating to the number of bugs per class.

> **NOTE** Studies that show 80 percent of the bugs being in 20 percent of the code include the following: Albert Endres, "An analysis of errors and their causes in system programs," *IEEE Transactions on Software Engineering* 2 (June 1975), 140–49; Lee L. Gremillion, "Determinants of program repair maintenance requirements," *Communications of the ACM* 27, no. 8 (August 1984), 826–32; Barry W. Boehm, "Industrial software metrics top 10 list," *IEEE Software* 4, no. 9 (September 1987), 84–85; and Shull and others, "What we have learned about fighting defects," *Proceedings of the 8th International Symposium on Software Metrics* (2002), 249–58.

Testing legacy code requires a different approach than when writing new code with tests. See chapter 9 for more details.

8.4.7 We work in several languages: is unit testing feasible?

Sometimes tests written in one language can test code written in other languages, especially if it's a .NET mix of languages. You can write tests in C# to test code written in VB.NET, for example. Sometimes each team writes tests in the language they develop in: C# developers can write tests in C# using NUnit or MbUnit, and C++ developers can write tests using one of the C++ oriented frameworks, such as CppUnit. I've also seen solutions where people who wrote C++ code would write managed C++ wrappers around it and write tests in C# against those managed C++ wrappers, which made things easier to write and maintain.

8.4.8 What if we develop a combination of software and hardware?

If your application is made of a combination of software and hardware, you need to write tests for the software. Chances are, you already have some sort of hardware simulator, and the tests you write can take advantage of this. It may take a little more work, but it's definitely possible, and companies do this all the time.

8.4.9 How can we know we don't have bugs in our tests?

You need to make sure your tests fail when they should and pass when they should. Test-driven development is a great way to make sure you don't forget to check those things. See chapter 1 for a short walk-through of TDD.

8.4.10 My debugger shows that my code works: why do I need tests?

You may be sure your code works fine, but what about other people's code? How do you know it works? How do they know your code works and that they haven't broken anything when they make changes? Remember that coding is just the first step in the life of the code. Most of its life, the code will be in maintenance mode. You need to make sure it will tell people when it breaks, using unit tests.

A study held by Curtis, Krasner, and Iscoe showed that most defects don't come from the code itself, but result from miscommunication between people, requirements that keep changing, and a lack of application domain knowledge. Even if you're the world's greatest coder, chances are that, if someone tells you to code the wrong thing, you'll do it. And when you need to change it, you'll be glad you have tests for everything else to make sure you don't break it.

> **NOTE** The study by Bill Curtis, H. Krasner, and N. Iscoe is "A field study of the software design process for large systems," *Communications of the ACM* 31, no. 11 (November 1988), 1268–1287.

8.4.11 Must we do TDD-style coding?

TDD is a style choice. I personally see a lot of value in TDD, and many people find it productive and beneficial, but others find that writing the tests after the code is good enough for them. You can make your own choice.

If this question arises from a fear of too much change happening at once, the learning can be broken up into several intermediate steps:

- Learn unit testing from books such as this, and use tools such as Typemock Isolator or JMockit so that you don't have to worry about design aspects while testing.
- Learn good design techniques, such as SOLID (which is discussed at the end of section 3.6 in chapter 3).
- Learn to do test-driven development. (A good book is *Test-Driven Development in Microsoft .NET* by James Newkirk.)

This way, the learning is easier and you can get started more quickly with less loss of time to the project.

8.5 Summary

Implementing unit testing in the organization is something that many readers of this book will have to face at one time or another. Be prepared. Make sure you have good answers to the questions you're likely to be asked. Make sure that you don't alienate the people who can help you. Make sure you're ready for what could be an uphill battle.

In the next chapter, we'll take a look at legacy code and examine some tools for working with it.

9
Working with legacy code

This chapter covers

- *Examining common problems with legacy code*
- *Deciding where to begin writing tests*
- *Surveying helpful tools for working with legacy code*

I once consulted for a large development shop that produced billing software. They had over 10,000 developers and mixed .NET, Java, and C++ in products, subproducts, and intertwined projects. The software had existed in one form or another for over five years, and most of the developers were tasked with maintaining and building on top of existing functionality.

My job was to help several divisions (using all languages) learn test-driven development techniques. For about 90 percent of the developers I worked with, this never became a reality for several reasons, some of which were a result of legacy code:

- It was difficult to write tests against existing code.
- It was next to impossible to refactor the existing code (or there was not enough time to do it).
- Some people didn't want to change their designs.
- Tooling (or lack of tooling) was getting in the way.
- It was difficult to determine where to begin.

Anyone who's ever tried to add tests to an existing system knows that most such systems are almost impossible to write tests for. They were usually written without proper places in the software (seams) to allow extensions or replacements to existing components.

There are several problems that need to be addressed when dealing with legacy code:

- There's so much work, where should I start to add tests? Where should I focus my efforts?
- How can I safely refactor my code if it has no tests to begin with?
- What tools can I use with legacy code?

This chapter will tackle these tough questions associated with approaching legacy code bases, by listing techniques, references, and tools that can help.

9.1 Where do you start adding tests?

Assuming you have existing code inside components, you'll need to create a priority list of components for which testing makes the most sense. There are several factors to consider that can affect each component's priority:

- *Logical complexity*—This refers to the amount of logic in the component, such as nested ifs, switch cases, or recursion. Tools for checking cyclomatic complexity can also be used to determine this.
- *Dependency level*—This refers to the number of dependencies in the component. How many dependencies do you have to break in order to bring this class under test? Does it communicate with an outside email component, perhaps, or does it call a static log method somewhere?
- *Priority*—This is the component's general priority in the project.

You can give each component a rating for these factors, from 1 (low priority) to 10 (high priority).

Table 9.1 shows a short list of classes with ratings for these factors. I call this a *test-feasibility table*.

Where do you start adding tests?

Table 9.1 A simple test-feasibility table

Component	Logical complexity	Dependency level	Priority	Notes
Utils	6	1	5	This utility class has few dependencies but contains a lot of logic. It will be easy to test, and it provides lots of value.
Person	2	1	1	This is a data-holder class with little logic and no dependencies. There's some (small) real value in testing this.
TextParser	8	4	6	This class has lots of logic and lots of dependencies. To top it off, it's part of a high priority task in the project. Testing this will provide lots of value but will also be hard and time-consuming.
ConfigManager	1	6	1	This class holds configuration data and reads files from disk. It has little logic but many dependencies. Testing it will provide little value to the project and will also be hard and time-consuming.

From the data in table 9.1, we can create the diagram shown in figure 9.1, which graphs our components by the amount of value to the project and number of dependencies.

We can safely ignore items that are below our designated threshold of logic (which I usually set at 2 or 3), so `Person` and `ConfigManager` can be

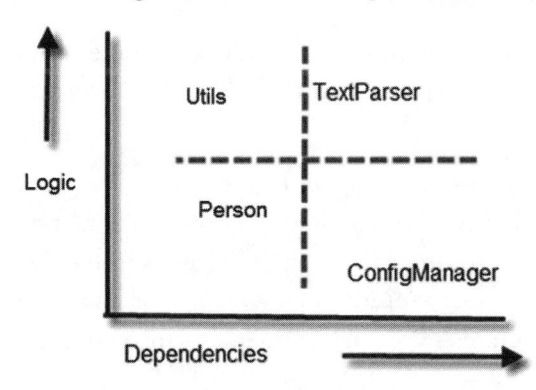

Figure 9.1 Mapping components for test feasibility

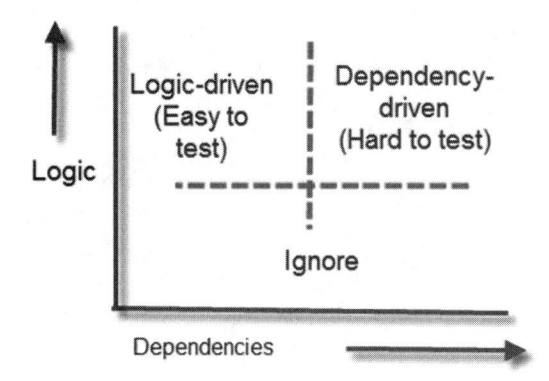

Figure 9.2 Easy, hard, and irrelevant component mapping based on logic and dependencies

ignored. We're left with only the top two components from figure 9.1. There are two basic ways to look at the graph and decide what you'd like to test first (see figure 9.2):

- Choose the one that's more complex and easier to test (top left).
- Choose the one that's more complex and harder to test (top right).

The question now is what path you should take. Should you start with the easy stuff or the hard stuff?

9.2 Choosing a selection strategy

As the previous section explained, you can start with the components that are easy to test or the ones that are hard to test (because they have many dependencies). Each strategy presents different challenges.

9.2.1 Pros and cons of the easy-first strategy

Starting out with the components that have fewer dependencies will make writing the tests initially much quicker and easier. But there's a catch, as figure 9.3 demonstrates.

Figure 9.3 shows how long it takes to bring components under test during the lifetime of the project. Initially it's easy to write tests, but as time goes by, we're left with components that are increasingly harder and harder to test, with the particularly tough ones waiting for us at the end of the project cycle, just when everyone is stressed about pushing a product out the door.

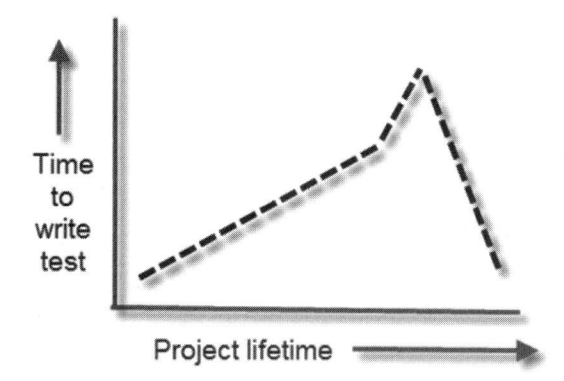

Figure 9.3 When starting with the easy components, the time to test gets longer and longer until the hardest components are done.

If your team is relatively new to unit-testing techniques, it's worth starting with the easy components. As time goes by, the team will learn the techniques needed to deal with the more complex components and dependencies.

For such a team, it may be wise to initially avoid all components over a specific number of dependencies (with 4 being a good place to start).

9.2.2 Pros and cons of the hard-first strategy

Starting with the more difficult components may seem like a losing proposition to begin with, but it has an upside, as long as your team has experience with unit-testing techniques.

Figure 9.4 shows the average time to write a test for a single component over the lifetime of the project, if you start testing the components with the most dependencies first.

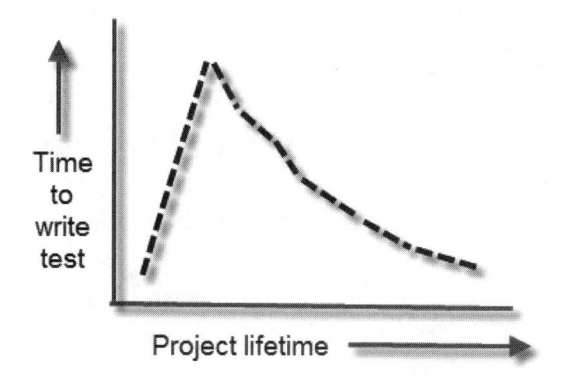

Figure 9.4 When you use a hard-first strategy, the time to test is long for the first few components, and then it gets shorter as more dependencies are refactored away.

With this strategy, you could be spending a day or more to get even the simplest tests going on the more complex components. But notice the quick decline in the time required to write the test relative to the slow incline in figure 9.3. Every time you bring a component under test and refactor it to make it more testable, you may also be solving testability issues for the dependencies it uses, or for other components. Specifically because that component has lots of dependencies, refactoring it can improve things for other parts of the system. That's why the quick decline appears.

The hard-first strategy is only possible if your team has experience in unit-testing techniques, because it's harder to implement. If your team does have experience, use the priority aspect of components to choose whether to start with the hard or easy components first. You might want to choose a mix, but it's important that you know in advance how much effort will be involved and what the possible consequences are.

9.3 Writing integration tests before refactoring

If you do plan to refactor your code for testability (so you can write unit tests), a practical way to make sure you don't break anything during the refactoring phase is to write integration-style tests against your production system.

I consulted on a large legacy project, working with a developer who needed to work on an XML configuration manager. The project had no tests and was hardly testable. It was also a C++ project, so we couldn't use a tool like Typemock Isolator to isolate components without refactoring the code.

The developer needed to add another value attribute into the XML file and be able to read and change it through the existing configuration component. We ended up writing a couple of integration tests that used the real system to save and load configuration data, and that asserted on the values the configuration component was retrieving and writing to the file. Those tests set the "original" working behavior of the configuration manager as our base of work.

Next, we wrote an integration test that showed that, once the component was reading the file, it contained no attribute in memory with the name we were trying to add. We proved that the feature was missing, and we now had a test that would pass once we added the new attribute to the XML file and correctly wrote to it from the component.

Once we wrote the code that saved and loaded the extra attribute, we ran the three integration tests (two tests for the original base implementation, and a new one that tried to read the new attribute). All three passed, so we knew that we hadn't broken existing functionality while adding the new functionality.

As you can see, the process is relatively simple:

- Add one or more integration tests (no mocks or stubs) to the system to prove the original system works as needed.
- Refactor or add a failing test for the feature you're trying to add to the system.
- Refactor and change the system in small chunks, and run the integration tests as often as you can, to see if you break something.

Sometimes, integration tests may seem easier to write than unit tests, because you don't need to mess with dependency injection. But making those tests run on your local system may prove annoying or time-consuming because you have to make sure every little thing the system needs is in place.

The trick is to work on the parts of the system that you need to fix or add features to. Don't focus on the other parts. That way, the system grows in the right places, leaving other bridges to be crossed when you get to them.

As you continue adding more and more tests, you can refactor the system and add more unit tests to it, growing it into a more maintainable and testable system. This takes time (sometimes months and months), but it's worth it.

Did I mention that you need to have good tools? Let's look at some of my favorites.

9.4 Important tools for legacy code unit testing

Here are a few tips on tools that can give you a head start if you're doing any testing on existing code in .NET:

- Isolate dependencies easily with Typemock Isolator.
- Find testability problems with Depender.
- Use JMockit for Java legacy code.
- Use Vise while refactoring your Java code.
- Use FitNesse for acceptance tests before you refactor.
- Read Michael Feathers' book on legacy code.
- Use NDepend to investigate your production code.
- Use ReSharper to navigate and refactor your production code more easily.
- Detect duplicate code (and bugs) with Simian.
- Detect threading issues with Typemock Racer.

Let's look at each of these in a little more detail.

9.4.1 Isolate dependencies easily with Typemock Isolator

Typemock Isolator was introduced in chapter 5, and it's the only commercial-grade isolation framework (which means it allows stubs and mocks) of the frameworks currently on the market. It's also different from the other frameworks in that it's the only one that allows you to create stubs and mocks of dependencies in production code without needing to refactor it at all, saving valuable time in bringing a component under test.

> **NOTE** Full disclosure: While writing this book, I also worked as a developer at Typemock on a different product. I also helped to design the API in Isolator 5.0.

In its latest version (5.2 at the time of writing this book), Isolator uses the term "fake" and removes completely the words "mock" and "stub" from the API. Using the new framework, you can "fake" interfaces, sealed and static types, nonvirtual methods, and static methods. This means you don't need to worry about changing the design (which you may not have time for, or perhaps can't for testability reasons). You can start testing almost immediately. There's also a free version of Typemock Isolator for open source projects, so you can feel free to download this product and try it on your own.

Listing 9.1 shows a couple of examples of using the new Isolator API to fake instances of classes.

Listing 9.1 Faking static methods and creating fake classes with Isolator

```
[Test]
 public void FakeAStaticMethod()
 {
    Isolate
    .WhenCalled(()=>MyClass.SomeStaticMethod())
    .WillThrowException(new Exception());

}

[Test]
 public void FakeAPrivateMethodOnAClassWithAPrivateConstructor()
 {
    ClassWithPrivateConstructor c =
       Isolate.Fake.Instance<ClassWithPrivateConstructor>();
    Isolate.NonPublic
          .WhenCalled(c,"SomePrivateMethod").WillReturn(3);
}
```

As you can see, the API is simple and clear, and uses generics and delegates to return fake values. There's also an API specifically dedicated for VB.NET that has a more VB-centric syntax. In both APIs, you don't need to change anything in the design of your classes under test to make these tests work, because Isolator uses the specialized *extended reflection* (or *profiler APIs*) of the .NET Common Language Runtime to perform its actions. This gives it much more power than other frameworks.

Isolator is a great framework if you want to start testing, you have existing code bases, and you want a bridge that can help make the hard stuff more agile. There are more examples and downloads at www.Typemock.com.

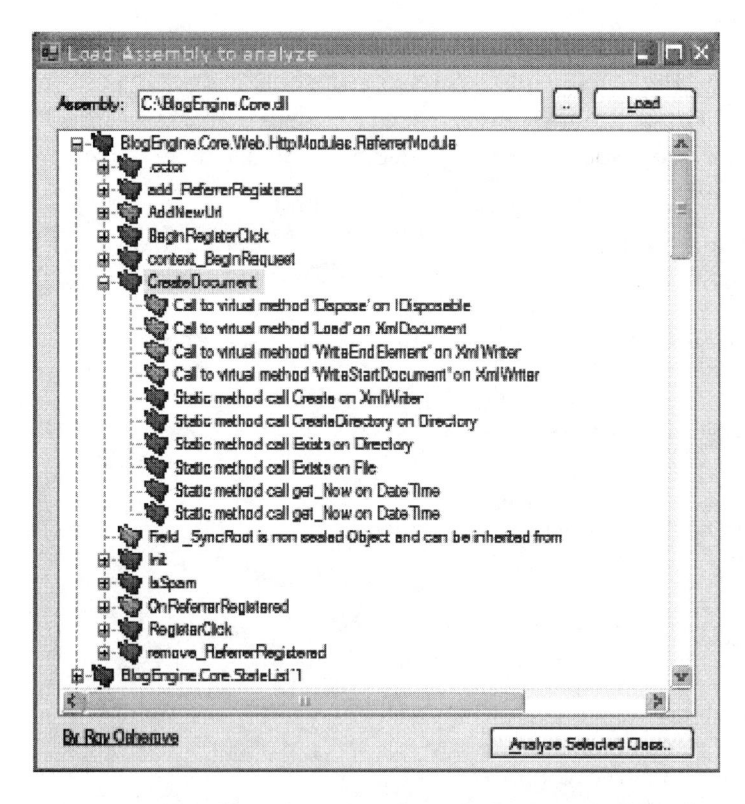

Figure 9.5 Depender is simple and easy to use.

9.4.2 Find testability problems with Depender

Depender is a free tool I've created that can analyze .NET assemblies for their types and methods, and can help determine possible testability problems in methods (static methods, for example). It displays a simple report for an assembly or a method, as shown in figure 9.5.

You can download Depender from my blog: http://weblogs.asp.net/rosherove/archive/2008/07/05/introducing-depender-testability-problem-finder.aspx.

9.4.3 Use JMockit for Java legacy code

JMockit is an open source project that uses the Java instrumentation APIs to do some of the same things that Typemock Isolator does in .NET. You don't need to change the design of your existing project to isolate your components from their dependencies.

JMockit uses a swap approach. First, you create a manually coded class that will replace the class that acts as a dependency to your component under test (say you code a FakeDatabase class to replace a Database class). Then you use JMockit to swap calls from the original class to your own fake class. You can also redefine a class's methods by defining them again as anonymous methods inside the test.

Listing 9.2 shows a sample of a test that uses JMockit.

Listing 9.2 Using JMockit to swap class implementations

```
public class ServiceATest extends TestCase    {
      private boolean serviceMethodCalled;

      public static class MockDatabase     {
         static int findMethodCallCount;
         static int saveMethodCallCount;

         public static void save(Object o)     {
            assertNotNull(o);
            saveMethodCallCount++;
         }

         public static List find(String ql, Object arg1)    {
            assertNotNull(ql);
            assertNotNull(arg1);
            findMethodCallCount++;
            return Collections.EMPTY_LIST;
         }
      }

      protected void setUp() throws Exception    {
        super.setUp();
        MockDatabase.findMethodCallCount = 0;
        MockDatabase.saveMethodCallCount = 0;
        Mockit.redefineMethods(Database.class,              ◁─┐ The magic
                      MockDatabase.class);                     happens here
      }

      public void testDoBusinessOperationXyz() throws Exception    {
         final BigDecimal total = new BigDecimal("125.40");

         Mockit.redefineMethods(ServiceB.class,
                         new Object()                       ◁─┐ The magic
                                                              happens here
```

```
        {
            public BigDecimal computeTotal(List items)
            {
                assertNotNull(items);
                serviceMethodCalled = true;
                return total;
            }
        });

        EntityX data = new EntityX(5, "abc", "5453-1");
        new ServiceA().doBusinessOperationXyz(data);

        assertEquals(total, data.getTotal());
        assertTrue(serviceMethodCalled);
        assertEquals(1, MockDatabase.findMethodCallCount);
        assertEquals(1, MockDatabase.saveMethodCallCount);
    }
}
```

JMockit is a good place to start when testing Java legacy code.

9.4.4 Use Vise while refactoring your Java code

Michael Feathers wrote an interesting tool for Java that allows you to verify that you aren't messing up the values that may change in your method while refactoring it. For example, if your method changes an array of values, you want to make sure that as you refactor you don't screw up a value in the array.

Listing 9.3 shows an example of using the `Vise.grip()` method for such a purpose.

Listing 9.3 Using Vise in Java code to verify values aren't changed while refactoring

```
import vise.tool.*;

public class RPRequest {
    ...
    public int process(int level, RPPacket packet) {
        if (...) {
            if (...) {
                ...
```

```
            } else {
                ...
                bar_args[1] += list.size();
                Vise.grip(bar_args[1]);                    ◄──┐ Grips
                packet.add(new Subpacket(list, arrivalTime));  an object
                if (packet.calcSize() > 2)
                    bar_args[1] += 2;
                Vise.grip(bar_args[1]);                    ◄──┐ Grips
            }                                                 │ an object
        } else {
            int reqLine = -1;
            bar_args[0] = packet.calcSize(reqLine);
            Vise.grip(bar_args[0]);
            ...
        }
    }
}
```

NOTE The code in listing 9.3 is copied with permission from http://www.artima.com/weblogs/viewpost.jsp?thread=171323.

Vise forces you to add lines to your production code, and it's there to support refactoring of the code. There's no such tool for .NET, but it should be pretty easy to write one. Every time you call the `Vise.grip()` method, it checks whether the value of the passed-in variable is still what it's supposed to be. It's like adding an internal assert to your code, with a simple syntax. Vise can also report on all "gripped" items and their current values.

You can read about and download Vise free from Michael Feathers' blog: http://www.artima.com/weblogs/viewpost.jsp?thread=171323.

9.4.5 Use FitNesse for acceptance tests before you refactor

It's a good idea to add integration tests to your code before you start refactoring it. FitNesse is one tool that helps create a suite of integration- and acceptance-style tests. FitNesse allows you to write integration-style tests (in Java or .NET) against your application, and then change or add to them easily without needing to write code.

Using the FitNesse framework involves three steps:

1. Create code adapter classes (called *fixtures*) that can wrap your production code and represent actions that a user might take against it. For example, if it were a banking application, you might have a `bankingAdapter` class that has withdraw and deposit methods.

2. Create HTML tables using a special syntax that the FitNesse engine recognizes and parses. These tables will hold the values that will be run during the tests. You write these tables in pages in a specialized wiki website that runs the FitNesse engine underneath, so that your test suite is represented to the outside world by a specialized website. Each page with a table (which you can see in any web browser) is editable like a regular wiki page, and each has a special "execute tests" button. These tables are then parsed by the testing runtime and translated into test runs.

3. Click the Execute Tests button on one of the wiki pages. That button invokes the FitNesse engine with the parameters in the table. Eventually, the engine calls your specialized wrapper classes that invoke the target application and asserts on return values from your wrapper classes.

Figure 9.6 shows an example FitNesse table in a browser.

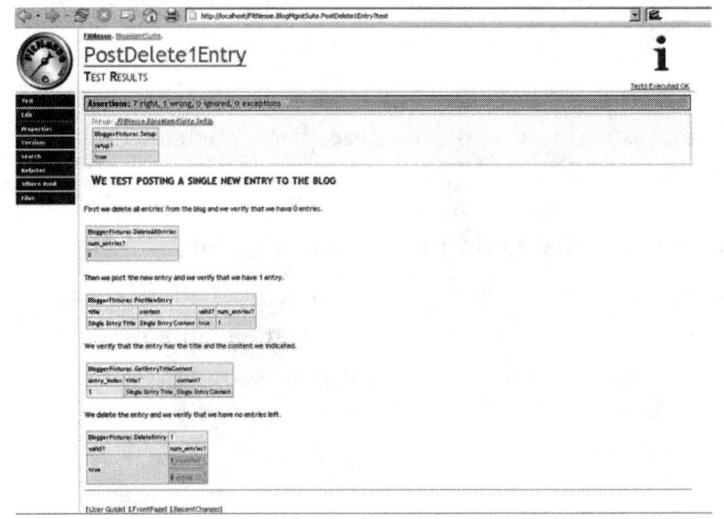

Figure 9.6 Using FitNesse for integration

You can learn more about FitNesse at http://fitnesse.org/. For .NET integration with FitNesse, go to http://fitnesse.org/FitNesse.DotNet.

9.4.6 Read Michael Feathers' book on legacy code

Working Effectively with Legacy Code, by Michael Feathers, is the only book I know that deals with the issues you'll encounter with legacy code (other than this chapter). It shows many refactoring techniques and gotchas in depth that this book doesn't attempt to cover. It's worth its weight in gold. Go get it.

9.4.7 Use NDepend to investigate your production code

NDepend is a relatively new commercial analyzer tool for .NET that can create visual representations of many aspects of your compiled assemblies, such as dependency trees, code complexity, changes between the different versions of the same assembly, and more. The possibilities of this tool are huge, and I recommend you learn how to use it.

NDepend's most powerful feature is a special query language (called CQL) you can use against the structure of your code to find out various component metrics. For example, you could easily create a query that reports on all components that have a private constructor.

You can get NDepend from http://www.ndepend.com.

9.4.8 Use ReSharper to navigate and refactor production code

ReSharper is one of the best productivity-related plugins for VS.NET. In addition to powerful automated refactoring abilities (much more powerful than the ones built into Visual Studio 2008), it's known for its navigation features. When jumping into an existing project, ReSharper can easily navigate the code base with shortcuts that allow you to jump from any point in the solution to any other point that might be related to it.

Here are some examples of possible navigations:

- When in a class or method declaration, you can jump to any inheritors of that class or method, or jump up to the base implementation of the current member or class, if one exists.

- You can find all uses of a given variable (highlighted in the current editor).
- You can find all uses of a common interface or a class that implements it.

These and many other shortcuts make it much less painful to navigate and understand the structure of existing code.

ReSharper works on both VB.NET and C# code. You can download a trial version at www.jetbrains.com.

9.4.9 Detect duplicate code (and bugs) with Simian

Let's say you found a bug in your code, and you want to make sure that bug was not duplicated somewhere else. With Simian, it's easy to track down code duplication and figure out how much work you have ahead of you, as well as refactoring to remove duplication. Simian is a commercial product that works on .NET, Java, C++, and other languages.

You can get Simian here:
http://www.redhillconsulting.com.au/products/simian/.

9.4.10 Detect threading issues with Typemock Racer

If your production code uses multiple threads, Typemock Racer may help you discover common but hard-to-detect threading problems in your existing code. It's a relatively new product that aims to find deadlocks and race conditions in your existing production code without needing to change it.

You can find out more about it at www.Typemock.com.

9.5 Summary

In this chapter, we talked about how to approach legacy code for the first time. It's important to map out the various components according to their number of dependencies, their amount of logic, and the project priority. Once you have that information, you can choose the components to work on based on how easy or how hard it will be to get them under test.

If your team has little or no experience in unit testing, it's a good idea to start with the easy components and let the team's confidence grow as they add more and more tests to the system. If your team is experienced, getting the hard ones under test first can help you get through the rest of the system more quickly.

If your team doesn't want to start refactoring code for testability, but only to start with unit testing out of the box, a tool like Typemock Isolator will prove helpful because it allows you to isolate dependencies without changing the existing code's design. Consider this tool when dealing with legacy .NET code. If you work with Java, consider JMockit for the same reasons.

I also covered a number of tools that can prove helpful in your journey to better code quality for existing code. Each of these tools can be used in different stages of the project, but it's up to your team to choose when to use which tool (if any at all).

Finally, as a friend once said, a good bottle of vodka never hurts when dealing with legacy code.

Appendix A

Design and testability

Changing the design of your code so that it's more easily testable is a controversial issue for some developers. This appendix will cover the basic concepts and techniques for designing for testability. We'll also look at the pros and cons of doing so and when it's appropriate.

First, though, let's consider why you would need to design for testability in the first place.

A.1 Why should I care about testability in my design?

The question is a legitimate one. In designing our software, we're taught to think about what the software should accomplish, and what the results will be for the end user of the system. But tests against our software are yet another type of user. That user has strict demands for our software, but they all stem from one mechanical request: testability. That request can influence the design of our software in various ways, mostly for the better.

In a testable design, each logical piece of code (loops, ifs, switches, and so on) should be easy and quick to write a unit test against, one that demonstrates these properties:

- Runs fast
- Is isolated, meaning it can run independently or as part of a group of tests, and can run before or after any other test
- Requires no external configuration
- Provides a consistent pass/fail result

These are the FICC properties: fast, isolated, configuration-free, and consistent. If it's hard to write such a test, or it takes a long time to write it, the system isn't testable.

If you think of tests as a user of your system, designing for testability becomes a way of thinking. If you were doing test-driven development, you'd have no choice but to write a testable system, because in TDD the tests come first and largely determine the API design of the system, forcing it to be something that the tests can work with.

Now that you know what a testable design is, let's look at what it entails, go over the pros and cons of such design decisions, and discuss alternatives to the testable design approach.

A.2 Design goals for testability

There are several design points that make code much more testable. Robert C. Martin has a nice list of design goals for object-oriented systems that largely form the basis for the designs shown in this chapter. See his "Principles of OOD" article at http://butunclebob.com/ArticleS.UncleBob.PrinciplesOfOod.

Most of the advice I include here is about allowing your code to have seams—places where you can inject other code or replace behavior without changing the original class. (Seams are often talked about in connection with the Open Closed Principle, which is mentioned in the Martin's "Principles of OOD" article.) For example, in a method that calls a web service, the web service API can hide behind a web service interface, allowing us to replace the real web service with a stub that will return whatever values we want, or with a mock object. Chapters 3–5 discuss fakes, mocks, and stubs in detail.

Table A.1 lists some basic design guidelines and their benefits. The following sections will discuss them in more detail.

Table A.1 Test design guidelines and benefits

Design guideline	Benefit(s)
Make methods virtual by default.	This allows you to override the methods in a derived class for testing. Overriding allows for changing behavior or breaking a call to an external dependency.
Use interface-based designs.	This allows you to use polymorphism to replace dependencies in the system with your own stubs or mocks.
Make classes nonsealed by default.	You can't override anything virtual if the class is sealed (`final` in Java).
Avoid instantiating concrete classes inside methods with logic. Get instances of classes from helper methods, factories, Inversion of Control containers such as Unity, or other places, but don't directly create them.	This allows you to serve up your own fake instances of classes to methods that require them, instead of being tied down to working with an internal production instance of a class.
Avoid direct calls to static methods. Prefer calls to instance methods that later call statics.	This allows you to break calls to static methods by overriding instance methods. (You won't be able to override static methods.)
Avoid constructors and static constructors that do logic.	Overriding constructors is difficult to implement. Keeping constructors simple will simplify the job of inheriting from a class in your tests.
Separate singleton logic from singleton holder.	If you have a singleton, have a way to replace its instance so you can inject a stub singleton or reset it.

A.2.1 Make methods virtual by default

Java makes methods virtual by default, but .NET developers aren't so lucky. In .NET, to be able to replace a method's behavior, you need to explicitly set it as virtual so you can override it in a default class. If you do this, you can use the Extract and Override method that I discussed in chapter 3.

An alternative to this method is to have the class invoke a custom delegate. You can replace this delegate from the outside by setting a property or sending in a parameter to a constructor or method. This isn't a typical approach, but some system designers find this approach suitable. Listing A.1 shows an example of a class with a delegate that can be replaced by a test.

Listing A.1 A class that invokes a delegate that can be replaced by a test

```
public class MyOverridableClass
{
    public Func<int,int> calculateMethod=delegate(int i)
                                         {
                                             return i*2;
                                         };
    public void DoSomeAction(int input)
    {
        int result = calculateMethod(input);
        if (result==-1)
        {
            throw new Exception("input was invalid");
        }
        //do some other work
    }
}

[Test]
[ExpectedException(typeof(Exception))]
 public void DoSomething_GivenInvalidInput_ThrowsException()
 {
     MyOverridableClass c = new MyOverridableClass();
     int SOME_NUMBER=1;

     //stub the calculation method to return "invalid"
     c.calculateMethod = delegate(int i) { return -1; };

     c.DoSomeAction(SOME_NUMBER);
 }
```

Using virtual methods is handy, but interface-based designs are also a good choice, as the next section explains.

A.2.2 Use interface-based designs

Identifying "roles" in the application and abstracting them under interfaces is an important part of the design process. An abstract class shouldn't call concrete classes, and concrete classes shouldn't call concrete classes either, unless they're data objects (objects holding data, with no behavior). This allows you to have multiple seams in the application where you could intervene and provide your own implementation.

For examples of interface-based replacements, see chapters 3–5.

A.2.3 Make classes nonsealed by default

Some people have a hard time making classes nonsealed by default because they like to have full control over who inherits from what in the application. The problem is that, if you can't inherit from a class, you can't override any virtual methods in it.

Sometimes you can't follow this rule because of security concerns, but following it should be the default, not the exception.

A.2.4 Avoid instantiating concrete classes inside methods with logic

It can be tricky to avoid instantiating concrete classes inside methods that contain logic because we're so used to doing it. The reason for doing so is that later our tests might need to control what instance is used in the class under test. If there's no seam that returns that instance, the task would be much more difficult unless you employ external tools, such as Typemock Isolator. If your method relies on a logger, for example, don't instantiate the logger inside the method. Get it from a simple factory method, and make that factory method virtual so that you can override it later and control what logger your method works against. Or use constructor injection instead of a virtual method. These and more injection methods are discussed in chapter 3.

A.2.5 Avoid direct calls to static methods

Try to abstract any direct dependencies that would be hard to replace at runtime. In most cases, replacing a static method's behavior is difficult or cumbersome in a static language like VB.NET or C#. Abstracting a static method away using the Extract and Override refactoring (shown in section 3.4.6 of chapter 3) is one way to deal with these situations.

A more extreme approach is to avoid using any static methods whatsoever. That way, every piece of logic is part of an instance of a class that makes that piece of logic more easily replaceable. Lack of replaceability is one of the reasons some people who do unit testing or TDD dislike singletons; they act as a public shared resource that is static, and it's hard to override them.

Avoiding static methods altogether may be too difficult, but trying to minimize the number of singletons or static methods in your application will make things easier for you while testing.

A.2.6 Avoid constructors and static constructors that do logic

Things like configuration-based classes are often made static classes or singletons because so many parts of the application use them. That makes them hard to replace during a test. One way to solve this problem is to use some form of Inversion of Control containers (such as Microsoft Unity, Autofac, Ninject, StructureMap, Spring.NET, or Castle Windsor—all open source frameworks for .NET).

These containers can do many things, but they all provide a common smart factory, of sorts, that allows you to get instances of objects without knowing whether the instance is a singleton, or what the underlying implementation of that instance is. You ask for an interface (usually in the constructor), and an object that matches that type will be provided for you automatically, as your class is being created.

When you use an IoC container (also known as a dependency injection container), you abstract away the lifetime management of an object type and make it easier to create an object model that's largely based on interfaces, because all the dependencies in a class are automatically filled up for you.

Discussing containers is outside the scope of this book, but you can find a comprehensive list and some starting points in the "List of .NET Dependency Injection Containers (IOC)" article on Scott Hanselman's blog: http://www.hanselman.com/blog/ListOfNETDependencyInjectionContainersIOC.aspx.

A.2.7 Separate singletons and singleton holders

If you're planning to use a singleton in your design, separate the logic of the singleton class and the logic that makes it a singleton (the part that initializes a static variable, for example) into two separate classes. That way, you can keep the single responsibility principle (SRP) and also have a way to override singleton logic.

For example, listing A.2 shows a singleton class, and listing A.3 shows it refactored into a more testable design.

Listing A.2 An untestable singleton design

```
public class MySingleton
    {
        private static MySingleton _instance;
        public static MySingleton Instance
        {
            get
            {
                if (_instance == null)
                {
                    _instance = new MySingleton();
                }

                return _instance;
            }
        }
    }
```

Listing A.3 The singleton class refactored into a testable design

```
    public class RealSingletonLogic              ◁———— Newly testable logic
    {
        public void Foo()
        {
            //lots of logic here
        }
    }
public class MySingletonHolder                   ◁———┐ Singleton
    {                                                 container
        private static RealSingletonLogic _instance;
        public static RealSingletonLogic Instance
        {
            get
            {
```

```
            if (_instance == null)
            {
                _instance = new RealSingletonLogic();
            }

            return _instance;
        }
    }
}
```

Now that we've gone over some possible techniques for achieving testable designs, let's get back to the larger picture. Should you do it at all, and are there any consequences of doing it?

A.3 Pros and cons of designing for testability

Designing for testability is a loaded subject for many people. Some believe that testability should be one of the default traits of designs, and others believe that designs shouldn't "suffer" just because someone will need to test them.

The thing to realize is that testability isn't an end goal in itself, but is merely a byproduct of a specific school of design that uses the more testable object-oriented principles laid out by Robert C. Martin (mentioned at the beginning of section A.2). In a design that favors class extensibility and abstractions, it's easy to find seams for test-related actions. All the techniques shown in this appendix so far are very much aligned with Robert Martin's principles.

The question remains, is this the best way to do things? What are the cons of such a method? What happens when you have legacy code? And so on.

A.3.1 Amount of work

In most cases, it takes more work to design for testability than not because doing so usually means writing more code.

You could argue that the extra design work required for testability points out design issues you hadn't considered and that you might have been expected to incorporate in your design anyway (separation of concerns, single responsibility principle, and so on).

On the other hand, assuming you're happy with your design as is, it can be problematic to make changes for testability, which isn't part of production. Again, you could argue that test code is as important as production code, because it exposes the API usage characteristics of your domain model and forces you to look at how someone will use your code.

From this point on, discussions of this matter are rarely productive. Let's just say that more code, and work, is required when testability is involved, but that designing for testability makes you think about the user of your API more, which is a good thing.

A.3.2 Complexity

Designing for testability can sometimes feel a little (or a lot) like it's overcomplicating things. You can find yourself adding interfaces where it doesn't feel natural to use interfaces, or exposing class behavior semantics that you hadn't considered before. In particular, when many things have interfaces and are abstracted away, navigating the code base to find the real implementation of a method can become more difficult and annoying.

You could argue that using a tool such as ReSharper makes this argument obsolete, because navigation with ReSharper is much easier. I agree that it eases most of the navigational pains. The right tool for the right job can help a lot.

A.3.3 Exposing sensitive IP

Many projects have sensitive intellectual property that shouldn't be exposed, but which designing for testability would force to be exposed: security or licensing information, or perhaps algorithms under patent. There are workarounds for this—keeping things internal and using the `[InternalsVisibleTo]` attribute—but they essentially defy the whole notion of testability in the design. You're changing the design but still keeping the logic hidden. Big deal.

This is where designing for testability starts to melt down a bit. Sometimes you can't work around security or patent issues. You have to change what you do or compromise on the way you do it.

A.3.4 Sometimes you can't

Sometimes there are political or other reasons for the design to be done a specific way, and you can't change or refactor it. Sometimes you don't have the time to refactor your design, or the design is too fragile to refactor. This is another case where designing for testability breaks down—when you can't or won't do it.

Now that we've gone through some pros and cons, it's time to consider some alternatives to designing for testability.

A.4 Alternatives to designing for testability

It's interesting to look outside the box at other languages to see other ways of working.

In dynamic languages such as Ruby or Smalltalk, the code is inherently testable because you can replace anything and everything dynamically at runtime. In such a language, you can design the way you want without having to worry about testability. You don't need an interface in order to replace something, and you don't need to make something public to override it. You can even change the behavior of core types dynamically, and no one will yell at you or tell you that you can't compile.

In a world where everything is testable, do you still design for testability? The answer is, of course, "no." In that sort of world, you're free to choose your own design.

Consider a .NET-related analogy that shows how using tools can change the way you think about problems, and sometimes make big problems a non-issue. In a world where memory is managed for you, do you still design for memory management? Mostly, "no" would be the answer. People working in languages where memory isn't managed for them (C++, for example) need to worry about and design for memory optimization and collection, or the application will suffer.

In the same way, by following testable object-oriented design principles, you might get testable designs as a byproduct, but testability should not be a goal in your design. It's just there to solve a specific problem. If a tool comes along that solves the testability problem for you, there will be no need to design specifically for testability. There are other merits to such designs, but using them should be a choice and not a fact of life.

The main problems with nontestable designs is their inability to replace dependencies at runtime. That's why we need to create interfaces, make methods virtual, and do many other related things. There are tools that can help replace dependencies in .NET code without needing to refactor it for testability. One such tool is Typemock Isolator (www.Typemock.com), a commercial tool with an open source alternative.

Does the fact that a tool like Isolator exists mean we don't need to design for testability? In a way, yes. It rids us of the need to think of testability as a design goal. There are great things about the OO patterns Bob Martin presents, and they should be used not because of testability, but because they seem right in a design sense. They can make code easier to maintain, easier to read, and easier to develop, even if testability is no longer an issue.

A.5 Summary

In this appendix, we looked at the idea of designing for testability: what it involves in terms of design techniques, its pros and cons, and alternatives to doing it. There are no easy answers, but the questions are interesting. The future of unit testing will depend on how people approach such issues, and on what tools are available as alternatives.

Testable designs usually only matter in static languages, such as C# or VB.NET, where testability depends on proactive design choices that allow things to be replaced. Designing for testability matters less in more dynamic languages, where things are much more *testable by default*. In such languages, most things are easily replaceable, regardless of the project design.

Testable designs have virtual methods, nonsealed classes, interfaces, and a clear separation of concerns. They have fewer static classes and methods, and many more instances of logic classes. In fact, testable designs are what SOLID design principles have stood for. Perhaps it's time that the end goal should not be testability, but good design instead.

Appendix B

Extra tools and frameworks

This book would not be complete without an overview of some tools and basic techniques you can use while writing code. From database testing to UI testing and web testing, this appendix lists tools you should consider. Some of them are used for integration testing, and some allow unit testing. I'll also mention some that I think are good for beginners.

The tools and techniques listed below are arranged in the following categories:

- Isolation frameworks
- Test frameworks
- Dependency injection and IoC containers
- Database testing
- Web testing
- UI testing
- Thread-related testing
- Acceptance testing

TIP An updated version of the following list can be found on the book's wiki site: ArtOfUnitTesting.com.

Let's begin.

B.1 Isolation frameworks

Mock or isolation frameworks are the bread and butter of advanced unit-testing scenarios. There are many to choose from, and that's a great thing:

- Moq
- Rhino Mocks
- Typemock Isolator
- NMock
- NUnit.Mocks

Here is a short description of each framework.

B.1.1 Moq

Moq is an open source newcomer to the world of mocking and has adopted an API that tries to be both simple to learn and easy to use. The API also follows the arrange-act-assert style (as opposed to the record-and-replay model) and relies heavily on .NET 3.5 features, such as lambdas and extension methods. If you're planning on working with .NET 3.5 exclusively, this is a relatively pain-free learning curve, but you need to feel comfortable with using lambdas.

In terms of features, it has fewer than most other mock frameworks, which also means it's simpler to learn.

You can get Moq at http://code.google.com/p/moq/.

B.1.2 Rhino Mocks

Rhino Mocks is a widely used open source framework for mocks and stubs. It's also the framework used throughout this book for examples, and it's discussed more in chapter 5.

Rhino Mocks is loaded with features and has recently moved to using the new arrange-act-assert syntax.

You can get Rhino Mocks at http://ayende.com/projects/rhino-mocks.aspx.

B.1.3 Typemock Isolator

Typemock Isolator is a powerful commercial isolation framework that tries to remove the terms "mocks" and "stubs" from its vocabulary in favor of a more simple and terse API.

Isolator differs from the other frameworks by allowing you to *isolate* components from their dependencies regardless of how the system is designed (although it supports all the features the other frameworks have). This makes it ideal for people who are getting into unit testing and want an incremental approach to learning. Because it doesn't force you to design for testability, you can learn to write tests correctly and then move on to learning better design, without having to mix the two together.

> **NOTE** Full disclosure: While writing this book, I've also been working at Typemock.

You can get Typemock Isolator at www.typemock.com.

B.1.4 NMock

NMock is an open source mocking framework that started out as a direct port of jMock. It used to be the de facto mocking framework until Rhino Mocks took its place in the open source world. The main reason it was dethroned is that it did not offer strong typing of method names. (You had to use strings to define expectations on methods.) Lately, it has been getting back into development, and the new 2.0 release marks a nice change in the API. It remains to be seen how well it will do against the current competition.

You can get NMock at www.NMock.org.

B.1.5 NUnit.Mocks

NUnit.Mocks is an ultra-small open source mocking framework that comes built into NUnit as a separate DLL. It initially started life as an aid for testing NUnit internally, and NUnit's authors still discourage people from using it in their own projects, because it may "disappear" in the future.

NUnit.Mocks is one of the simplest frameworks to learn with, but I don't recommend using it for anything other than a learning tool.

You can get NUnit.Mocks as part of the installation of NUnit at http://nunit.com.

B.2 Test frameworks

The test frameworks are the bases from which we start writing our tests. Like mock frameworks, there are many to choose from, and this competition has brought lots of innovation with it. Here are some of the available frameworks:

- Microsoft's Unit Testing Framework
- NUnit
- MbUnit
- Gallio
- xUnit
- Pex

Let's look at each in turn.

B.2.1 Microsoft's Unit Testing Framework

Microsoft's Unit Testing Framework (also known as MSTest) comes bundled with any version of Visual Studio .NET 2008 professional or above. It includes basic features that are similar to NUnit, but it runs a little slower. The upcoming versions of Visual Studio (2010) will add a lot of power to this framework, but you can use it today as easily as NUnit.

One big problem with this framework is that it's not as easily extensible as the other testing frameworks. To see how cumbersome it is to add a simple attribute, see the discussion of YUnit on MSDN at http://code.msdn.microsoft.com/yunit.

One big plus for this framework is that it's integrated into the Visual Studio Team System tool suite and provides good reporting, coverage, and build automation out of the box. If your company uses Team System, I highly suggest using MSTest as your test framework because of the good integration possibilities.

You can get MSTest with Visual Studio.

B.2.2 NUnit

NUnit is currently the de facto test framework for unit test developers in .NET. It's open source and is in almost ubiquitous use among those who do unit testing. I cover NUnit deeply in chapter 2. NUnit is easily extensible and has a large user base and forums. I'd recommend it to anyone starting out with unit testing in .NET. I still use it today.

You can get NUnit at http://nunit.com.

B.2.3 MbUnit

MbUnit is fully open source, and the "mb" stands for "model-based" testing. It started out as a competitor to NUnit but soon zoomed past NUnit in terms of features and abilities.

MbUnit is easily extensible and supports lots of interesting test attributes, such as Repeat and Timeout. MbUnit has its own UI and console runners that also support running tests written in NUnit. If you're looking for something more in your current test framework, MbUnit is a good step up from NUnit. I almost never have to use such features myself, but if you're mixing integration testing and unit testing with the same framework, MbUnit is a good fit.

You can get MbUnit at www.mbunit.com.

B.2.4 Gallio

Gallio is an open source platform for running tests written in most (if not all) unit test frameworks in .NET, from NUnit to MSTest. Gallio is also extensible, and you can create your own custom test runner using it. It has plugins for Visual Studio .NET, which can highlight coding errors relating to tests and other things. It's still not in very popular use, but it's built by the same people who maintain MbUnit, and it's a fully working, robust product that seems to have been in an endless beta cycle for the past year or so.

You can get Gallio at www.gallio.org.

B.2.5 xUnit

xUnit is an open source test framework, developed in cooperation with one of the original authors of NUnit, Jim Newkirk. It's a minimalist and elegant test framework that tries to get back to basics by having fewer features, not more, than the other frameworks, and by supporting different names on its attributes.

What is so radically different about it? It has no setup or teardown methods, for one. You have to use the constructor and a dispose method on the test class. Another big difference is in how easy it is to extend.

Because xUnit reads so differently from the other frameworks, it takes a while to get used to it if you're coming from a framework like NUnit or MbUnit. If you've never used any test framework before, xUnit is easy to grasp and use, and it's robust enough to be used in a real project.

For more information and download see www.codeplex.com/xunit.

B.2.6 Pex

Pex (short for program exploration) is an intelligent assistant to the programmer. From a parameterized unit test, it automatically produces a traditional unit test suite with high code coverage. In addition, it suggests to the programmer how to fix the bugs.

With Pex, you can create special tests that have parameters in them, and put special attributes on those tests. The Pex engine will generate new tests that you can later run as part of your test suite. It's great for finding corner cases and edge conditions that aren't handled properly in your code. You should use Pex in addition to a regular test framework, such as NUnit or MbUnit.

You can get Pex at http://research.microsoft.com/projects/pex/.

B.3 IoC containers

IoC (Inversion Of Control) containers can be used to improve the architectural qualities of an object-oriented system by reducing the mechanical costs of good design techniques (such as using constructor parameters, managing object lifetimes, and so on).

Containers can enable looser coupling between classes and their dependencies, improve the testability of a class structure, and provide generic flexibility mechanisms. Used judiciously, containers can greatly enhance the opportunities for code reuse by minimizing direct coupling between classes and configuration mechanisms (such as by using interfaces).

We'll look at the following tools:

- StructureMap
- Microsoft Unity
- Castle Windsor
- Autofac (Auto Factory)
- Common Service Locator Library
- Spring.NET
- Microsoft Managed Extensibility Framework
- Ninject

Let's look briefly at each of these frameworks.

B.3.1 StructureMap

StructureMap is an open source container framework that has one clear differentiator from the others. Its API is very fluent and tries to mimic natural language and generic constructs as much as possible.

StuctureMap has a relatively small user base, and the current documentation on it is lacking, but it contains some powerful features, such as a built-in automocking container (a container that can create stubs automatically when requested to by the test), powerful lifetime management, XML-free configuration, integration with ASP.NET, and more.

You can get StructureMap at http://structuremap.sourceforge.net.

B.3.2 Microsoft Unity

Unity is a latecomer to the DI container field, but it provides a simple and minimal approach that can be easily learned and used by beginners. Advanced users may find it lacking, but it certainly answers my 80-20 rule: it provides 80 percent of the features you look for most of the time.

Unity is open source by Microsoft, and it has good documentation. I'd recommend it as a starting point for working with containers.

You can get Unity at www.codeplex.com/unity.

B.3.3 Castle Windsor

Castle is a large open source project that covers a lot of areas. Windsor is one of those areas, and it provides a mature and powerful implementation of a DI container.

Castle Windsor contains most of the features you'll ever want in a container and more, but it has a relatively high learning curve due to all the features.

You can learn about Castle Windsor at www.castleproject.org/container/ and download the Castle project at www.castleproject.org.

B.3.4 Autofac

Autofac is a fresh approach to IoC in .NET that fits well with the C# 3.0 syntax. It takes a rather minimalistic approach in terms of APIs. The API is radically different from the other frameworks, and requires a bit of getting used to. It also requires .NET 3.5 to work, and you'll need a good knowledge of lambda syntax. Autofac is difficult to explain, so you'll have to go to the site to see how different it is. I recommend it for people who already have experience with other DI frameworks.

You can get it at http://code.google.com/p/autofac/.

B.3.5 Common Service Locator Library

The Common Service Locator (CSL) was born out of a need to create a common infrastructure in applications for getting instances of things. Using the advice of the leading open source container frameworks, Microsoft created a shared library that can help abstract away the actual container your application might use. The CSL sits in front of the container of your choice, be it Unity, StructureMap, or Castle.

You don't need to use the CSL, but the concept of abstracting away the choice of container in your application is a useful one. Most application authors were doing this anyway, so using CSL is one step in making it more of a recommended design pattern.

You can get the Common Service Locator library at www.codeplex.com/CommonServiceLocator.

B.3.6 Spring.NET

Spring.NET is an open source container framework. It's one of the oldest and is a port of the Java Spring Container libraries. It has a lot of abilities, but many consider it to be a sort of dinosaur among the other frameworks, with an API that isn't as easy to use, and configuration that isn't as friendly as it could be.

You can get Spring.NET at www.springframework.net.

B.3.7 Microsoft Managed Extensibility Framework

The Managed Extensibility Framework (MEF) isn't actually a container, but it does fall in the same general category of providing services that instantiate classes in your code. It's designed to be much more than a container; it's a full plugin model for small and large applications. MEF includes a lightweight IoC container framework so you can easily inject dependencies into various places in your code by using special attributes.

MEF does require a bit of a learning curve, and I wouldn't recommend using it strictly as an IoC container. If you do use it for extensibility features in your application, it can also be used as a DI container.

You can get MEF at www.codeplex.com/MEF.

B.3.8 Ninject

Ninject is a latecomer to the DI field, but it has a simple syntax and good usability. There isn't much else to say about it except that I highly recommend taking a look at it.

You can find out more about Ninject at http://ninject.org/.

B.4 Database testing

How to do database testing is a burning question for those who are starting out. Many questions arise, such as, "Should I stub out the database in my tests?" This section provides some guidelines.

First, let's talk about doing integration tests against the database.

B.4.1 Use integration tests for your data layer

How should you test your data layer? Should you abstract away the database interfaces? Should you use the real database?

I usually write integration-style tests for the data layer (the part of the app structure that talks directly to the database) in my applications because data logic is almost always divided between the application logic and the database itself (triggers, security rules, referential integrity, and so on). Unless you can test the database logic in complete isolation (and I've found no really good framework for this purpose), the only way to make sure it works in tests is to couple testing the data-layer logic to the real database.

Testing the data layer and the database together leaves few surprises for later in the project. But testing against the database has its problems, the main one being that you're testing against state shared by many tests. If you insert a line into the database in one test, the next test can see that line as well.

What we need is a way to roll back the changes we make to the database, and thankfully there's good support for this in the current test tools and the .NET framework.

B.4.2 Use rollback attributes

The three major frameworks—MbUnit, NUnit, and xUnit—support a special `[Rollback]` attribute that you can put on top of your test method. When used, the attribute creates a special database transaction that the test code runs in. When the test is finished, the database transaction is rolled back automatically, and the changes to the database vanish.

To learn more about how this works, see an MSDN article I wrote a while back, called "Simplify Data Layer Unit Testing using Enterprise Services" at http://msdn.microsoft.com/en-us/magazine/cc163772.aspx.

If you aren't interested in using the `[Rollback]` attributes the frameworks provide, you can use the simple class introduced in .NET 2.0 called `TransactionScope`.

B.4.3 Use TransactionScope to roll back

For examples on how to use the `TransactionScope` class in your setup and teardown code, see a blog article called "Even Simpler Database Unit Testing with TransactionScope" at http://www.bbits.co.uk/blog/archive/2006/07/31/12741.aspx.

Some feel that another good option is to run the tests against an in-memory database. My feelings on that are mixed. On the one hand, it's closer to reality, in that you also test the database logic. On the other hand, if your application uses a different database engine, with different features, there's a big chance that some things will pass or fail during tests with the in-memory database, and will work differently in production. I choose to work with whatever is as close to the real thing as possible. Usually that means using the same database engine.

B.5 Web testing

"How do I test my web pages?" is another question that comes up a lot. Here are some tools that can help you in this quest:

- Ivonna
- Team System Web Test
- NUnitAsp
- Watir
- WatiN
- Selenium

The following is a short description of each tool.

B.5.1 Ivonna

Ivonna is a unit-testing framework that abstracts away the need to run ASP.NET-related tests using a real HTTP session and pages. It does some powerful things behind the scenes, such as compiling pages that you want to test and letting you test controls inside them without needing a browser session, and it fakes the full HTTP runtime model.

You write the code in your unit tests just like you're testing other in-memory objects. There's no need for a web server and such nonsense.

Ivonna is being developed in partnership with Typemock and runs as an add-on to the Typemock Isolator framework. You can get Ivonna at http://sm-art.biz/Ivonna.aspx.

B.5.2 Team System Web Test

Visual Studio Team Test and Team Suite editions include the powerful ability to record and replay web requests for pages and verify various things during these runs. This is strictly integration testing, but it's really powerful. The latest versions also support recording Ajax actions on the page, and make things much easier to test in terms of usability.

You can find more info on Team System at http://msdn.microsoft.com/en-us/teamsystem/default.aspx.

B.5.3 NUnitAsp

NUnitAsp is an open source framework that's no longer being supported but is still used in many places. It allows you to write tests against live HTTP page objects.

Most people end up using NUnitAsp for acceptance testing. In those cases, it would be better to use frameworks such as Watir and WatiN, described next.

You can get NUnitAsp at http://nunitasp.sourceforge.net/.

B.5.4 Watir

Watir (pronounced "water") stands for "Web application testing in Ruby". It's open source, and it allows scripting of browser actions using the Ruby programming language. Many Rubyists swear by it, but it does require that you learn a whole new language.

You can get Watir at http://wtr.rubyforge.org/.

B.5.5 WatiN

WatiN (pronounced "what-in") is a product inspired by Watir. You don't need to know Ruby to use WatiN, but it offers much the same scripting abilities as Watir.

You can get WatiN at http://watin.sourceforge.net/.

B.5.6 Selenium

Selenium is a suite of tools designed to automate web app testing across many platforms. It has existed longer than all the other frameworks in this list, and it also has an API wrapper for .NET.

Selenium is an integration testing framework, and it's in wide use. It's a good place to start. But beware: it has many features and the learning curve is high.

You can get it at http://selenium.openqa.org/.

B.6 UI testing

UI testing is always a difficult task. I'm not a great believer in writing unit tests or integration tests for UIs because the return on such tests is low compared to the amount of time you invest in writing them. UIs change too much to be testable in a consistent manner, as far as I'm concerned. That's why I usually try to separate all the logic from the UI into a lower layer that I can test separately with standard unit-testing techniques.

Nevertheless, there are several tools that try to make the UI-testing job easier:

- NUnitForms
- Project White
- Team System UI Tests

Here is a short rundown of each tool.

B.6.1 NUnitForms

NUnitForms is an open source framework that allows you to instantiate Windows Forms classes and check values of controls inside them. It has specific APIs for getting controls in a form and asserting values against them, but it will only work for simple controls.

More complex controls aren't supported and the framework doesn't seem to be in active development anymore, so I recommend not using it. Instead, I recommend Project White (discussed next) for WinForm testing.

You can get it at http://nunitforms.sourceforge.net/.

B.6.2 Project White

Project White is, in a way, a successor to NUnitForms, in that it supports a richer set of application types (WPF, WinForm, Win32, and Java JWT), and sports a newer API with better usability. Unlike NUnitForms, White is more of an integration-test framework, because it allows spawning separate processes that it tests against.

White uses the UIAutomation API (part of Windows) to do its bidding, which gives it much more power. You can think of it as Selenium or WatiN for WinForms.

You can get White at http://www.codeplex.com/white.

B.6.3 Team System UI Tests

The upcoming version of Visual Studio Team System will support a new kind of test—a UI test. You'll be able to record actions on UI windows and play them back and verify assertions during test runs. As with all Team System tools, its main advantage will be its integration with other Team System tools, reports, source control, and servers.

You can learn more about Team System at http://msdn.microsoft.com/en-us/teamsystem/default.aspx.

B.7 Thread-related testing

Threads have always been the bane of unit testing. They're simply untestable. That's why new frameworks are emerging that let you test thread-related logic (deadlocks, race conditions, and so on), such as these:

- Typemock Racer
- Microsoft CHESS
- Osherove.ThreadTester

I'll give a brief rundown of each tool.

B.7.1 Typemock Racer

Typemock Racer is a managed framework for multithreaded code testing that helps visualize, detect, and resolve deadlocks and race conditions in managed code. You use it by putting an attribute on top of an existing test method, and the engine does all the work. It also allows full thread visualization during debugging of a threaded test.

> **NOTE** Full disclosure: during the writing of this book, I've been part of the developer team at Typemock.

Racer is a commercial product that works with all flavors of Visual Studio (including Express) and all test frameworks. You can get it at www.Typemock.com.

B.7.2 Microsoft CHESS

CHESS is an upcoming tool that will be offered by Microsoft with Visual Studio 2010. (It's currently offered only as part of MS Research.) Much like Typemock Racer, CHESS attempts to find thread-related problems (deadlocks, hangs, livelocks, and more) in your code by running all relevant permutations of threads on existing code. These tests are written as simple unit tests.

CHESS currently supports native code, but a managed .NET version should be coming out soon as part of Visual Studio Team System (a commercial product).

You can get CHESS at http://research.microsoft.com/projects/CHESS/.

B.7.3 Osherove.ThreadTester

This is a little open source framework I developed a while back. It allows you to run multiple threads during one test to see if anything weird happens to your code (deadlocks, for example). It isn't feature-complete, but it's a good attempt at a multithreaded test (rather than a test for multithreaded code).

You can get it from my blog, at http://weblogs.asp.net/rosherove/archive/2007/06/22/multi-threaded-unit-tests-with-osherove-thread-tester.aspx.

B.8 Acceptance testing

Acceptance tests enhance collaboration between customers and developers in software development. They enable customers, testers, and programmers to learn what the software should do, and they automatically compare that to what it actually does. They compare customers' expectations to actual results. It's a great way to collaborate on complicated problems (and get them right) early in development.

Unfortunately, there are few frameworks for automated acceptance testing, and just one that works these days! I'm hoping this will change soon. Here are the tools we'll look at:

- FitNesse
- StoryTeller

Let's take a closer look.

B.8.1 FitNesse

FitNesse is a lightweight, open source framework that makes it easy for software teams to define acceptance tests—web pages containing simple tables of inputs and expected outputs—and to run those tests and see the results.

FitNesse is quite buggy, but it has been in use in many places with varying degrees of success.

You can learn more about FitNesse at www.fitnesse.org.

B.8.2 StoryTeller

StoryTeller is a response to FitNesse, which has existed for a long time but presented many usability and stability problems for users. It's an open source framework, still in development, that attempts to create a more compelling UI and usability story than FitNesse. There aren't many details on it yet, but hopefully it will be out soon. It will support running tests written for FitNesse.

The project page is at http://storyteller.tigris.org/, but most of the real details are found on the author's blog: http://codebetter.com/blogs/jeremy.miller/archive/tags/StoryTeller/default.aspx.

Index

Symbols
.dll 32
.NET 21, 25, 56, 69, 100, 151
   extension methods 129, 269
   Moq framework 100, 126
   NMock 100
   Rhino Mocks 100
   Typemock 100
.NET mock object frameworks 129

A
AAA *See* arrange-act-assert model
AAA-style stubs 128
abstract class 259
abstract test class 159
abstract test driver class pattern 159
abstract test infrastructure class pattern 152
abstractions 263
acceptance testing 268, 283
acceptance-style test 251
accidental bugging 9
Act action 30
action attributes 34
action-driven testing 83
actions *See* test actions
Adapt Parameter 96
Addison-Wesley 227, 231
agent of change 220
agile 142, 234
Ajax 279
analyzer object 188
annotated method 79
anonymous delegate 120, 124–125
anonymous method 124, 249

anti-patterns 192
   constrained test order 192
   external-shared-state corruption 198
   hidden test call 194
   shared-state corruption 196
API 168
   See also interface
API changes 174
Arrange action 30
arrange-act-assert model 103, 126
arrange-act-assert style 269
arrange-act-assert syntax 269
art of unit testing 52
ArtOfUnitTesting 268
ASP.NET 274, 278
Assert 31, 35–36, 38, 42–43
Assert action 30
Assert class 31
assert failures 180
assert messages 209, 212
   best practices 212
   repetition 213
assert utility class 168
assert utility method 168
Assert.AreEqual 31
Assert.AreSame 31
Assert.IsTrue 31
Assertion *See* test assertion
assertion logic 188
assumptions 205, 209
attributes
   Category 39
   ExpectedException 38
   Ignore 38
   SetUp 34–35

attributes *(continued)*
  TearDown 34–35
  Test 30
  TestFixture 30
  TestFixtureSetUp 36
  TestFixtureTearDown 36
  See also NUnit & unit-testing framework
Auto Factory *See* Autofac
Autofac 62, 261, 274–275
automated build 142–143, 146–147, 169, 225
  types 144
automated test 6, 11, 28, 30, 141
automocking container 274

B
base class 75, 159, 163–165
Beck, Kent 4
Beizer, Boris 227
best practices 172, 230
blockers 220
bottom-up change 223
brittle test 94, 97, 107, 206
  less brittle test 207
broken test 38, 175, 182
build break 142
build process 142–143, 228, 234
business logic 8

C
C# 124, 236
C++ 25, 100, 236, 239, 244, 265
  mockpp 100
call chains 96
callback 120, 132
calling test 196
Castle 275
  See also Microsoft Castle
Castle Windsor 62, 261, 274–275
Category 39
champions 220, 226
CHESS 282
class 5, 8, 148
  methods 5, 148
class extensibility 263
class library 28
class under test *See* system under test
classic object-oriented design 81
classic testing 6
code adapter classes 252

code churn 228
"Code Churn Perspective" article 228
Code Complete 228
code consistency 225
code coverage 180, 273
code design 208
code duplication 254
  refactoring 254
code integration 142
code integrity 224
code library 24
code quality 18, 231, 234
code reuse 151, 156
code smell 208
code under test *See* system under test
code with logic 23, 28
collaborator 50, 208
collections 209
Common Language Runtime 247
Common Service Locator 274–275
Communications of the ACM 235–237
Complete Guide to Software Testing, The 7
components 5, 240–241
  complex 243
  easy 243
  mapping 241
  priority list 240
  rating 240
composite object hierarchy 62
concrete class 259
Conditional attribute 79
conditional compilation 69, 79
  #if and #endif 80
  when to use 69
configuration class 168
configuration data 241
Configuration property 95
ConfigurationManager 152
ConfigurationManagerTests 152
conflicting test 176–177
console application 5, 13
constructor injection 58–59, 64–65, 260
  parameters 63
  when to use 63
constructors 258
  static constructors 258
containers 62
  Autofac 62
  Castle Windsor 62

containers *(continued)*
   container object 62
   factory methods 62
   Microsoft Unity 62
   Ninject 62
   Spring.NET 62
   StructureMap 62
continuous integration 144, 225
continuous integration build 144
correctness 4
CppUnit 25, 236
CQL 253
CRUD (create, retrieve, update and delete) 159
CruiseControl.NET 143
CSL *See* Common Service Locator
Curtis, Bill 237
custom header 159
cyclomatic complexity 240

D

data access 8
data helper 8
data layer 277
data objects 259
database testing 268, 276
data-holder class 241
DBConfiguration 95
debug switch 68
debugging 19, 32, 146, 225
   bug-fixing time 228
   bugs 10, 18–19
   bugs per class 235
   reopening bugs 228
decision-making code *See* logical code
decoupled design 132
defects 228
delegates 247, 258
dependencies 11, 40, 52–53, 62–63, 65, 80, 132, 240–241, 243
   breaking 55
   direct dependency 51, 54, 260
   external dependency 87
   fake dependency 58, 69
   injecting fake dependencies 97
   injection with properties 64
   non-optional 61, 63
   production dependencies 75
   relevant 62
   replacing 73

dependency driven 242
dependency injection 64, 245, 261, 268
Dependency Inversion Principle 78
dependency level 240
Depender 246, 248
derived class 71–72, 156, 158–159, 163–164, 166
Design Patterns 68
development stages 232
DI container 275
DI frameworks 275
domain logic 61
dos and don'ts of introducing unit testing 219
driving force 229
DRY ("don't repeat yourself") principle 151, 184
duplicate code 246
duplicate test 173, 177, 185
duplication 182, 184, 186
   factory methods 187
   removing 186, 196
   setup method 188
   See also duplicate test
dynamic fake 102
dynamic fake object
   definition 102
dynamic languages 266
dynamic mock object 102, 104, 137
dynamic mocks 99
dynamic stubs 99
   combining with mocks 112
dynamically generated object 104

E

easy-first strategy 242
   pros and cons 242
EasyMock 100
Eclipse 165
Eclipse for Java 22
empirical evidence 235
encapsulation 77
   See also object-oriented
end assert 208
end functionality 174, 182
end result 83, 90, 158, 208
Endres, Albert 236
entry points for test-driven development 222

event notification 26
event recognition 26
events 121
  event source 124
  event-related actions 121
  event-related assertions 132
  EventsVerifier 125
  registering for an event 121
  testing event triggering 124
  triggering an event 123
exceptions 14, 24, 38, 179, 199
  ArgumentException 36
  deliberate exceptions 33
  expected exceptions 36
  stack trace 24
  unhandled exception 33
Execute Tests button 252
execution path 36
expectations 104, 109, 135
  assertion 105
  best practices 136
  expectations on mocks 105
  expectations on stubs 105
  mockEngine.Verify(mockObject) 105
  mockEngine.VerifyAll() 105
  MockRepository.GenerateStub 105
  MockRepository.StrictMock 105
  MockRepository.Stub 105
  MockRespository.DynamicMock. 105
  Moq framework 126
  nonstrict mocks 106
  order of method calls 109
  overspecifying 136
  recording stage 109
  simulated object 104
  strict mocks 106
  stub object 111
  Verify(mock) 105
  verifying 111
expected object 119
ExpectedException 38, 44, 49
  expected exception message 38
  See also exceptions
extended reflection PIs 247
extensions 240
external dependency 50, 89, 258
  definition 50
external resource 44, 168, 196–197
external-shared-state corruption 192

Extract and Override 71, 73, 75, 81
  when to use 74, 77

F

factories 68
factory class 168
  fake factory 69
  faking 70
  implementation 68
factory method 72, 151, 163–165, 167–168
  virtualizing 76
factory pattern 66
failing test 18, 32–33, 36, 174, 178, 191, 200, 245
fake class 249
fake component 95
fake dependency 70
  See also dependencies
fake exception 129
fake methods 134
fake objects 44, 68, 84, 97, 108, 110, 189, 191
  return values 108
fake result 75
fake values 247
fakes 50, 90, 135, 191
  when a mock object 90
  when a stub 90
faking 69–70
  fake result 75
  fake returning a fake 71
  layers 69
fast tests 39
fast-running test 144
Feathers, Michael 10, 55, 73, 96, 183, 246, 250–251, 253
feedback 10
FICC properties 257
filesystem 50, 51, 53
  configuration file 52
  FileExtensionManager 53–54, 56
final functionality 7
final result *See* final functionality
FinalBuilder 143
FitNesse 246, 251, 283
  download 253
  usage 252
FitNesse engine 252
  wrapper classes 252

FitNesse table 252
fixture 36, 252
flow diagrams 224
folder structure 145
FUD (fear, uncertainty, and doubt) 220
full objects 119, 203

G
Gallio 271–272
generic implementation 15
generics 152, 166, 247
GlobalUtil 95
goals 227
good test 171
good unit test 3
   See also unit test
Gremillion, Lee L. 236
gripped items 251
groups
   test-code coverage report 226
guerrilla-style implementation 223
GUID (globally unique identifier) 116

H
Hanselman, Scott 62, 261
hardcoded strings 209
hard-first strategy 242, 244
   pros and cons 243
hardware 236
hardware simulator 236
Haskell programming language 25
helper classes 8, 117, 170
   Contains 117
   EndsWith 117
   Like 117
   StartsWith 117
   Text 117
helper frameworks 63
   See also containers
helper methods 15–16, 162, 186, 188, 190–191, 198, 215, 258
Hetzel, Bill 7
hidden test call 192
   duplication 195
   flow testing 195
   laziness 195
   problems 195
   solutions 195
HTML tables 252

HUnit 25
Hunt, Andy 151

I
IDE *See* integrated development environment
IEEE Software 236
IEEE Transactions on Software Engineering 236
IExtensionManager 58
Ignore 38
ignored test 38–39
independent test 34
indirect testing 40
indirection 52–53, 71, 181
   layers 70
infrastructure API 167
inheritance 151, 157
   See also test class inheritance
inheritance patterns 165
initial state 196
injecting 58
injection 55, 89
   constructor injection 58
   factory class 66
   getting stub before method call 66
   local factory 71
   properties 64
   See also stub
insiders 220
integrated development environment 22
integrating test-driven development 219
integration process 144
integration test 7–8, 45, 50–51, 169, 244
   failure points 8
   hidden 146
   problems 51
   slow-running tests 145
integration testing 3, 7, 151, 168, 268, 272
   definition 8
   drawbacks 9
   See also integration test
integration testing framework 280
integration zone 147
   See also safe green zone
integration-style test 244, 251, 277
   process 245
intellectual property 264
IntelliJ IDEA 165
intellisense 210

interaction testing 82–83, 137
  action-driven testing 83
  comparison with state-based testing 83
  definition 83
interactive user dialogs 14
interface 52
  custom implementation 58
  extraction 55
  IExtensionManager 58
  interactive 53
  original implementation 58
  receiving as a property 55, 58
  receiving at constructor level 55, 58
  underlying implementation 52–53
  See also stub
Interface Segregation Principle 78
interface-based design 260
internal method 183
InternalsVisibleTo 78, 80
invalid test 173, 176
inversion of control 62
inversion of control containers See containers
Inversion of Control principle 63
IoC 275
  See also inversion of control
IoC containers 63, 261, 268, 273
  See also containers
IP See intellectual property
Iscoe, N. 237
isolated test 256
isolation frameworks 268
  See also mock object frameworks
Isolator See Typemock
Ivonna 278
IWebService 104

J
Java 25, 100, 131, 239, 248, 258
  EasyMock 100
  jMock 100
  legacy code 250
  Vise 250
Java JWT 281
Java Spring Container 276
jMock framework 100, 131, 270
JMockit 237, 246, 248–250
  test sample 249
Johnson, Mark 227
Jones, Capers 231
JUnit 25, 192

K
Krasner, H. 237

L
lambda syntax 275
lambdas 128, 134, 269
leftover state 34
legacy code 9, 132, 236, 239, 246, 254
  definition 10
  problems 240
legacy code tools
  when to use which 246
legacy project 244
legacy system 51
license.txt 26
Liskov Substitution Principle 78
lists 209
Load event 122
local factory 71
log files 25
LogAn project 25, 29
LogAnalyzer 35, 41, 50, 67, 87, 105, 152
  interaction with web service 89
LogAnalyzerTests 152
logger dependency 152
LoggingFacility 152
logical code 12
logic-driven 242
long-running test 144

M
magic values 137
maintainability 4, 44, 63, 81, 89, 94, 96, 141,
    150, 171, 176–177, 181, 185, 195, 216,
    231, 233
maintainable test 11, 16, 18, 25, 33, 61, 97,
    175, 188, 203, 205, 215
maintenance mode 237
management 224
manual mocks 94, 96, 98, 103, 113
  problems 96, 100
manual stubs 94, 96
  problems 96
Martin, Robert C. ("Bob") 78, 257, 263, 266
MbUnit 192, 236, 271–272, 277
  parameterized test 201
  RowSet attribute 201
McConnell, Steve 228
McGraw-Hill 231

MEF *See* Microsoft Managed Extensibility
    Framework
Meszaros, Gerard 50, 88, 149, 205
method 28
method behavior 182
method constants 181
method contract 182
method logic 36
method parameters 181
method strings 133
Microsoft 274–275, 282
Microsoft Castle 275
Microsoft CHESS 281
    See also CHESS
Microsoft Managed Extensibility
    Framework 274, 276
Microsoft Press 228
Microsoft Unity 62, 261, 274
missing test 181
mock classes 132
mock email service 91
mock frameworks 74
mock object 44, 82, 85, 87, 89–90, 99, 105,
    108, 135, 189, 257
    asserts 85
    combining with stubs 89, 97
    definition 84
    difference with stub 84, 97
    dynamic mocks 99
    expectations 105
    how many per test 94
    LastCall 108
    mock object frameworks 85
    nonstrict mocks 106
    optimal mocks per test 136
    return values 108
    reusing 89
    setters 94
    strict mocks 106
    using mocks too much 97
    what to test 136
mock object frameworks 98–99, 121, 126
    advantages 100, 134
    arrange-act-assert 126
    definition 100
    parameter constraints 115
    Rhino Mocks 99
    smart stubs 110
    when not to use 135

mock service 124
mockpp 100
MockRepository
    StrictMock 103
mocks 50, 269
    See also mock object
model-based testing 272
module 24
Moq framework 100, 126, 130, 134, 269
MSBuild 143
MSDN 271, 277
MSTest 271
multiple aspects 202
multiple asserts 94, 179–180, 198, 202–203
multiple method calls 134
multiple tests 15, 177, 200, 202
multiple threads 254
multithreaded test 179, 282
Myre, Glenford 235

N
namespace 32, 39, 145, 147
naming convention 210
NAnt 143
NCover 180, 234
NDepend 246, 253
    download 253
    query language 253
new test 180
Newkirk, James ("Jim") 237, 272
nightly build 147, 225
Ninject 62, 261, 274, 276
NMock 100, 131, 269–270
NMock2 131
    difference with Rhino Mocks 131
nonsealed classes 258, 260, 267
nonstrict mocks 106–107, 136
nontestable design 262, 266
NUnit 21, 24–27, 29–30, 32, 35, 49, 102,
    156, 192, 199, 271–272, 277
    actions 34
    assembly 29, 32
    Assert class 30
    attribute scheme 29
    attributes 26, 29, 34–36, 44
    automated test 30
    Categories tab 40
    color scheme 33
    getting started 26

NUnit *(continued)*
  GUI 26, 32–33, 39
  initial state 34
  installing 26
  open source license 26
  parameterized test 201
  Row attribute 201
  RowSet attribute 201
  Run button 32, 40
  Selected Categories 40
  SetUp attribute 34
  special attributes 34
  TearDown attribute 34
  test actions 30
  Test attribute 30
  test class 30
  test method 30
  Test Not Run tab 39
  TestFixture attribute 30
  typename 32
  unit test runner 26
  version 26
NUnit.Extensions.dll 201
NUnit.Framework namespace 31
NUnit.Mocks 130, 133, 269–270
  limitations 131
NUnitAsp 279
NUnitForms 280–281

O

object calls 82
object configuration methods 167
object model 167
object-oriented 52, 66, 77–78, 151, 182, 257, 263, 266
  encapsulation 77
  object-oriented design 78
Open Closed Principle 78, 257
ordered mocks 109
organizational change 223
  bottom-up 223
  top-down 223–224
organizational culture 219
organizational structure 228
Osherove.ThreadTester 281–282
outside consultant 224
  advantages 224
overriding 203
overspecification 205

overspecified test 206–207
  features 205

P

parameter constraints 115–116, 132
  combining constraints 118
  helper classes 116
  parameter object properties 118
  string constraint 116
parameter injection 58
parameter object refactoring 62
parameter verification 120, 134
parameterized test 199, 202
parser class 162
partial code test 23
patent issues 265
Peer Reviews in Software: A Practical Guide 227
Pex 271, 273
phishing 95
pilot project 223, 232
  statistics 232
pilot test 222
political support 229
polymorphism 258
Poole, Charlie 131
posters 225
Pragmatic Programmer, The 151
presenter class 122
"Principles of OOD" article 257
priority 240, 244
private method 182
problem output 14
Proceedings of the 8th International Symposium on Software Metrics 236
production bug 173
  fixing 173
production class 13
production code 18, 29, 33, 66, 70, 72, 75, 79, 123, 136, 141, 148, 173, 180, 264
  See also production class
production server 143
productivity 231
profiler APIs 247
program exploration *See* Pex
Programming Productivity 231
progress metrics 228
project 148
  See also testing project
project failure
  causes 229

project feasibility 222–223
Project White 281
properties 12, 64
property injection 65
    when to use 65
protected method 182
public functionality 206
public properties 94

Q
QA engineer 220, 233, 235
QA process 233
QA team 233

R
readability 4, 61, 79, 89, 94, 96, 98, 128, 130, 135, 149–150, 170, 177–178, 209, 216
    assert messages 209, 212
    definition 171
    importance 171
    mock object initialization 215
    separation of asserts and actions 214
    setup and teardown method 214
    test naming 210
    variable naming 211
readable test 11, 18, 25, 33, 67, 156, 188, 190, 203
    best practices 209
real object 90
real test 159
real-world scenarios 45
record-and-replay model 102, 104, 126, 269
    difference with arrange-act-assert model 128
recording stage 122
redefine class 249
Red-Green-Refactor 33
Refactor from DevExpress 165
refactored test 176
refactoring 17–18, 55, 87, 95, 132, 150, 152, 154, 165, 168, 173, 177, 180, 186, 190, 200, 208, 239, 244, 250
    automated tools 134
    definition 19, 55
    maintainable state 186
    over-refactoring 190
    Vise 250–251
refactoring pattern
    extracting an interface 55

refactoring phase 244
regression 9
reinvention 230
renaming 173, 177
Repeat 272
repeatable test 6, 22
repetition 137
replaceability 260
ReSharper 165, 246, 253, 264
    download 254
    navigations 253
ReSharper for .NET 134
result-driven testing 83
    end result 83
return values 212
Rhino Mocks 99–100, 107, 110, 114, 116, 126, 132, 137, 269
    arrange-act-assert model 103
    comparison with other .NET mock object frameworks 129
    introduction 102
    Mock Repository 103
    ordered mocks 109
    parameter constraints types 117
    record-and-replay model 102
    Rhino.Mocks.Dll 102
    single parameter method 121
    smart stubs 110
    stub object properties 111
roles 259
Rollback attribute 277
Ruby 265, 279
runtime 98–99, 102, 249

S
safe green zone 147, 169, 180
Scrum 226
sealed classes 78
seam 58, 67–68, 70–71, 74, 80
    target layer 70
    See also seams
seams 55, 68, 74, 240, 257, 260, 263
    creating 58
    definition 55
    hiding 69
    multiple 259
    seam 67–68, 70
    seam statements 69
security 260, 264

selection strategy 242
Selenium 278, 280–281
semantics 174, 264
    changes 175, 185
    See also test semantics
SetUp 35, 45, 49, 187
    See also NUnit
setup action 34
setup code 151
setup method 152, 154, 156–157, 162, 170, 186, 189, 196, 198, 273
    best practices 190
    initializing objects 189–190
    maintainable 190
    wrong use 188
    See also setup action
shared class 188
shared factory method 186
shared resources 196, 198
shared-state corruption 192
    causes 197
    maintainability 197
    manifestation 196
    problems 197
    solutions 198
    test subsets 197
Simian 246, 254
    download 254
similar tests 177
simple objects 49
simple unit test 12, 27
single asserts 200
single responsibility principle 262, 264
single unit 9
singletons 198, 258, 261
slow tests 39
slow-running test 144
Smalltalk 4, 265
smart factories See inversion of control
smart stubs 110
software 236, 256
Software Assessments, Benchmarks, and Best Practices 231
software development 4, 23
software module 8
Software QA Quarterly, The 227
SOLID 78, 237, 267
Solution Explorer 128
source control 142, 144, 147

Spring.NET 62, 261, 274, 276
SRP See single responsibility principle
state sharing 36
state verification See state-based testing
state-based testing 40, 82–83, 137
    comparison with interaction testing 83
    definition 40
    result-driven testing 83
    when to use 84
static languages 266
static method 183, 258, 260
static state 198
statics 67, 258
StoryTeller 283
strict mocks 106
    failure 106
    StrictMock method 107
structured test 16, 22, 24
StructureMap 62, 261, 274–275
stub 54, 58, 66
    asserts 85
    combining with mock object 89
    definition 50
    difference with mock object 84
    getting before method call 55, 66
    injecting stub implementation 55, 58
    injection 80
    receiving before method call 58
    setters 94
    stub analyzer 60
    stub extension manager 57
    stub injection 58
    stub manager 57
    stub method 71
    stub object 61
stub chains 95
stub class 57, 61, 72
    configurability 57
    StubExtensionManager 53
    See also stub
stub loggers 167
stub method 71
stub object 71
    See also stub
stubbing See faking
StubLogger 152
stubs 49, 82, 87, 102, 108, 124, 136, 269
    combining with mocks 97
    difference with mocks objects 97

stubs *(continued)*
  dynamic stubs 99
  fake values 110
  how many per test 94
  preference over mock objects 209
subclass 164
subteam 222
superclass 165
swap approach 249
swap class 249
system initialization methods 167
system state 167
system test 144
system testing 168
system under test *See* unit testing

T
T generic type 167
target server 143
tasks 144
TDD 17–18, 227, 235, 257
  See also test-driven development
team formation 222
team support 230
Team System tools 281
Team System UI Tests 280–281
Team System Web Test 278
TeamCity 143
TearDown 35, 45, 49
  See also NUnit
teardown action 34
teardown code 151
teardown method 196, 198, 273
  See also teardown action
technical definition 5
techniques 268
template test class pattern 158
test actions 30
test API 150
test assembly 146
test assertion 30, 38, 43
  assert class 24
  assert message 24, 31
  assert method 24
test blockage 191
test bug 173, 178
  debugging 174
  fixing 174
test categories 39

test class 27–28, 30, 36, 43–44, 103,
    148–149, 154, 164
  test class hierarchy 170
  See also class
test class inheritance 151
  abstract test driver class 151
  abstract test infrastructure class 151
  template test class 151
test class patterns 148–149
  one-test-class-per-class pattern 149
  one-test-class-per-feature pattern 150
test code 30, 210
  semantics 74
test code coverage 227
  code coverage tools 227
  sample report 234
test code coverage report 225
test complexity 178
test conditions 29
test constructors 36
test design 16, 18, 237
  guidelines 257
  interface-based design 258
  object-oriented 266
test destructors 36
test development
  time consumed 242
test feasibility table 240
test fragility 178, 205
test frameworks 268, 271
test hierarchies 141
test isolation 182, 191, 198
  flow testing 193
  importance 193
  laziness 193
  multiple asserts 200
  test design 193
test layers
  advantages 70
  disadvantages 70
test loading 29
test logic 41, 178
test mapping 148
test method 13, 27–28, 30, 40, 44, 57, 159,
    164–165
  expected behavior 29
  method name 29
  multiple 150
test name 210

test naming 18, 28, 33, 179
  naming conventions 28
test order 192
test output 205
test pass 18
test path 242
test pattern names 50
test project 44, 145, 149
test quality 177
test result 40
test review 172, 191, 221
test run 32, 34, 36, 67, 252
test runner 14, 24, 199
  test results 24
test semantics 173, 184
Test Spy 88
test state 36, 196–197
test stubs 44
test subsets 193, 195
test suite 252
testability 45, 53, 55–56, 78, 150, 244, 247, 256–257, 263, 270, 273
  alternatives 265
  complexity 264
  designing code 238
  problems 248
testable design 78, 81, 256–257, 262–263
  properties 256
testable object-oriented design (TOOD) 78, 81
testable system 257
test-code coverage report 226
test-driven development 3, 16–18, 33, 182, 219, 225, 236, 257
  incremental 17
  style choice 237
  technique 18
Test-Driven Development in Microsoft .NET 237
test-driven development techniques 239
test-first 16
TestFixtureSetUp 36
TestFixtureTearDown 36
testing guidance 151, 159
testing project 29
test-inhibiting design 51
third-party tools 25
Thomas, Dave 151
threading problems 254
thread-related testing 268, 281

threads 50
three pillars 172
threshold of logic 241
Timeout 272
TOOD *See* testable object-oriented design
tooling 239
tools 268
top-down change 223–224
ToString() 203
traditional coding *See* traditional development
traditional development 18
TransactionScope 277–278
triggers 144
trustworthiness 171, 215
trustworthy test 172, 180
  definition 171
  guidelines 172
try-catch 199, 202
Typemock 100, 126, 128–129, 137, 237, 244, 246, 248, 260, 266, 279
  expectations 132
Typemock code
  download 254
Typemock Isolator 97, 269
  See also Typemock
Typemock Racer 246, 254, 281–282

U
UI testing 268, 280–281
UIAutomation API 281
UIs 280
unit test 3, 6, 11, 23, 45, 126, 141, 169
  actions 30
  automation 10, 24
  core techniques 138
  ease of development 11
  ease of running 180
  fast tests 39
  fast-running tests 145
  final definition 11
  frameworks 22
  good unit test 5–6, 9–11
  human factor 146
  initial state 34
  lifecycle 34
  multiple tests 57
  properties of a good unit test 6
  quickness 10

unit test *(continued)*
  removing 173
  running a test 24
  setup methods 34
  slow tests 39
  status 24
  test placement 141
  tools 44
  unit 4
unit testing 4–5, 83
  classic definition 4
  coding 233
  designing for testability 266
  effect on release date 232
  GUI 6
  implementation 230, 232–233, 238
  metrics 234–235
  overall time reduction 233
  system under test (SUT) 4
  time added 231
  time consumed 232
  tough questions 231
unit-testing framework 11, 22–24, 145, 268
  attributes 24
  base classes 24
  benefits 22
  interfaces 24
  list 24
  xUnit framework 25
unit-testing technique 18, 243–244
Unity 274–275
  See also Microsoft Unity
Unix 22
unreadable test 177
user interface (UI) 5
utility class 150, 167, 241
utility method 141, 150, 167, 176, 183

V
valid test 175
validation check 41
value to the project 241
variable naming
  importance 211
VB.NET 124, 236, 260
verbosity 201
  MbUnit 201
  NUnit 201
versioning info 159
view class 122
virtual by default 258
virtual method 71–72, 75, 96, 134, 258–260, 267
virtualizing 76
Vise 246, 250–251
Visual Build Pro 143
Visual Studio 79, 128, 134, 149, 165, 253, 271
Visual Studio .NET 22, 272
Visual Studio 2008 26
Visual Studio Team Foundation Server 143
Visual Studio Team System 271, 281–282
Visual Studio Team System Test
  Edition 180
Visual Studio Team Test 279
VS.NET 253

W
WatiN 278–279, 281
Watir 278–279
web service 49, 61, 74, 83, 87, 89–90, 113, 129, 257
  MockWebService 87
  stub 90
web testing 268, 278
whiteboards 225
Wiegers, Karl 227
wiki page 252
Win32 281
WinForm 281
Working Effectively with Legacy Code 10, 55, 73, 96, 183, 253
WPF 281
wrapper classes 96

X
xUnit 25, 271, 273
xUnit framework 25
xUnit Test Patterns 50, 88, 149, 205

Y
YUnit 271